THE AGE OF
MANIPULATION

THE AGE OF MANIPULATION

THE CON IN CONFIDENCE
THE SIN IN SINCERE

WILSON BRYAN KEY, PH.D.

MADISON BOOKS

The 1993 Edition is
Published by Madison Books
4720 Boston Way
Lanham, Maryland 20706

Distributed by National Book Network

The paper used in this publication meets the minimum
requirements of American National Standard for
Information Sciences—Permanence of Paper for
Printed Library Materials, ANSI Z39.48–1984. ∞™
Manufactured in the United States of America.

Library of Congress Cataloging-in-Publication Data
Key, Wilson Bryan, 1925–
The age of manipulation : the con in confidence, the
sin in sincere / Wilson Bryan Key.
p.   cm.
Originally published: New York : H. Holt, © 1989.
Includes bibliographical references and index.
1. Mass media—Psychological aspects.
2. Advertising—Psychological aspects.
3. Manipulative behavior.   4. Subliminal projection.
I. Title.
P96.P75K39   1992
302.23—dc20   92–15630 CIP

ISBN 0–8191–8653–8 (pbk. : alk. paper)

R.D. Laing's The Politics of the Family was published by CBC
Learning Systems of Toronto, Ontario. Excerpt used by
permission.

Illustration Credits
Figure 1: © August Bullock, 1979, artwork by Nelson Carrick;
Subliminal Sex® T-shirts is a registered trademark.
Figures 2, 3, 4, 17, 18, 19, 20, 21, 22: TV stills by Cliff Roth.
Figure 29: Art Institute of Chicago.

For my dearest wife, Jan, and our pixie, Christina—lovely ladies who share and enrich my life. They have never doubted impossible things are always possible when part of the good fight.

"There is no use in trying," said Alice; "one cannot believe impossible things."

"I dare say you haven't had much practice," said the Queen. "When I was your age, I always did it for half an hour each day. Why, sometimes I've believed as many as six impossible things before breakfast."

Lewis Carroll
Alice's Adventures in Wonderland

CONTENTS

Foreword: The Battle of Beliefs   ix
Author's Warning   xvii

PART ONE   SUBLIMINAL MEDIA TECHNOLOGY:
Bending Minds in Pursuit of Power and Profit

1   For Those Who Think They Think for Themselves   3

2   How to Get Inside the Open Mind—Undetected   35

3   The Underside of Consciousness   64

PART TWO   LANGUAGE AND CULTURE:
The Tools of Indoctrinability

4   Media—The Brainwashing Laundromat   93

5   How We Know That We Know That We Know   115

The Logic of Illogic
The Logic of Identification
The Logic of Excluded Middles
The Logic of Contradiction

6   The Real Thing—Symbolic Realities   148

7   Cause and Effect—The Greatest Illusion of All   164

8   The Expectations of Stereotypes   180

9   Self-Fulfilling Prophecies   205

10 The Self-Sealing World of Objectivity   227

11 The Permanently Closed Mind   249

Epilogue   265

Appendix   267

Bibliography   269

Index   283

Illustrations follow page 140.

FOREWORD

THE BATTLE OF BELIEFS

Orwell's 1984 actually occurred around 1934. We were just too busy to notice.

Marshall McLuhan

Genius is the capacity to see ten things, where the ordinary person sees only one, and the person of talent, two or three.

Ezra Pound

Over fifteen years have passed since Wilson Bryan Key first warned us to "Watch ourselves!" much as the Greek god Zeus once cautioned Narcissus. Narcissus had narcotized himself by endlessly staring at his mirrored image in a pond. He never realized the idealized reflection's identity and fell deeply in love with it. As in the ad-media mirror in the U.S., the reflected image was always kind, noble, brave, wise, fair, good, generous, beautiful, and truthful. Narcissus eventually perished because he could not sort out reality from fantasy.

Since the first edition of *Subliminal Seduction* in 1973, and Dr. Key's two subsequent books on subliminal persuasion, few other subjects have had as great an impact upon large reading audiences. It would be difficult to find a college student since 1973 who has not read, or at least heard of, these books. They are still required reading in many high schools and universities. Their message has spread far beyond classrooms into Senate committee hearings, into regulatory agency rulings, and even into international discourse on media ethics.

Like the Ouroborus (the snake that bites its own tail) from ancient Greek mythology, the books have become paradoxes. Dr. Key has raised the world's awareness about advertising media's rape-of-the-mind rip-offs. His warnings have also provided technical primers on how to manipulate human behavior. Though the ad industry publicly denounced the books and attempted to discredit the author, his writings are widely used by ad agencies, media research psychologists, and others who labor in the Machiavellian orchards of deceit and human exploitation.

Most of us are constantly pressured to change our behaviors. As consumers, we are endlessly enticed by advertisers to buy products, brands, and services in their merciless pursuit of our discretionary incomes. As voters, we are incessantly persuaded and hounded toward some point of view by politicians who compete for power over our lives and profits for their sponsors. As social and ethical beings, we are bombarded by religious and ideological zealots of countless persuasions to become their *true* believers and their generous and obedient slaves. Some of these efforts are overt, clearly perceivable, on the table, so to speak. Others are far more subtle, even invisible to the conscious mind. Virtually all these attempts to solicit our patronage and change our behavior are effective in one measure or another. Even those of us who resist are changed by our resistance. Collectively, these efforts have made the U.S. into an ideological wasteland, with increasing numbers of people desperate to find something—often anything—of value to believe in. This desperation makes them uniquely vulnerable to the industries that manufacture and manage their belief systems.

Most people—especially in our media-managed culture—are unaware of the masterful strategies utilized to direct their destinies. Most are educated to ignore their participation in the collective cultural conscious, which makes them susceptible to indoctrination. Vulnerability to manipulation was imposed early upon Western cultures by centuries of conditioning in the logic and language systems described by the philosophers of ancient Greece. The illusion is still popularly cherished that humans individually—all on their own—are in total control of their own thoughts, values, and behaviors. We believe that we think entirely for and by ourselves. This fantasy feeds a self-perception that is currently perilous to human survival and adjustment—an intellectual Achilles' heel.

It is easy to become distracted by the riotous illustrations in Dr. Key's books. They are simultaneously hilarious and exquisitely painful. Readers often appear uncertain whether to laugh or cry. The pictures unmask the incredible vulnerability of people to persuasion technologies, the pompous pretensions of morality, piety, convictions, and ideologies that allow us to be manipulated in any direction worthy of an investment in time, money, and power. They reveal that the slogan "truth in advertising" was just another damned lie dreamed up by an ad hustler. They also strip the camouflage the society's leadership have developed to veil their incalculable greed, their merciless misuse of human hopes for decency, honesty, and fairness. The ad-media industries loudly and continuously proclaim what they have altruistically done *for* us. We should long ago have inquired about what they were doing *to* us. The illustrations may mask the more significant, underlying nature of the linguistic-cultural system that permits and makes acceptable the media rip-off. Media critics have often concentrated upon the trees and missed the forest.

Aside from the sheer entertainment provided by this exposé of obscenity masked as respectability, of naïve gullibility masked as sophistication, of lies and deceits masked as truth, perhaps the most significant portions of the text are the probes into archetypal structures of both language and culture. The use and misuse of Aristotle's laws of logic (which are not really laws at all) are rarely criticized today by a society persuaded that it has achieved so many ultimate truths. These sections of the book are, by themselves, worth the purchase price.

One of the greatest enigmas throughout history continues to be the nature of the human mind. Evidence on how the brain receives, processes, stores, retrieves, and communicates to other brains is incomplete, hypothetical, and inconclusive. Voluminous research by a vast number of scientists and philosophers has attempted to construct order from the complexity and seeming chaos of the mentation and language processes. Chaos, doubt, and uncertainty still prevail in spite of everything. The operations of the human brain have nothing even remotely to do with those of an electronic computer, though this has long been a profitable ploy of the industries involved in producing computers. There are infinitely more questions about the brain and how it functions than there are answers. It appears that this imbalance may persist indefinitely.

In most areas of disciplined inquiry, researchers do not work or theorize in a vacuum. The so-called scientific method is inextricably involved with language, culture, and both conscious and unconscious human motives. The ways in which a problem is perceived; how the hypotheses, syntheses, and methods are stated; which evaluative procedures are applied; and the principles and concepts utilized for theorization all guide evaluations and conclusions both consciously and unconsciously. The notion of objectivity is as mythological as were the gods atop Mount Olympus. Conclusions, scientific or otherwise, must be expressed in simplistic, linear, fragmented verbal or mathematical abstractions.

Reality is infinitely complex, multiple, integrated, constantly changing, and subject to the vagaries of human perception. Verbal language, and even mathematics, is simplistic, definition-limited, orderly, sequential, rigid, and nonchanging. Languages have in themselves nothing directly to do with the realities they attempt to describe, except possibly in the remote vagaries of human perceptual abstraction. Words, things, and the human perceptual uncertainties involved in each ensure that truth, if such an abstraction could be meaningful, may always remain just beyond the grasp of human intellect. Functional, pragmatic, tentative, verbal, or mathematical generalization appears the closest humans may ever approach to an ultimate, definitive—though always tentative—truth about anything.

Were the above problem widely recognized, there would exist a much lower probability that humans will vaporize themselves in some proud and patriotic attempt to save the world from whatever mass neurosis may be current. If Dr. Leakey is correct, the human species has been around some 4½ million years. Thus, every isolated event perceived by humans is merely a tiny drop in a very large ocean. Simple survival and adjustment as worthy, tolerant, loving, unselfish beings might even be permitted to evolve as a fundamental doctrine of human existence. The doctrine should remind each of us, every morning as we look into the mirror, that in spite of the thousands of gods, philosophies, sciences, and unquestionable "truths" humans have created with language throughout their history, no one has as yet discovered how to make even a worm.

Marshall McLuhan called those elements within an individual's environment, with which he or she interacts consciously and unconsciously, the "environmental surround." There are always so many perceptual particles within this surround that no individual could conceivably concentrate consciously upon everything at the same time. Conscious awareness, therefore, is always fragmented. Because visual, auditory, tactile, gustatory, and olfactory perceptions are innumerable, continuous, and overlapping, the conscious mind cannot deal simultaneously with all of them. The ability to isolate, concentrate, or abstract a small portion of the perceptions available at any given moment into a linear, logical, definition-oriented language process is considered the basis for evaluations of *intelligence*—whatever that may mean from day to day and from person to person.

The process appears to be a concentration upon a small portion of perceptions to the exclusion of competing ones. Consciously perceived reality is usually a vast oversimplification, an abstraction, of actual perceivable reality. The myriad of perceptions that conscious awareness has deemphasized, set aside, placed out of focus, subordinated to ground, and/or repressed, remain in the brain's unconscious storage for varying periods of time. Perhaps some perceptions are stored permanently.

You can experience the process by stopping to consciously consider the perceptual stimulation going on while you read these pages. If your concentration on these words is intense enough, most of the peripheral perceptions will register only at an unconscious level until your attention is diverted from figure (the words) to some portion of ground (peripheral perceptions). Perceptions, of course, can be internally generated as well as externally stimulated, as your concentration wanders from these words to a momentary thought of a well-turned ankle you perceived while crossing the campus this morning. Or, the words may diminish in your attention as they elicit associations with other subjects, authors, and arguments.

These peripheral unconscious perceptions can often be brought to consciousness later through such techniques as hypnosis or narcosynthesis. Under hypnosis, subjects often recall in great detail perceptions of license plates and other minutiae that were unavailable consciously. Numerous experiments have even recovered conversations heard during surgery under anesthesia. All the sensory inputs appear to function continuously, with prodigious quantities of information pouring into the brain, but only small bits and pieces surfacing in conscious awareness. Perception is *total* and *instantaneous* at the nonconscious level but extremely limited at a conscious level.

For 2,000 years the environmental surround of Western cultures has focused consciously on what seems logical, linear, rational, connected, verbal, arithmetic, and symmetrical. The traditional language-logic system was initially defined by Aristotle, though the ideas reach as far back as Hammurabi's Code around 3000 B.C. The verbal-arithmetic description of the physical world by Newton, the symmetrical view of spatial relationships in the geometry of Euclid, the neat, systematic, reasonable, logical views of reality began to explode by the early twentieth century. These language-organized certainties slowly came to seem mere fantasy. Very little within human perception any longer appeared certain, permanent, unassailable. Organized views of language and culture began to evolve as wishful thinking, projection, and construction. Powerful contributions from writers such as Marx, Darwin, and Freud further assaulted conventional wisdom. Traditional language-logic and order tumbled into shambles. New, far more subtle views of the human animal slowly eroded away the certainties of the earlier, more simplistic modes of thought.

Non-Aristotelian logic entered science, art, and philosophy.

Non-Euclidean geometry devastated traditional ways of viewing spatial relationships. Non-Newtonian physics became the basis for quantum mechanics and relativity, the new science of nuclear and electron particles. Considerations of the human unconscious rendered obsolete earlier platitudes about human perception and motives. The world responded to the new modes of thought, logic, and their threat to vested interests, conventional wisdom, and the status quo with confused defensiveness.

The old ways never relinquish their grip easily or painlessly. They had evolved to represent the vested interests of Western civilization. The new modes of thought and reason were threatening, often violently so. Religious, social, political, economic, scientific, and philosophical vested interests fought tenaciously to suppress change and innovation. Yet slowly, inexorably, the best, most logical of all worlds came to be perceived by more and more as the worst and most illogical.

Anyone alive today will complete his or her life experience in the middle of this largely unseen revolution in ideas, concepts, values, traditions, ideologies, and human relationships. The fantasies of certainty, permanence, and simplicity have become obsolete, often tragically. Comprehension of *process* and *change* has become a survival imperative. The imperative is also driven by the continuing crises attributable to exponential world population growth, the depletion of natural resources, the inequitable and unacceptable distribution of power and wealth, the devastation of environment by pollution and greed, and the most frightening specter of all hovering as a dark shadow over the earth's struggling populations—devastation by nuclear accident or warfare.

It appears, therefore, vital to survival that humans learn to overcome—at least in some measure—their vulnerability to manipulation. If democracy and freedom are ever to evolve into meaningful abstractions beyond the self-serving, dishonest, platitudinous rhetoric of political campaign speeches, humans must largely break out of traditional modes of thought. This will be painful, most painful. Simplistic *common sense* may constitute the world's most dangerous perceptual illusion. Common sense is often uncommonly deceptive and should always be considered with a stern admonition to *beware*!

Those who still adamantly reject the prevalence of subliminal manipulation technology fall into two general categories: those whose vested interests lie in the continuing exploitation and manipulation of humans, including many who exploit commercial, religious, and political fanatacism; and those who reject the notion of subliminal persuasion because they hate, distrust, and dislike whatever is new. The new has usually been perceived as threatening, subversive, and heretical.

Dr. Key has done a masterful job of exploring the continuing search for truth through which humans may survive their follies, foibles, and technologies. His insights into the world's propaganda battle of beliefs may contribute significantly to the struggle for world peace and understanding. The search for truth, of course, is a far different matter than the discovery of an *eternal* truth. Once an *eternal* truth is discovered, learning, progress, growth, and freedom become restricted, biased, and narrowly focused. Human options inevitably are diminished. After all, if a truth were really true, for all time, in all places, for all peoples, there would be little need to believe in it, propagandize it, struggle over it, and murder in its name.

Watch yourselves!

Dr. Bruce R. Ledford
Professor of Media
Auburn University
Auburn, Alabama

AUTHOR'S WARNING

Readers can make practical use of this book in two ways. The ideas and information can be used by anyone in a media-dominated environment to protect themselves against exploitation by picture and word symbols. Readers should be able to achieve greater autonomy—freedom upon which to act or believe. Certainly they should free themselves in some measure from the dehumanizing effects of media merchandising upon their personalities and relationships.

The second practical use of the book is for readers preoccupied only with media-propagated self-indulgence. It should prepare them for profitable careers in advertising and public relations. Indeed, since *Subliminal Seduction* appeared in 1973, subliminal techniques have become far more persuasive, sophisticated, technologically advanced, and more profitably applied to anesthetize the U.S. population against the intrusion of reality into their daily lives. Few advertising or media people are unfamiliar with my three earlier books. Many appear so informed they could pass rigorous examination on the subject. In public, however, they steadfastly maintain innocence, repeating ad nauseam that subliminal perception does not exist. The standard industry defense alleges my "dirty mind" was responsible for the entire controversy. Ad executives, professors, and other assorted media apologists refuse to discuss the more than 500 published research studies that confirm the effects of subliminal stimuli on ten measureable areas of human behavior.

The books were intended as exposés, critiques, revelations about the most dangerous affront to sanity, freedom, and survival that now threatens the earth's population. Subliminal indoctrination may prove more dangerous than nuclear weapons. The substitution of cultural fantasies for realities on a massive, worldwide scale threatens everyone in this precarious period of human evolution. Present odds appear to favor total devastation.

The paradox of a book actually serving what it attacks is not unusual in the history of ideas. Any enterprising capitalist will carefully study new intellectual developments in the socialist world to learn about weaknesses in both socialist and capitalist economics just as executives, managers, and leaders in socialist countries carefully study Western capitalism. The study of competition and critics is the first rule of survival. At the same time, it is necessary to attack or pretend to attack competition at every opportunity.

Nothing in human perception—which includes everything humans know or think they know consciously and unconsciously—is what it appears to be. Part I of this book deals with pictures, ads for the most part, in an update of the three earlier books. Part II concerns language and culture, and their effective brainwashing of populations to prefer fantasies over realities.

Media industries are great fun to molecularize—to take apart in small, revealing pieces. Their dissected anatomy embarrasses the manipulators and frightens their victims. There is much to be learned from them about how humans think or do not think. Ad media demonstrate human venality and gullibility at its worst and reveal how languages, pictures, and cultures serve more to enslave than to enlighten, unless audiences are educated to discriminate between fantasy (how we wish the world existed) and perceptual reality (that limited fraction of reality available to conscious perception).

Advertising operates from an almost universal simplistic human motive—to sell, to sell, to sell. By comparison, both fine art and literature are created out of motivational complexity—diffuse, contradictory, and paradoxical. Deeper artistic insights involve the artist's unique perceptions of the world. This may be why creative artistic productivity often survives through centuries as meaningful human experience.

The manipulative motives of advertising and public relations produce images for momentary conscious perception, repression, and unconscious memory storage. They are created to be unacknowledged, consciously insignificant audience experiences. This, indeed, can be termed the Age of Manipulation.

Humans often do not appear to have learned much from the thousands of years in world experience behind them. In the U.S., history is perceived to have begun with John Wayne at the Alamo or, for the young, with the Beatles. Our culture, arranged to optimize the return on media investments, rarely permits learning from experience. This may constitute modern man's Achilles' heel.

This book is intended to change the way individuals perceive the world in which they live. If it succeeds, nothing will ever again be quite the same.

Part One

SUBLIMINAL MEDIA TECHNOLOGY

BENDING MINDS IN PURSUIT OF POWER AND PROFIT

1 | FOR THOSE WHO THINK THEY THINK FOR THEMSELVES

We are all at the mercy of influences over which we are consciously unaware and over which we have virtually no conscious control.

> Robert Rosenthal, *Pygmalion in the Classroom*

The people want to be deceived, let them be deceived. *Populus vult decepi, decipiatus.*

> Cardinal Carlo Caraffe to Pope Paul IV

In many ways creativity and mental illness are opposite sides of the same coin.

> Anton Ehrenzweig, *The Hidden Order of Art*

This book is about the human misuse of humans. High-technology mass persuasion has achieved levels of sophistication far beyond what most individuals imagine. Most still desperately cling to the delusion that they think for themselves, determine their own destinies, exercise both individual and collective *free will* (the great myth that underlies democratic ideology); that advertising works in the interest of the consumer; and—perhaps the greatest self-deception of all—that they can easily discriminate between fantasy and reality. This book attempts to throw the proverbial monkey wrench into these worn, nonsensical platitudes.

The following insights can be utilized to fight off the daily assault of misrepresentations so devastating to freedom and autonomy. By consciously knowing how the rascals get inside your head, you at least have the option to fight back. Technologies of exploitation appear far more developed in capitalist than in socialist nations, though the question is academic. Technology is never a successful secret. It remains available to anyone with time, money, and motivation. The *engineering of consent* assaults human perception at both conscious and unconscious levels, especially the latter. Once the group or collective unconscious is programmed into what has been called culture, virtually any bill of goods can be sold at conscious levels.

Psychological indoctrination also exists through language structures, cultural assumptions, and highly malleable perspectives toward the self, the world, and perceived relationships with what is casually accepted as reality. In terms of survival and adjustment, these may be far more significant than the obscene imagery embedded in advertising.

This book examines efforts to make the end justify the means—a perversion that never disappears in human evolution. Not long ago, the U.S. appeared willing to destroy the populations of Vietnam, Cambodia, and Laos to save them from communism. Communism, of course, is an idea and, like most ideas, is interpreted differently throughout the world. The folly of sacrificing millions to the perception of an idea should be apparent but is not. Humans are uniquely dangerous because their perceptual blindness does not permit them to know they are dangerous. There are zealots in world governments willing to justify mass murder in the name of fanatic, ideological fantasies. This willingness to betray the human spirit through arrogance, ignorance, "absolute" knowledge, dehumanization, and the mindless pursuit of profit and power should, but rarely does, frighten us.

Humans appear difficult to frighten; they forget so easily. Mankind's most ennobling pursuit throughout history has been the search for truth. Each time, however, truth was believed to have been discovered, tragic mischief resulted. Converts to the latest version of *truth* usually end up as victims along with the unbelievers whom they have victimized. *Truth* is a product of human perception.

It Takes One to Know One

The heritage of U.S. commercial mass-communication media dates back at least to the Greek philosopher Protagoras (485–410 B.C.). Protagoras was the most famous of the sophists, known for his dictum, "Man is the measure of all things." Having pondered the relativity of human perceptions and judgments, Protagoras was eventually accused of heresy, his books were burned, and he died in exile.

Early Greek sophists were professional teachers of rhetoric, then considered, in the words of Aristotle, to be *"all the available means of persuasion." Sophist* originally meant a "clever" or "skilled" person. Sophists were attacked by Plato and Aristotle for not seeking *objective truths*. The sophists' only concern, according to their critics, was victory in debate—a victory they were allegedly prepared to use dishonest means to achieve. In the interest of their clients, who paid high fees, sophists supposedly attacked traditional values in Greek society. This was their fatal mistake. They are remembered today almost entirely through their critics who tell us that sophists cared only for success and power, not *truth*. Sophists sought to understand the structure of human societies, relationships between words and things, between observers and their observations, and between reality and perceptions of reality. Protagoras was widely known for his ethical and moral preoccupations. Critics, however, claimed sophist doctrines were dishonest and blamed them for weakening Greek moral fiber. The sophists perceived no permanently enduring truth, no divinely sanctioned law, and no eternal, transcendental code of values. The sophist movement disappeared in Greek philosophy by the third century B.C., but had a powerful effect upon succeeding centuries of philosophy, science, and scholarship as an anti-thesis (something to oppose). *Sophistry* today is a term used for fallacious reasoning or argument.

Plato, though antagonistic to the sophists, accepted their view that all perceptions are relative to time, place, and the situation of the perceiver. Aristotle, however, sought to verify objective truths. Aristotelian logic has served the ruling elites of Western society for over 2,000 years. Aristotle demonstrated, through verbal syllogistic logic, the existence of truth. During the Middle Ages, Catholic scholastic philosophers adapted Aristotelian logic to justify and validate papal authority, social hierarchies, slavery, canon law, and theological doctrine, and most importantly, to verify the existence of God. Aristotelian logic became the foundation of Western religious, social, economic, legal, and philosophical reasoning. Protagoras was forgotten, his sophist perspectives ignored or treated as evil and false. Had the views of Protagoras been useful to the power elites who controlled societies over the two millenia, as useful as Aristotle's, civilization would have taken a far different course—perhaps one marked by far less bloodshed.

The sophists were the earliest known exponents of perceptual, cultural, and epistemological relativism. The measure of things, in their view, was not God or abstract, scientific, philosophical truth, but human beings, their needs, and their search for happiness. Sophistic relativism offended many as a recipe for moral anarchy, a denial of enduring truth, and a perceived threat to the power elite of the day.

Sophistry has flourished in the twentieth century under other labels, definitions, and socioeconomic rationalizations. It became far more sophisticated, and sophists learned not to talk about being sophists. They learned to affect publicly a pretense of accepting "objective reality." For sophistry to succeed in an Aristotelian world, it must not be perceived as sophistry. Thus, the modern media technician must disguise his technology under a mantle of credible truths. Media must reach the most desirable demographic and psychographic audience characteristics on behalf of its clients. What appears credible to one stratum may appear specious to another. Appeals must sell products, ideas, and individuals regardless of actual product merit or substance.

The communication industry operates on the sophistic basis that all things are relative, that credibility and sales are the criteria of effectiveness, that truth is an adaptable, malleable, even expendable commodity. Truth, as every media employee knows, can be created, ignored, adapted to any purpose, modified, or turned upside down. Truth becomes credibility and is validated in the eyes of the beholder instead of within a rigorous structure of confirmable facts. This relativistic perspective, however, must never be permitted to surface consciously within the audience.

In the training of professional communication technicians, effort is made to sidestep personal conviction or commitment to a cause, perspective, ideal, or even personal preference. "Professional objectivity" is offered as an ideal that disposes, in fantasy at least, of human bias. Media technicians work for any product, brand, politician, or individual who can hire them.

U.S. media executives operate in a milieu of sophistic relativism, constantly measuring work and cost-effectiveness against sales, votes, or attitude and opinion change. Truths are manufactured to order; audience-perceived realities are manipulated to appear as objective realities. Media technicians cannot, however, develop credible illusions and fantasies accidentally. They must *know* what they are doing. They also must disguise from audiences what they are doing, or that they are doing anything beyond the superficially obvious. Audiences are never permitted backstage; illusions are easily destroyed, and media illusions are worth a great deal of money.

This book uses an almost classical sophist perspective to unmask the cynical sophistry of mass-communication media. It is unconcerned with the obvious, consciously perceived world in which humans think they live out their lives. What appears conscious, logical, and reasonable has little persuasive significance. These explorations probe influences humans do not consciously perceive—*the subliminal*. The goal is to render more of the subliminal consciously apparent.

The Subliminal Strategies

There are six audiovisual techniques through which subliminal information can be communicated, hidden from conscious awareness, that appear frequently in ad media. Categories invariably overlap. Any single visual or audio example may include an assortment of the categories. Unexpected creative innovation may demand new, revised categorization. But the basic categories are:

1. Figure-Ground Reversals (syncretistic illusions)
2. Embedding
3. Double Entendre
4. Tachistoscopic Displays
5. Low-Intensity Light and Low-Volume Sound
6. Lighting and Background Sound

Figure-Ground Reversals

Visual and auditory perceptions can be divided into *figure*—content, foreground, subject—and *ground*, background supportive to figure, the environment in which the figure occurs. Areas peripheral to figure are usually taken for granted, unnoticed, and considered irrelevant. Humans constantly, unconsciously, distinguish between figure and ground, separating the two. Conscious attention focuses upon figure, while background is subordinated, perceived unconsciously. When a threatening distraction appears in ground, ground becomes figure. To alert, perceptually sensitive individuals, probing every possible dimension of a percept for new, meaningful information, figure and ground can appear in a constant state of flux. At a low level of sensitivity, figure and ground remain rigidly fixed, static, locked-in.

The famed vase or faces explained the idea for generations in introductory psychology textbooks. Other widely known figure-ground (or syncretistic) illusions include the old woman or young woman, duck or rabbit, vanity (a beautiful woman before her mirror) or death (a skull), and the famous Rubens profiles—a series of drawings where one illusion is perceived on one side of a line and another on the other side. Less than 1% of the adult U.S. population has syncretistic vision—the ability to perceive both sides of these illusions (figure and ground) simultaneously. Experiments suggest, however, that figure-ground is easily perceived while in a hypnotic trance. Most people appear to have a latent, unconscious potential for syncretistic vision.

For several centuries at least, artists have known that ground is as important to meaning and visual experience as figure. In many famous paintings, ground often carries the most significant information, the data necessary to make sense, significance, or meaning out of the picture. Advertising artists eventually learned that figure could be reduced to banality—a safe, uncontroversial, nonchallenging presentation of information. Ground, on the other hand, could contain the really exciting proposition, the vital data perceived unconsciously. One simple example of visual figure-ground reversal is the cartoon painting of four plants (fig. 1).

Blossoms in a Garden

The painting was developed by a San Francisco attorney, August Bullock. Several designs printed on the Subliminal Sex® T-shirts sold through Macy's stores in California and Georgia and through Bamberger's in New Jersey. The two plants on the left appear in intimate proximity. The left plant has wound a tendril gently around the plant on its right. Were the plants people, they would appear affectionately involved.

With a little imagination, the two flowers on the left appear to have gender—boy and girl. Flowers are important symbolic as well as biological entities—even though symbolism is rarely studied in the U.S. There are good reasons why humans, especially women, like flowers—even pictures of flowers. Flowers are the reproductive organs of the plant.

By contrast, the third plant with the big head is separated from the two loving plants on the left—lonely, alienated, trying to make out with the plant on the far right, which has lost its flower. The above describes *figure* in the painting—obviously about the birds and the bees. A bluebird perches on a leaf at left and a bee bumbles about on the bottom right. *Ground*, on the other hand, involves the white background. Search the white areas for information. Study the ground between each flower carefully before reading further.

Just above the grass between the two plants at left, the white ground curves upward to the right—forming the letter S. Once the S is perceived consciously, the two other letters usually appear. The E is formed by the ground between the second and third plants. The X appears between the third and fourth plants.

Similar simple figure-ground reversals are regularly utilized in advertising art. The emotional, dramatic information is in ground, available at an unconscious level of perception. The figure information, what the picture is superficially about, is banal, unthreatening, taken for granted.

The SEX was instantly perceived within the brain unconsciously. Perception occurs in microseconds. The portions of perception that surface consciously process much more slowly. Conscious perception, in this case, focused upon the flowers. Unconscious perception saw the word for the most powerful drive system in the human psyche.

Perception involves both conscious and unconscious inputs into the brain. The systems apparently interconnect, but can function separately. The unconscious is believed responsible for powerful basic attitude and belief systems. With a little ingenuity—and there is much ingenuity available in the pursuit of power and profit—the simple figure-ground technique is applied to sexualize everything in the society from presidents to fingernail polish. Roughly 5% of individuals tested saw the hidden SEX immediately.

Another example of figure-ground reversal appeared in the TV commercial for Wrigley's chewing gum. From the still, it is easy to perceive that this young man is up to no good (fig. 2). In the next scene (fig. 3), the young woman almost drops the picnic basket. After juggling it for a moment, the young man helps her keep the basket from falling. The audience focal point in the brief scene concentrates upon the basket—the *figure*, the primary action. But, in the background, the emotionally significant information appears—the man's hand reaches beneath the basket to pat the female's genitalia. In the final brand identification frame, Wrigley's advises, "Get the Little Lift!" Indeed! (fig. 4)

Auditory Figure-Ground Reversals

Figure-ground relationships also appear in sound. Composers developed orchestration techniques over five centuries ago that could be described as subliminal. When an orchestra plays a chord, each musician holding a single component of the chord, only the aggregate is perceived by the audience. Individual instruments and their notes in the chord are not consciously differentiated. However, a one-note variation in the chord can be detected.

Traditional polyphonic composition employs four voices as full harmonic sound, though there can be more or less than four. Figure-ground, in this case, might be composed of four levels, only one of which is likely to be perceived consciously as figure at any one moment in time. Nonmusicians usually perceive only one voice, melody, or melodic harmony. Musicians often can consciously hear two voices. Some individuals can perceive three. Very few consciously perceive all four voices. The complexity of consciously perceiving all the voices, often running counter to one another, is staggering.

In a musical score, however, all the voices can be read on paper, vertically and horizontally. As they appear vertically, the notes—one above the other—are perceived simultaneously at one time interval. Horizontally, as the score progresses, you can follow as each voice pursues an independent melodic direction in time. But human hearing welds the voices into a unified time continuum. Unconsciously, the brain appears to perceive each one independently, is able to discriminate one from another. Consciously, the four-voice continuities are experienced collectively.

Perceptions of Genius

The young Mozart once heard a polyphonic choral composition sung by the Vatican's Sistine Chapel Choir. The complex score

11

had been a guarded secret of the Church for many decades. After one hearing, Mozart transcribed the complete score from memory. He was able to perceive each of the four voices separately and collectively, vertically and horizontally.

Ludwig van Beethoven's Ninth Symphony is arguably the most magnificent and complex single composition in Western music, and Beethoven wrote it after becoming totally deaf. He never heard the work performed. Synesthesia, which most individuals perform unconsciously, means a perception of one sense that stimulates another sense. In this case, Beethoven's auditory sense was stimulated by his visual perception of the written score. In effect, he saw how it would sound. Most individuals can demonstrate synesthesia during hypnotic trance, but Beethoven did it consciously.

This perceptual sensitivity is most often found in creative individuals, in musicians, poets, painters, sculptors, or writers. Perceptual sensitivity can, apparently, be taught only up to a modest point. But such perceptually liberating education has often been considered subversive or countercultural. Perceptual flexibility usually provides a wide range of multiple options.

Most world educational systems teach people to concentrate conscious focus only at one level of perceptual experience—a one-dimensional bias. There are strong ideological, economic, political, and even religious motives involved. Once individuals move beyond simplistic, one-dimensional perception, they become extremely difficult to control and to fit into preconceived group norms.

British psychoanalyst Anton Ehrenzweig theorized that flexible, multidimensional perception, which often appears among children under eight, might be sustained throughout life by an early introduction to abstract, nonlinear art forms in painting, music, sculpture, and literature. He believed it possible to extend the delightful perceptual flexibility of children before socialization up through maturation into adulthood, perhaps throughout life.

But, perceptual flexibility presents enormous problems of peer-group conflict in high-tech conformist cultures, such as those of the U.S., Japan, most of Europe, and the U.S.S.R. Young people are commercially managed into group identifications, values, and behaviors under the pretense of individualized preferences. Much of this consumer conditioning is engineered via popular arts and culture, which derive from advertising and promotion. Radio, television, newspapers, magazines, popular music, clothing fashions, artifacts, recreations, and inexhaustible entertainments—are all perceived by the audience at a simplistic level. They appear honest, straightforward, direct: "What you see is what you get!" Nothing in the world is this simplistic.

Monolithic perception, of course, is an illusion created for consumers. The reality, known, researched, and manipulated by the merchandising media, is perceptually complex. Simplistic *seeing* and *getting* are perceptual constructs custom-manufactured only for overprotected, nongrowth-oriented children, highly vulnerable to manipulation, who eventually become the adult victims in a media-dominated society.

The victims can be observed as they scream and shout hysterically at rock concerts and later in life at religious revival meetings. They mindlessly absorb the ads in television, magazines, and newspapers. They endlessly shop fashions in supermarkets and department stores. They proudly defend consumption of junk foods, tobacco, alcohol, drugs, and other media-hyped addictive substances. They are usually fantasy-defined by media as the "in crowd." Their reality is usually that of the losers, the used, the persuaded, the patsies, the appropriated.

Embedding

The U.S. Treasury Department's Bureau of Alcohol, Tobacco, and Firearms—which supposedly regulates ads in these areas—included in its August 6, 1984, "New Rules and Regulations" (*see* Appendix) a definition of subliminal embedding. "One prevalent form of subliminal technique was described as the insertion of words or body forms (embeds) by the use of shadows or shading, or the substitution of forms and shapes generally associated with the body. . . . The consumer does not perceive them at a normal level of awareness, and thus is given no choice whether to accept or reject the message, as is the case with normal advertising. ATF holds that this type of advertising technique is false and deceptive, and is prohibited by law." The ruling applies only to alcoholic beverage ads—spirits, beer, and wine.

Subliminal techniques had earlier been declared by the Federal Communication Commission "contrary to the public interest because they are clearly intended to be deceptive." The Federal Trade Commission also prohibited the use of subliminal techniques (*see* Key, *The Clam-Plate Orgy*, pp. 132–49), as did the voluntary advertising and broadcasting industries' codes of ethics. It would appear, from all the time, money, and effort expended on subliminal persuasion by regulatory agencies, that the nation is safe from such nefarious manipulation and pollution. The rules prohibiting repressed media content, however, have been ignored. None of the regulations have ever been enforced.

Embedding, at first, appears as though an artist cleverly hid obscene or taboo images within a picture. Human perception can be considered both *total* (everything sensed transmits to the brain) and *instantaneous* (the speed of electron flow through neurons). In a visual percept, as little as $^1/_{1000}$ of the total percept registered in the brain actually surfaces in consciousness. The remainder lies dormant within memory. Embeds enhance perceptual experience of the picture, intensifying responses such as EKG, EEG, GSR—heart rate, brain rhythms, and galvanic skin response. Emotionalized, repressed information remains in the memory system for long periods, perhaps for a lifetime. In embedded pictures, nothing is actually hidden—certainly not by the artist. Once viewers learn perceptual flexibility, the embeds are readily available to consciousness. *The only thing hidden, in embedded media is what viewers or listeners hide from themselves.* Repression appears to be a compulsive process, probably initiated to protect oneself from unsettling information that would provoke anxiety.

The Erect Emerald

The Tanqueray emerald ad (fig. 5) appeared in numerous national periodicals, including *Time* magazine. Somerset Importers of New York spent an estimated $3–4 million to publish the ad. As with most ads, this layout was designed to be read in fractions of a second. Ads are not expected to be studied by readers. The copy is rarely read. The Tanqueray copy is similar to that in medical journal pharmaceutical ads. Printed in small type, it is wordy, difficult to read and comprehend. Ad designers know few readers will actually read these texts—very few in this case, because to do so would require a prodigious investment of time, concentration, and eyestrain.

The copy, a complex explanation of the Tanqueray contest, was designed as a credibility device. The unread copy supplies a raison d'être, a logical excuse for the expensive full-page, four-color ad. The $25,000 emerald prize makes the whole thing appear logical. Credible logic conceals from consciousness what is really going on.

The pouring gin, emerald, and glass are, of course, painted, not a photograph of the real thing. Artists must offer credible assumptions to viewers. The viewer must believe the stream of gin flows down from the top upon the emerald, then splashes into the glass, or the painting will make no sense, and nonsensical art will be rejected.

But let's suspend the law of gravity; it does not apply to painted illusions. Once you determine what the artist wants you to perceive, you can reverse or invert the artist's expectations. Instead of gin pouring down from above, think of the gin stream flowing upward to just below the letter *p* (a meaningful letter) in *pour*.

A formidable, erect, male genital has been embedded into the gin stream (fig. 31). Of course, alcoholic beverage ads never inform gullible consumers that anyone who drinks enough gin becomes incapable of such an erection. Ad fantasies aside, alcohol is probably the most powerful enemy of sex humans have yet invented. Alcoholic beverages are widely consumed to avoid sexual intimacy. Alcoholic fantasies conceal absurd, pathetic, and most destructive realities.

In addition to the erect penis, one of the screaming faces frequently embedded in alcohol ads appears in the green emerald triangle, just below the gin stream (fig. 30). The face, presumably, depicts the emotional state of another satisfied Tanqueray consumer. Below the triangle appears a lion's head, the king of beasts who for centuries has symbolized sexual endurance and power. This ad was designed for people who are convinced they think for themselves, but cannot distinguish between fantasy and reality.

Should anyone still believe there are things the ad media will not do in support of alcohol consumption—a dangerous, addictive drug responsible for numerous illnesses and deaths—the Tanqueray ad demonstrates avaricious trickery at its worst.

Betty Crocker Is Super Moist

Super Moist cake mixes are Betty Crocker products of the General Mills Corporation of Minneapolis. The two-page "*MMMMMMMMM Moister*" ad (fig. 6) appeared in national periodicals, including *Reader's Digest*, *TV Guide*, and various women's magazines. This four-color ad involved at least a $5 million investment in publishing space. Reading time would be one or two seconds. In tests, one in eight readers paused to ponder the copy. People who read ads are like money in the bank to advertisers, but they are not really necessary. These few readers may consciously reflect upon the secondary head, "There have been moist layer cakes before. But now there's Super Moist!" The copy advises, quite factually as it turns out, that the preparation "has a special pudding in the mix to make it unbelievably moist." Unbelievably? Yes! But that comes later.

There is something dissonant about the slice of cake on the fork. Dissonance, something illogical, appears in many ads. It seems to act as a priming device for subliminal content, setting up the unconscious mentation system for a more profound message—all quite invisible to conscious perception. Look at the slice of cake. Either that slice is the size of a postage stamp or the fork is the size of a hay fork. You cannot have it both ways.

The Betty Crocker ad is a painting that probably represents over a $30,000 investment in art production. Logically, the artist should have constructed the fork and the cake in a reasonably proportionate relationship. The dissonance was intentional. The only other conclusion suggests gross incompetence by the executives who invested all that money in a defective ad.

By this time, the reader has strained painfully over the cake mix ad, trying to find out what is hidden in the picture. Most will discover nothing exciting, only the obvious. Don't strain! Relax! Let your eyes play over the picture. Remember, nothing was really hidden by the artist. Readers hide (repress) taboo information from themselves. At some level of knowing, you already know what lies perceptually repressed in the ad.

Considerable skill was involved in painting the cake, although the artist expected that none of the tens of millions of consumers who saw the ad would consciously deal with reality. This is an art of *concealment*, where viewers predictably conceal from conscious awareness, rather than an art of *exposition*. The contents of the ad are banal—little here of intellectual challenge at the conscious level. From what lies on the perceptual surface, it is impossible to justify the millions of dollars invested.

Notice casually, do not strain, what has been sculptured into the icing on the cake (fig. 32). Any standard anatomy text will confirm that the shape painted into the icing is an accurate tumescent female genital. "Super Moist," at the portrayed state of excitation, constitutes a normal physiological event.

Curiously, male genitalia in ads are usually directed to male audiences. Female genitalia are directed toward females. By conventional logic, it should be the other way around. But genital embedding appears to be most effective when arousing, unconsciously, powerful taboo associations. The modus operandi appeals to latent homosexuality, guilt, and fear of taboo violation. The chocolate icing on the cake makes the old ethnic stereotype of Aunt Jemima appear a tempest in a teapot. The promise of Betty Crocker is really the icing on the cake.

Double Entendre

Double entendre, or double meaning, is frequently used in the fine art of persuasion. "The most carefully-poured Scotch in the world," by Chivas Regal (fig. 7) is a typical example. A man's hands tenderly pour Chivas into the glass—hardly subject matter to thrill the critical perceptions of affluent, well-educated readers. The ad is a composite painting, complex, expensive, and time-consuming to manufacture. The glass, ice cubes, bottle, pouring whiskey, and hands have been painted separately and assembled. Notice the discrepancy in the sizes of the hands and the bottle. Think a moment about the act of pouring whiskey from a bottle. Have you ever watched anyone pour with their hands in this position? The only thing held this way is a penis while standing before a urinal. The most tenderly poured Scotch, indeed. This Chivas ad appeared in such magazines as *Playboy*, *Time*, *U.S. News & World Report*, *Newsweek*, etc.—a multimillion-dollar corporate investment in alcohol marketing.

In another example of double entendre, where double-talk embeds within double-talk, the American Association of Advertising Agencies published a black-and-white flyer in the spring of 1986 (fig. 8). AAAA, a national propaganda lobby, had long been troubled over growing public awareness of subliminal advertising, and the ad was designed to dismiss the issue. The ad also implied support for alcoholic-beverage advertising, presently under attack by U.S. federal and state legislators, the American Medical Association, the National Institute of Alcohol Abuse and Addiction, the National Institutes of Health, and numerous other groups. The AAAA ad copy alleged "that since 1957 people have tried to find breasts in the ice cubes." The copy continued, "if you really searched you probably could see the breasts. For that matter, you could also see Millard Fillmore, a stuffed pork chop and a 1946 Dodge. So-called subliminal advertising," the ad concluded, "simply doesn't exist. Overactive imaginations, however, most certainly do. If anyone claims to see breasts, they're in the eyes of the beholder." The subhead is particularly interesting: "ADVERTISING; ANOTHER WORD FOR FREEDOM OF CHOICE."

AAAA mailed thousands of these posters to U.S. universities in an attempt to quash concerns over subliminal advertising. Subliminal perception is validated by over 500 published scientific papers (*see* Dixon, *Subliminal Perception*). Researchers have affirmed the effects of subliminal stimuli upon ten measurable areas of human behavior. One of these is *purchasing behavior*, a subject well researched by the ad industry.

Careful analysis failed, as the AAAA promised, to find female breasts, Millard Fillmore, a stuffed pork chop, and a 1946 Dodge in the expensive painting. Nevertheless, a collection of grotesque faces, animals, a shark, and other bizarre imagery was discovered, some of them anamorphic (figs. 33–37), and an erect penis (fig. 38). The painted cocktail was so exhaustively embedded it easily qualifies under the U.S. Treasury Department's new ATF rulings (*see* Appendix), which prohibit subliminals in alcohol advertising. The original painting was, apparently, reduced from color to black-and-white, and some of the subtle details are obscured. Nevertheless, the logic is classic Madison Avenue. *Trust us! We wouldn't lie to you!*—even though that is precisely what they do for a living.

A simple photograph of ice cubes, including a cherry, could be produced for several hundred dollars. A sophisticated painting such as the AAAA ad is very expensive, and the consumer absorbs the costs—in more ways than one. Advertisers could not justify the initial investment if subliminals did not enhance sales, increasing both consumers and consumption. And, increased alcohol consumption directly parallels increased alcohol-related pathology—correlations discovered by World Health Organization research in a dozen nations.

Double entendre audio is also widespread. As with the visual examples, double meanings appear to enrich significance in virtually any symbolic stimuli. Michael Jackson's rock-music extravaganza *Thriller* reportedly sold some 22 million copies. The album spawned a number of rock videos that advertised the record album.

The "Beat It!" scenario is disarmingly simple. A group of young men (women are completely absent) enter a large room. They are aggressive, uptight, angry, looking for a fight. Two begin a knife fight, their combat crudely choreographed as a ballet. Michael Jackson bravely intercedes. They finally put away their knives and everyone then participates in a precision dance routine, Jackson leading the chorus. The lyric "Beat it!" repeats over and over. There appeared only one other recognizable line in the lyric, "No one wants to beat it!" The voices are loud, hysterical, screaming, led by the high-pitched, effeminate voice of Michael Jackson.

Roughly 300 university students were asked how many times they had listened to "Beat It!" Of the 97% who had heard the song: 28% had heard it from 1 to 25 times; 21% from 26 to 50 times; 26% from 51 to 100 times; and 25% over 100 times. The 51% of students who had heard "Beat It!" over fifty times were considered aficionados and used for further testing. If anything was significant about "Beat It!" they appeared most likely to know. On an anonymous questionnaire, half the aficionados confessed they had no idea what the title "Beat It!" meant. The remainder attempted to rationalize the title as, "the music beat or rhythm," "beat up or fight with someone," "we're beating it or them (getting away with something)," "putting it or them down (criticizing)," or "beat the system."

Poorly Kept Secrets

For the past fifty years, "beat it" has been a euphemism for male masturbation. Not one of the aficionados (roughly one-third female and two-thirds male) mentioned sexual implications about "Beat It!" The survey was repeated several times with similar results. The students had repressed, or hidden from conscious awareness, the reality of "Beat It!" Michael Jackson's megahit portrayed young men at a group homosexual masturbation session. The group was beating it, letting loose tensions: when the choreography is viewed in slow motion, each time the dancers pass their right hands across their genital areas their hands jerk in perfect unison.

When someone does not consciously know something they should reasonably be expected to know, it is usually significant. Young people tend to be secretive about masturbation. The carefully kept secret, however, is well known to everyone.

The writer, director, choreographer, composer, photographers, musicians, and performers in "Beat It!" consciously had to know what they were doing in the costly rock-video production. They also had to predict (accurately) that audiences would not consciously deal with the group jack-off, would repress reality. Unconsciously perceived information of this taboo nature ensures a deep, meaningful emotional response, and continued memory. During the survey, once the subject of *group homosexual masturbation* became consciously perceived, the students appeared almost unanimously turned off to the recording. Many commented they felt nauseous when they thought of it.

Tachistoscopic Displays

Patented in 1962 by Dr. Hal Becker, a Tulane University Medical School professor, the high-speed tachistoscope is a flashing projector used with a cine screen or light box to flash words and pictures at high speeds. Several researchers found $1/3000$ second most effective with audiences. Although a small percentage of people can consciously perceive tachistoscopic flashes at this speed, most people see them only subliminally.

Tachistoscopic projection is rarely used commercially. The high-speed flashes cannot be edited into film or videotape. Tachistoscopes were useful in early experiments with subliminal stimuli (*see* Key, *Subliminal Seduction*, pp. 22–23) and are still occasionally involved in psychiatric experiments (*see* Key, *The Clam-Plate Orgy*, pp. 101–2) and for ad-copy testing. Visual recognition varies at different speeds in relation to content. Conscious recognition appears slower for some content than for others. Emotional words, for example, were more resistant to conscious awareness than were neutral words (*see* Dixon, *Subliminal Perception*, pp. 167–69). Ad designers often use tachistoscopes to determine how far they can safely go with subliminal taboo themes.

Slower tachistoscopes have been heavily used for many years. They operate much like a camera shutter—from $\frac{1}{10}$ to $\frac{1}{150}$ second—with slower flashes that are consciously apparent. During World War II, tachistoscopes were used in military training for airplane, ship, tank, and weapon identification. The device is also widely used in foreign-language courses for vocabulary development.

Slow tachistoscopic cuts *can* be edited into film or videotape, and are extensively used in commercials and dramatic productions. They produce *quick cuts*, also called *metacontrast* or *backward masking*. Quick cuts are consciously visible but are masked by the next quick cut or attention-diverting continuity. Masked cuts are subliminal because they cannot be recalled, but their information will have a lingering effect upon audience perception, not unlike post-hypnotic suggestion.

Visually, for example, metacontrast can be used to intensify foreboding, tension, fear, or even humor and laughter. The quick cut, followed by a diversion, plants an emotional predisposition or feeling without the audience being aware of precisely why they experience that emotion. Metacontrast is frequently utilized in motion pictures, video dramas, and TV commercials. Particularly watch pharmaceutical and soft-drink commercials. Rock video has turned metacontrast manipulation into an art form.

Reaction shots, in which actors react to the speech or actions of others, offer a host of possibilities with which to manipulate audiences. Reaction shots are rarely recalled, though they were consciously perceived. Audiences unconsciously identify with the reaction shots more strongly than with the actual speech or actions.

Low-Intensity Light and
Low-Volume Sound

More effective than tachistoscopic displays is low-intensity light and, its audio counterpart, low-volume sound. Several years ago, a Coca-Cola research executive explained how to make a subliminal induction device far more effective, cheaper, and more difficult to detect than a tachistoscope (*see* Key, *Subliminal Seduction*, p. 23). He wired a rheostat into the light cord of a slide projector. Once a slide was projected over a motion picture, light could be reduced to a level just below where the slide image was consciously apparent. Numerous experiments were also conducted at subliminal projection levels one candlepower above the ambient light in a room (*see* Key, *The Clam-Plate Orgy*, pp. 100–102). These early experiments were primitive compared with subliminal techniques developed later.

Very little photography is published in media without retouch work. Relax and focus visually upon a particular area of a face, scanning irregularities in skin tones, or backgrounds. After roughly ten seconds of relaxation, leisurely scan, allowing the eyes to wander in their own direction. One of the three letters *S, E,* or *X* will appear. When one of the letters appears, look sequentially for the other two. With a little practice at relaxed perceptual probing, anyone can soon consciously perceive dozens of *SEX*es embedded in the illustrations. These are low-intensity light embeds, the same technique used in film or video tape. Subliminal stimuli can be embedded in artwork through several techniques—engraving, airbrush retouch, or doctored film emulsions. *SEX*es can be embedded individually or in a mosaic pattern with stripped-in fine dot screens used on one or more of the color separations in film emulsion or engraved plates.

Many letter combinations convey the idea of *SEX*. Quite often, the *SEX* may not include all three letters. Abbreviations such as

SE, ZX, XE, EX, or names such as *NEXSON* or *EXXON* appear. Subliminal *SEX*, however, probably has little to do with girl-in-a-bikini *SEX*. Advertisers have indiscriminately sexualized virtually everything they publish or broadcast with subliminal *SEX*es. In the Betty Crocker "*MMMMMM* Moister" ad (fig. 6), several *SEX*es are lightly painted into the cake texture, and *SEX*es appear in the Seagram's Crown Royal (fig. 15) painted background.

With perceptual systems constantly under bombardment, individuals may have difficulty learning relaxed perception. The experience can be frustrating, which makes it even more difficult. Human perception becomes more inhibited as physiological tensions increase. Tension increases as humans become more susceptible to subliminal persuasion. The threshold—an imaginary line that divides conscious and unconscious perception—elevates in response to tension and anxiety; it lowers, and more information becomes consciously available, as tensions decrease and individuals become more relaxed.

If Looks Could Kill

A chilling example of subliminal embedding appeared on the April 21, 1986, cover of *Time* magazine—"Target Gaddafi" (fig. 9). Signed by an artist named Hirsch, the acrylic painting portrayed a stern, foreboding Muammar Gaddafi, described in the cover story as "Obsessed by a Ruthless, Messianic Vision." Much of the cover story had been researched and written in anticipation of the U.S. attack on Libya, the issue appearing on newsstands throughout the world a week after the April 14th air strikes against Tripoli and Benghazi.

A magazine cover is an ad for the publication. It has one function—to sell. *Time* covers, like other periodical covers, are embedded with subliminal information, readily perceivable to anyone familiar with the techniques. Every so often, however, merchandising zeal overwhelms discretion.

Just above Gaddafi's left eye (fig. 39) appears an obvious, clearly defined, large *X*. Starting under the right eyebrow next to the nose, the *S* extends upward across the forehead almost to the hairline. The *S* is interrupted by the white, overprinted *I* in *Gaddafi*.

The letter *E* appears obscure at first, but can be perceived after a few seconds of relaxed viewing. The horizontal bottom line of the *E* blends into the top right edge of the left eyebrow. In addition, numerous small *SEX*es appear embedded throughout.

Whose SEX Is Largest?

The *Time* cover portrait of the Ayatollah Khomeini on the November 26, 1979 issue, during the Iranian hostage crisis, was similarly embedded. A large *SEX* was lightly airbrushed across the forehead of the Iranian leader's portrait. The cover included a small inset photograph of then President Jimmy Carter. Numerous small *SEX* embeds very lightly appeared across Carter's face. The acrylic painting portrayed Khomeini as dark, powerful, and threatening. By comparison, Carter's expression is grim, tight-lipped, and defensive. Strong lighting on Carter's photo made him appear pale, even sickly. It is safe to assume the Khomeini *Time* cover sold well, especially among those readers convinced Carter was a passive blunderer. The Ayatollah Khomeini's *SEX* was much larger, far more formidable than the smaller, unimposing *SEX*es of the president.

The Gaddafi cover went beyond the simplistic subliminal comparison of one leader's *SEX* against the other's. The word *KILL*, in large capital letters, was embedded across Gaddafi's right cheek. Once consciously perceived, the four-letter word stands out like the fabled sore thumb.

Subliminal embedding initiates extremely subtle, powerful effects. Norman Dixon, the British experimental psychologist, commented, "It may be impossible to resist instructions which are not consciously experienced." Several students who had not read the Gaddafi cover issue were individually hypnotized by this author. Each was shown the cover and asked to carefully examine the portrait details before they were hypnotized. Under hypnosis, subjects are perceptually very sensitive. In the trance, they were asked to open their eyes and again study the portrait. The students were then awakened and asked, "What is Gaddafi thinking about?" They each replied without hesitation, "Kill!" One student first said "Revenge!"; her second choice was "Kill!" She reported that

"Kill" had actually been her first choice but that she rejected it as too farfetched and overdramatic.

In October 1986, six months after the April attack on Libya, *Washington Post* journalist Bob Woodward obtained a copy of a seven-page memorandum from the U.S. Department of State's Office of Intelligence and Research. The classified memo proposed that "a sequenced chain of real and illusory events might generate enough pressure to make Gaddafi believe his aides disloyal, that there was strong opposition to him internally in Libya, and that U.S. forces were about to launch another attack upon Libya (*see* Woodward, *Veil*, pp. 471–77). The plan was to provoke Gaddafi into actions that might cause his assassination.

The disinformation campaign against Gaddafi was supported by CIA Director William J. Casey, Vincent M. Cannistraro, a veteran CIA operations officer and director of intelligence on the NSC staff, Howard R. Teicher, director of the Office of Political-Military Affairs in the NSC, and White House National Security Affairs Adviser John M. Poindexter, later fired by President Reagan for his lies and misconduct in the Iran-Contra affair. Senior representatives from the CIA, State Department, and White House had endorsed the plan on August 7 at 4:30 P.M. in a White House Situation Room meeting.

Secretary of State George P. Shultz first admitted, then later denied, that he approved of putting out misleading information to confuse Gaddafi and the U.S. public. Other Reagan administration officials averred that the disinformation campaign was intended only to mislead foreign journalists, not Americans. Nevertheless, for two months U.S. news publications widely published and broadcast the fake stories, which quoted unnamed administration sources asserting Libya and the U.S. were again on a "collision course," elaborated upon the instability of Gaddafi's regime, and claimed the U.S. planned joint action with France to expel Libyan forces from Chad. When the State Department memo surfaced in early October, President Reagan strongly denied such a plan was approved. "We are not telling lies," he said, "or doing any of these disinformation things we were cited with doing." The president's casual honesty and direct eye contact reiterated, *Trust me, I wouldn't lie to you!*

Whether *Time*'s April cover stemmed simply from the desire

for increased circulation and ad revenue or from cooperation with the government is irrelevant. The cover's effect was to increase the emotional support of *Time*'s readers (some 25 million) for the attack upon Libya. Specific factual justifications for the military action were promised by Reagan, but never released. As justification for the attack on Libya, U.S. administration spokesmen named Gaddafi instigator of an April 5th discotheque bombing in West Berlin in which a U.S. serviceman was killed and numerous others injured. Months later, the discotheque bombing was attributed to a Syrian-based terrorist group. Once sufficient hysteria was generated, virtually any military act appeared justified. But then, the U.S. population has been taught to think it thinks for itself.

In the United States, news information is sold, merchandised, and manipulated in support of commercial and corporate interests. The validity of such public information should have been questioned long ago. Legislative committees could subpoena the artist and editorial executives who manufactured, supervised, purchased, and published the Gaddafi cover if they wished to know more about media manipulations of public opinion.

Dr. Hal Becker, who patented the high-speed tachistoscope, manufactures and sells audio processors that insert subliminal messages into music sound tracks. His Mark III-B Programmable Subliminal Audio Processor monitors and rectifies the changing volume of the consciously audible signal. Through an electronic analog multiplier, the rectified audible signal controls the subliminal input's low-volume level. Audible and subliminal signals are then mixed. Dr. Becker explained that the subliminal input so closely parallels the volume changes in the audible music that it would be impossible to prove the message contained subliminal information.

Similarly, Becker's Mark III Video Subliminal Processor inserts videotaped subliminal imagery into a standard video microwave signal. The subliminal video is set at a candlepower level slightly above the consciously apparent picture. Subliminal input may be words, phrases, silhouettes, half-tone black-and-white or color pictures, or combinations of all of them. This author observed the video processor in Becker's laboratory. It was ingenious. Dr. Becker inserted a videotape with subliminals into regular video transmissions going into his receiver. He could elevate the subliminal picture so it could be consciously perceived, then fade it down into the lights, shadows, and color blends and separations of the standard broadcast signal.

While watching the demonstration, I was troubled by unsettling thoughts about how easily the U.S. could insert such material via satellite into Soviet network TV. And, in turn, how the Soviets could subliminally hype U.S. TV, perhaps injecting lively thoughts into the banality of situation comedies or talk shows.

Becker sells his audio processor for subliminal antitheft indoctrination in supermarkets and department stores. The system reduced theft roughly 40% in one large supermarket chain, which also experienced a related 60% reduction in annual employee turnover. Becker successfully reduced workman's compensation claims via subliminal safety indoctrination. His antitheft program significantly reduced in-store arrests. After eight months, one store manager reported a complete turnaround in cashier shortages, staff turnovers, and negative employee attitudes, and was able to reduce stock handlers by 50% while maintaining the same level of efficiency. Cashier shortages dropped from an average $125 weekly to less than $10. Customer complaints about cashiers virtually disappeared. Merchandise damaged by stock handlers was down one-third. Pilferage dropped from $50,000 every six months to less than $13,000. In another supermarket chain, employee turnover dropped one-half during eleven months.

Becker also designs subliminal programs for physician and hospital waiting rooms. They reduced patient steam-ups (60% in one study), fainting from needle insertions (to nearly zero), and smoking (by 50% to 70%). He successfully operated a weight-control clinic in New Orleans for over a decade, in which subliminally embedded videotapes reinforced a rigorous diet program. The program, recognized by the New Orleans Medical Association, received most patients through physician referral. Becker emphasized he has not used subliminal technology in advertising, politics, or religion. His equipment is available only to qualified professionals through restrictive-use covenants. Becker believes subliminal indoctrination could reduce motor vehicle accidents, crime, and substance abuse, with great potential in therapy, education, and training. Not everyone, however, is convinced.

Becker appears genuinely concerned about the ethics of subliminal persuasion. But there is a paradox involved. If you tell someone they will be exposed to subliminals, the effectiveness is impaired. If you do not tell them, you may have violated legal and ethical rights under the Constitution (*see* Goodkin and Phillips). The discussion of ethics may be academic, since the advertising industry has intensively indoctrinated consumers subliminally for over half a century. Ad violations have consistently been ignored by the federal government; perhaps worse, the population has passively permitted the subliminal indoctrination to continue. As the *Christian Science Monitor* has said of Becker's inventions, "The real threat in a free society is that such attempts at thought control— or behavioral modification, as its promotors call it—would be tolerated at all. . . . This technique is an invasion of thinking. It could easily be put to political or oppressive purposes."

Security Through Subliminals

Another entrepreneur who has developed behavior modification systems is David Tyler, president of Proactive Systems of Portland, Oregon. Tyler's subliminal tapes adjust low-volume sound levels to changes in room noise levels. Proactive Systems, Inc., is primarily involved in theft-prevention. Tyler perceives himself as a social benefactor, preventing customers from being arrested for theft, employees from being entrapped and fired, and store owners from losing the present five cents of every retail dollar to theft. Tyler even envisions lower prices after subliminal indoctrination makes everyone honest—a worthy, though unlikely, goal. Like McDonald's, "He Does It All for Us!"

Proactive Systems, Inc., has also developed subliminal indoctrination for self-esteem enhancement, pain management in cardiac recovery rooms after open-heart surgery, stress management in stockbrokerage firms and a chemical company, and a tranquilizing program for a children's hyperactivity clinic. Proactive claims their installations, most on the West Coast, produce an average reduction in theft of 50% in department, clothing, grocery, and drug stores. Dr. Becker estimated in 1984 that there were probably around 300 such store installations in the U.S. Tyler insists he requires full public disclosure from clients, except in theft prevention.

Another entrepreneurial scheme to exploit subliminal persuasion technology was developed by Stimutech, Inc., of East Lansing, Michigan. Their marketing executives discovered millions of home computers were stored in attics and garages. The computers had been heavily merchandised, possibly with subliminals, and millions of families had invested in them, convinced that they were indispensable to an up-to-date household. After a few months of steadily decreasing use, most families discovered what the merchandisers had known from the beginning: home computers are expensive and, except as toys, useless in the home. After the media-hyped initial enthusiasm waned, home computers ended up in storage (they were too expensive to discard). Their owners made up one of the most ideal markets conceivable. By the time they had stored their computers in the garage for a year, they felt stupid, embarrassed, and defensive, receptive to any new product that would vindicate the investment.

Stimutech's Expando-Vision is a computer-video system that flashes subliminal messages to the subconscious. Only a small investment ($89.95 for an Electronic Interface Device) connects the idle computer to a TV set; the computer then controls the light and speed intensity of the inserted messages, holding them at subliminal levels. Subliminal videotapes are inserted into the E.I.D. Stimutech began its marketing program with eight videotapes: weight control/exercise, smoking control/calm nerves, stress control/positive thinking, drinking control/responsibility, athletic confidence/golf, study habits/memory power, career/success motivation, and, the ultimate tape for males beseiged by ERA and the masturbatory manipulations of men's magazines, sexual confidence.

Expando-Vision, like other simple answers to complicated questions, will probably work on *some* people, *some*times, under *some* conditions. The variable *some* is, of course, unknowable and extremely complex. Expando-Vision, apparently, worked profitably for the promoters. Beyond that lies enormous uncertainty. Some people quit smoking and, in an unconscious search for a replacement addiction, end up alcoholics or compulsive eaters. To achieve significant change in compulsive behaviors, physicians or licensed psychologists should be consulted, perhaps those skilled in clinical hypnosis. The objective of most therapy is to increase an individual's will power, autonomy, and sense of responsibility, not to provide an electronic crutch that may conceal critical symptoms.

Anorexia nervosa and bulimia are severe, often fatal eating disorders. They involve perceptual reality distortions. Individuals perceive themselves obese, even when they approach death by self-starvation. These are among the illnesses where media hype, subliminal ad indoctrination, and cultural manipulations about the desirability of thin bodies appear as powerful causative factors. Should an anorexia nervosa patient acquire a subliminally embedded weight-reduction tape, the result could be terminal.

Something to Sell

Both Becker and Tyler testified during a House Committee on Science and Technology hearing chaired by Rep. Dan Glickman that they did not believe subliminals could be effectively utilized in advertising—in direct contradiction to the wide range of applications they cited for their commercial gadgetry. Though this author's writings were referred to abundantly in written submissions to the committee, the use of subliminal technology in ads and commercial media was ignored during the seven hours of testimony.

Becker and Tyler diligently rationalized their use of subliminal stimuli. Becker claimed there has been no proven case of significant harm to anyone from subliminals. Dr. Charles Kamp of the Federal Communications Commission testified there is doubt among scientists that subliminal techniques are effective. He further emphasized that the FCC had not received a complaint for years. From 1966, he added, complaints about subliminals were no more than one-half of 1% of all complaints. Becker, curiously, reported he was not at liberty to discuss Defense Department research on subliminal persuasion.

Dr. Howard Shevrin, a University of Michigan Medical School psychologist, cited the work of Soviet experimenters who have developed a reliable lie-detection technique utilizing subliminal

EEG response within milliseconds of an exposure to stimuli (*see* Kostandov and Arzumanov). New York University psychologist Dr. Lloyd Silverman testified in considerable detail about successful therapeutic experiments with subliminal stimuli. Both Shevrin and Silverman are highly respected medical experimenters who have worked with subliminal phenomena over the past twenty-five years. They told the committee they would oppose as potentially dangerous the commercial applications offered by Becker and Tyler. Neither Shevrin nor Silverman mentioned ad-media applications of subliminal technology. Shevrin, however, compared the social consequences of subliminal persuasion to the discovery of nuclear weapons.

Congressman Glickman repeatedly asked about subliminals in advertising. The question was denied or sidestepped by each witness. Glickman finally concluded, "It [subliminal persuasion] is obviously not in widespread use today in commercial sectors of our economy, according to the testimony we have heard" (U.S. House of Representatives, p. 134).

The hearing was an interesting exercise in how to simultaneously investigate and not investigate an issue. It would be intriguing to know if agreements were made as to what would and would not be discussed. The omission of advertising was far too complete to be convincingly accidental.

Lighting and Background Sound

Two essential film and video production elements not consciously perceived by audiences are lighting and sound backgrounds. Both are carefully structured to engineer response to action and dialogue. Both are usually supportive or reinforcing to the consciously perceived material in a scene. Whenever lighting or sound backgrounds intrude into conscious awareness, they become distractions and detract from the collective perception.

Film or video sound without background sound or music seems emotionally flat and painfully slow-paced. Even on locations, it is usually difficult to obtain the precise background sound mix appropriate to a particular scene. Sound must be manufactured to order. Background sound is usually assembled in layers. Generic street sound may involve an aggregate of indistinct peripheral conversations, children playing, auto-bus-streetcar traffic, bird chirpings, distant thunder, footsteps, wind, distant sounds such as ships, foghorn, and police, fire, or ambulance sirens. These sound layers are usually recorded separately and mixed. A wide variety of sound dimensions—intensities, speeds, interrelationships, and tonal qualities—can be manufactured to fit a scene. The layers are mixed to a precise illusion of reality, or more correctly, audience expectations of reality. If well constructed, the illusion is more emotionally satisfying than would be the actual reality, but remains subliminal throughout.

Once the background sound mix is created for a scene, music may be integrated for dramatic emphasis, suspense, or emotional audience priming for a developing action. Silences are also a dimension of sound. There are dozens of distinct electronic silences, each producing a definable audience response. Sounds and silences can be alternated for an extensive array of audience effects. None of this, if well constructed, will ever be consciously considered by audiences.

Lighting in film or video is another of the powerful subliminal effects constructed into the media illusion of reality. As with sound, the audience remains unaware that lighting has been constructed. Maris Janson shared an Oscar for his work in lighting the movie *Chariots of Fire*. It was a difficult job because much of the film was shot outdoors. Natural lighting is rarely consistent, not to mention rarely exactly what scenes require. Janson controlled audience mood, emotion, tension, tranquillity, and anxiety with lighting technology he described as subliminal. The most difficult problem, he explained, was to prevent the lighting from intruding on audience awareness, which would ruin its effect. Janson modified audience-perceived meanings, significance, and emotional reactions through subtle lighting changes; for example, a consciously unnoticed shadow crossing an actor's face can prime the audience to expect a dramatic interlude.

Shadow lengths and subtle shadings of light and dark unconsciously manage emotional intensities. They can establish time order in a scene, or create feelings about a character who is lit differently than others. Backgrounds are lit unevenly to intensify depth illusions or action sequences. Every minute portion of a scene, as recorded on camera, is carefully studied for appropriate lighting. Foreground and background lighting can be integrated with backlighting and key lighting for a variety of effects.

Lighting, like sound, is constructed to provide audiences with credible illusions. If well engineered, the fantasy of reality appears far more real than actual reality. Fantasy (engineered perception) becomes more attractive, desirable, emotionally engaging, and meaningful than reality (unmanipulated perception).

The black-and-white, light and shadow, "Body by Soloflex" ads (figs. 10, 11, and 12) recently appeared as a series in a variety of national periodicals such as *Time*, *Newsweek*, and *GQ*. Market research discovered that in the New York male homosexual community, the ads became poster icons. They were framed and prominently displayed in apartments. Apparently, Soloflex focused their ad campaign upon men with strong latent homosexual tendencies. As the overt male homosexual community is believed to be less than 10% of the population, the expensive ads could not have been justified if directed only at this limited audience.

In the first ad (fig. 10), a young man takes off his undershirt. Half the model's face is in shadow, suggesting something about him is hidden. A rather ominous shadow, just left of the model's navel, emanates from above the top of his designer jeans, in the shape of a large, erect male genital. The shadow has been airbrushed into the artwork. What male could resist the promise of Soloflex?

The second ad (fig. 11) shows another young model standing with his left thumb hooked in a pocket. The thumb is often used as a phallic symbol in art, in this case passive and waiting. His eyes are hidden from the viewer by sunglasses. In Western cultures, hidden eyes usually imply hidden thoughts. On this model's abdomen, growing out of his trousers just above the belt buckle, appear two large erect genitals, deftly airbrushed into the photograph. Apparently, after six months of Soloflex, men are promised two prodigious penises. The promise of Soloflex appears unlimited, especially for sexually harassed American males who can never live up to media's expectations.

"No Pain, No Gain," is the copy line for the third Soloflex ad

33

(fig. 12). A young man sits on an exercise bench in shorts, legs widely spread to expose the genital area. The model's left shoulder is strangely discolored, as though burn-scarred, disfigured. Similarly, airbrushed in, in the shoulder just above the armpit, is a slit (fig. 40). The shoulder, viewed out of context, looks like the buttocks and anal opening, adding new significance to "No Pain, No Gain." Soloflex has utilized similiar sex-role ambiguities in their TV advertising.

2 | HOW TO GET INSIDE THE OPEN MIND — UNDETECTED

Nothing can be brought to an end in the unconscious. Nothing is past or forgotten.

Sigmund Freud, *The Interpretation of Dreams*

If you do not specify and confront real issues, what you say will surely obscure them. If you do not alarm anyone morally, you yourself remain morally asleep. If you do not embody controversy, what you say will be an acceptance of the drift of the coming human hell.

C. Wright Mills, *The Power Elite*

Hypocrisy which takes the form of a denial of hypocrisy is *hypocrisy squared*.

Lionel Rubinoff, *The Pornography of Power*

The effects of subliminal stimuli have been verified on at least ten measurable areas of human behavior. British psychologist Norman Dixon, in evaluations of over 500 scientific studies, concluded, "behavior can be determined by external events over which we can affect no [conscious] control" (Dixon, *Subliminal Perception*, p. 322). The ten areas of behavior are:

1. Dreams
2. Memory
3. Conscious Perception
4. Emotional Response
5. Drive-Related Behavior
6. Perceptual Threshold
7. Verbal Behavior
8. Adaptation Levels or Judgmental Values
9. Purchasing Behavior
10. Psychopathology

Validating studies published over the past sixty years on these ten measurable effects were summarized in my three earlier books. Avoiding a review of this basic information, this chapter only updates current developments.

In the cultural grip of media, modern societies blindly stumble from one crisis or disaster to another with the fantasized conviction that they know *what* they are doing, *where* they are going, *how* they will survive, *who* is in control, and *why* everything works or does not work as it should. These unconsciously reinforced fantasies actually threaten survival.

The list of subliminal effects powerfully demonstrates that humans can be programmed into almost any group perceptual construction or cultural perspective (synonymous concepts) by those who control media. Group behavior is measurable and believed predictable in terms of statistical probabilities. Media provide the system through which economic markets are controlled. Not everyone in any given culture is controllable. Humans become most vulnerable when the battle of beliefs supports basic cultural indoctrinations. Limiting factors at present are motivation, time, and money—not technology. Highly developed technologies of human engineering, propaganda, and mind control have been available for many years. Technological refinements and innovations continue to proliferate.

Population segments most susceptible to media management usually think they think independently, critically, clearly, and can readily discriminate between truth and falsity, reality and fantasy. The self-perception of autonomy is a basic indocrinational priming tool. Humans who think they think for themselves often do not. The better primed by cultural values, the more vulnerable to manipulation.

Bucking the System

There will be dissidents, disbelievers, deviants, heretics, subversives, and critics who struggle against mainstream conditioning for a variety of reasons. They are very important to the survival and growth of any cultural system. Deviant minorities may try to understand the mechanisms of perceptual construction and attempt to change the system. They may even openly oppose primary cultural systems. Like the sophists, however, they will eventually be discredited by the majority and its power elite.

Perception, not the labels used to describe the nonverbal perceptual process, cannot be divided into simplistic categories such as conscious (cognitive) and unconscious (subliminal). Conscious-unconscious must be viewed on a scale of more-or-less, rather than either-or. Perception, as it affects the brain and body, is totally integrated. All portions of the brain interconnect with all parts of the body. Body and mind are inextricable. A physical condition influences perception and vice versa. Perception (information flow from the senses into the brain) can be described as instantaneous and total. No one, however, knows how the brain functions; this knowledge may, indeed, be unknowable. There are only theories—hundreds of them. Theories are not truths. They must be useful only in some context to justify their existence.

Logic, reason, feelings, and conscious and unconscious motives flow in an endless stream both from memory and from the sensory inputs. The brain also manufactures or conditions perceptions independently of perceived realities. Conscious awareness appears a minute fragment of what is available in the memory. Sensory bias consciously shifts from one experience to another, one perception to another. Were this focus—consciousness or cognitive awareness—not possible, countless perceptual distractions would cause confusion and overwhelm attention.

The *subliminal*, the *unconscious*, or whatever anyone wishes to call it, appears to function as a culture machine. It is the repository of more-or-less basic, enduring belief and attitude systems, cultural values, predispositions, and basic assumptions. By comparison, *opinions* are consciously available, transitory, and superficial. Programmed from infancy with basic assumptions, unconsciously supported ideas are usually taken for granted. When assumptions surface, they should always be questioned. Unfortunately, formal education in most cultural systems concentrates on acceptance (fitting in with the majority's basic assumptions rather than questioning them). Few ever achieved the Ph.D. by questioning the system that grants Ph.D.s.

Instinctual or inherited predispositions for certain behaviors also appear to underly human relationships. These predispositions integrate invisibly into culture-language systems. Innate behaviors in humans often surface in unconscious, basic assumptions and biases. Nobel Laureate Konrad Lorenz (*Civilized Man's Eight Deadly Sins*, pp. 76–78) included among inherited behaviors the *sense of justice* (genetically anchored reactions against asocial behaviors), *morality* (mechanisms that inhibit species nonsurvival behaviors), and *altruism* (willingness to self-sacrifice on behalf of family or society).

To this list, Harvard sociobiologist Edward Wilson (*see* Wilson, p. 552) adds male dominance systems, scaling of responses in aggressive interactions, prolonged maternal care with socialization of the young, and matrilineal family organization. Several genetically acquired traits unique to humans include complex language, elaborate cultures, sexual activity continuous through menstrual cycles, formalized incest taboos, marriage exchange rules with recognition of kinship networks, and cooperative labor division between males and females. Wilson concluded that such inherited traits as a sense of *justice, morality*, and *altruism* can disappear from populations in as few as ten generations, only two or three centuries.

Conditioning of the human unconscious through available technology can, over a relatively brief period, reorganize, change, or diminish inherited predispositions. Such changes were observable in the total propaganda environment of Nazi Germany with comparatively primitive technology. The tragic Iks, a mountain tribe of central Uganda, within a few generations lost all traces of humanistic values. They presently border on extinction through self-indulgence, greed, and indifference to human suffering. The Icien evolution appeared owing to natural disasters coupled with inept and corrupt governmental policies and the tribe's increasing isolation (see Turnbull). The technology is available to make of the world's peoples anything desirable—the proverbial Utopia or a human garbage can filled with the refuse caused by self-indulgence, insatiable greed, and an unquenchable thirst for material acquisitions. It should be apparent that modern societies, pursuing mindless exploitation of human and natural resources, actually ensure their demise, perhaps even eventual extinction.

Dreams

Research originating with the 1917 findings of Viennese neurosurgeon Otto Poetzle shows that subliminally induced information appears in dreams. Dreams had long been considered products of the unconscious. Conveyed by hypnosis and tachistoscopes (high-speed light projectors), subliminal content was later recovered from dreams, often in symbolic form. A penis appeared in subsequent dreams as a banana, asparagus was modified into a symbolic green tie pin. Dreams thus provide an insight into how the brain transforms unconsciously perceived data into symbols, often to camouflage taboo ideas.

Researchers estimate that the eyes alone make some 100,000 fixations daily. Only a small fragment of these fixations are consciously experienced, but most appear to register in the brain, presumably retained at some level of memory. Dream content, during rapid-eye-movement (REM) dreams in deep sleep periods, appears solely to comprise subliminal perceptions. Poetzle called the process his *Law of Exclusion*: consciously acquired stimuli excluded from dreams.

Emotional significance appears to be the basic criterion for repression or exclusion from conscious awareness. Individuals with rigid, moralistic, religious perspectives, for example, appear especially vulnerable to the obscene subliminal embeds used by advertisers (*see* Dixon, *Subliminal Perception*, p. 168). Such individuals often appear highly repressed, with perceptual defenses tightly in control of daily experience. Few groups in the U.S. population appear so preoccupied with sexual or death taboos, for example, as religious fundamentalists—a fact of life regularly exploited by TV evangelists and other assorted hucksters.

Anyone who can relax via autohypnosis, meditation, or even through deep breathing, can learn consciously to discover subliminal content. In commercial uses of subliminals, however, the object is to prevent discovery. Readers are not supposed to discover genitalia in ad ice cubes. So tension is media-induced in numerous ways—data overload makes it difficult to focus upon any one portion of the perceptual experience, tension is intensified prior to commercial breaks on radio and television, and bad news (riots, wars, famines, violence, or scandals) is positioned adjacent to good news (advertising) in newspapers and magazines. Rock music is an intriguing example of engineered repression, with tension induced by high volume, hysterical, screaming performers, and visual spectacles. Very few fans understand the lyric content, which is perceived directly at the unconscious level.

Poetzle's early dream research with posthypnotic suggestions also demonstrated a time-delay mechanism in the human mentation process. Curiously, it is rare to find a U.S. psychologist familiar with the Poetzle research. Poetzle is a frequent subject of discussion, however, among ad researchers. Subliminal perceptions appear to trigger behavior, after a time period, when exposed to a related secondary conscious perception. For example, a day, week, or month after momentarily perceiving the Oscar Mayer sliced meat ad (fig. 13), conscious perception of the Oscar Mayer package in a supermarket could trigger the conscious thought that these meats are healthy and powerful. A purchase decision would be made without conscious awareness of the taboo hidden symbolism in the ad perceived earlier.

Poetzle's theorization attempted generally to describe a complex process within the human brain. Advertiser concerns, of course, focus simply upon sales effectiveness. The ability of subliminal stimuli to provoke delayed-action behavior, similar to posthypnotic suggestion, appears well documented in experimental literature (*see* Hilgard; Kroger and Fezler; and Dixon, *Subliminal Perception*), and verifiable in advertising and marketing studies of comparative ad effectiveness. All the ads included as illustrations in this book were million-dollar ads—single displays for which at least a million dollars was invested, often much more. These ads were successful. They sold enough product to justify sizable investments of corporate capital.

Memory

One of the most dramatic effects of subliminal stimuli upon behavior involves memory. Once subliminal embeds are perceived unconsciously, it appears impossible to forget them. Memory is generally believed to involve at least two general storage areas—conscious and unconscious. Numerous theories include a third stage—the preconscious. Other theories conceive separate memory systems for emotional and nonemotional information, or short- and long-term memory systems. Recent research has focused upon the right and left brain hemispheres' specialized memory functions. The major difficulty in memory studies is the brain's complexity—and, of course, the inevitable paradox of attempting to study a system from within the system under study. There appears a limit to the degree of understanding achievable about the human brain and language systems.

In any respect, current research into memory has barely scratched the surface. Memory involves hormonal, electrical, and chemical processes, interrelationships that function concurrently at microsecond speeds, through billions of microscopic neuron systems. The senses, around forty depending upon classifications and definitions, continuously input information into the brain. Hot and cold, for example, transmit through separate neuron systems. What humans are consciously aware of at any given instant, as conscious perceptual bias shifts from one sensory input system to another, is a tiny fragment of the totality of information available. Some of this massive input is probably dumped from the system as irrelevant, while other portions are retained for varying periods, some conceivably throughout a lifetime.

The very limited portion of memory of which humans are consciously aware as they speak, think, or write appears to function with time delays between preconscious memory storage and conscious communication. The voice, for example, pronounces words five to seven words after their apparent selection within the brain. Prior to speech, memory appears to sort, select, comparatively evaluate meaning, organize syntax and pronunciation—an unperceivable complexity of concurrent, high-speed functions. This has been called the *abstracting process.*

According to the industry house organ *Advertising Age,* the average North American perceives some 1,000 ads daily. A majority of these contain subliminal stimuli of one type or another. McCann-Erickson, one of the world's largest ad agencies, estimated total U.S. ad investments during 1986 at $101.9 billion, and annually increasing about 15%. That means over $155 billion in 1989. All of this is ultimately added to the price of advertised products, of course, and paid for by consumers. Residual effects of this massive brain conditioning are prodigious.

On the surface, ads appear innocent, harmless, even insipid. They are engineered to communicate this perception. Ads are not innocent, however. The unconscious memory possesses enormous storage capacity. Students who participated in my subliminal advertising research over the past fifteen years discovered surprising memory abilities. After a decade, they often recalled not only specific ads they had studied (quite an accomplishment when you consider the 1,000 ads that pass into perception daily), but also how the ads were studied, the embedded content discovered, and an array of associated detail such as the names of other individuals involved, clothing worn, lunches, and other peripheral events.

Conscious Perception

Conscious memory and perception appears limited largely by what individuals or groups attempt to perceptually avoid, defend themselves against, repress, deny—what is excluded from conscious, immediate awareness. This often appears the opposite of what logic might lead you to believe. Very little perceptual experience is what it appears to be. Overt censorship, either actual or symbolic, such as book-burning, is the best publicity a book or an author can ever hope to achieve. A prominent position on the Catholic *List of Prohibited Books* virtually ensures successful sales. Basic promotional strategies in the merchandising of obscene, drug-pushing rock music involve attempts to provoke suppression or censorship by moralists, outraged parents, or government bureaucrats. The music industry exploits moral opposition very profitably. Similarly, the more authority figures oppose drug use, the more widespread addiction becomes. President Reagan's antidrug program was designed to reach the nondrug-using population, not individuals actually involved or with a high probability of involvement. Drug-oriented high school students made jokes about the simplistic, trite, "Just Say No!" The campaign had been designed for reasons other than a meaningful attempt to deter drug consumption.

This author was intrigued to discover his three earlier books listed as contraband in both the U.S.S.R. and the People's Republic of China. The books, of course, are readily available in both countries via clandestine sources. Show-business personalities such as Jim Bakker, Pat Robertson, Jimmy Swaggart, and Jerry Falwell promote themselves to their massive audiences—who already agree with them—by attacks upon sin and disbelievers. They change nothing, except possibly their financial positions. Indeed, they ensure continued popularity for virtually anything they attack with stormy right-wing diatribes. Threats of eternal damnation mean little to those under attack; perhaps they even provide incentives to persist in what they are doing. This, of course, provides an inexhaustible resource for continued attacks against sin. The asserted belief in God is virtually meaningless without constant threats from the devil. Fund-raising abilities would collapse if stated objectives were accomplished. The evangelists' failure to change the world is actually the basis for continued financial success. It helps to know the real name of the game.

Emotional Response

In other words, what is not said is often far more important to a comprehension of perceivable reality than what is said. Strongly affirmative positions conceal the variety of alternate options that underlie fixed stated positions. For example, public declarations of religious faith, born-again revelations, and confessions of sin, wrongdoing, and repentance have nothing whatsoever to do with God, Christianity, daily life behaviors within society, or altruistic deeds. Such declarations are public posturing of self-righteousness, virtue, and the elevation of self above others who have not yet seen the light. Similarly, public declarations of zealous anticommunism do not fight communism. They are merely public display of what some audiences will perceive as patriotism, virtue, honesty, and goodness. If the communist menace suddenly disappeared, many U.S. politicians would become unemployable. They would have to quickly come up with a new menace. Such posturing changes little in the real world. Moralistic rhetoric, however, often contributes to successful strategy in the struggle for power and profit. Portions of the U.S. population appear peculiarly vulnerable to such stagecrafted entertainments.

Subliminal embedding can make celebrities, models, automobiles, food products, or any other merchandisable object more attractive, exciting, desirable, flavorful, and appealing. Modern media usually avoid confronting the audience with factual realities at the level of conscious perception. Fantasies are far more involving than unembellished perceptions. Reality is often perceived as boring, to be avoided as much as possible. Superficial, passive banalities in ads have been constructed purposely. Specific, factual information invites critical audience response—a threat to sales effectiveness. Blandness, or the appearance of blandness, is usually best for competitive products such as Betty Crocker cake mix (fig. 6).

News information should be equally suspect. Merchandised news media in the U.S. is accepted at face value. The "Target Gaddafi" *Time* cover (fig. 9), with the *SEX* and *KILL* embeds, made the issue—and the fantasy of Gaddafi—more exciting and emotionally significant. Simply expressed, what is consciously perceived by individuals, groups, or even nations often has little or nothing to do with the physical, biological, and social realities the perceptions represent.

There is nothing hidden in any of the illustrations in this book. The embeds are easily perceived by anyone who has learned to manage their perceptual defenses. The hiding (i.e., *perceptual de-*

fense) is accomplished by viewers who hide salacious information from themselves. This is a difficult, unsettling idea. The fantasy of free will is a basic myth in democratic ideology. Numerous psychologists, notably the behaviorists, rejected the notion of perceptual defense completely until it was substantiated by the discovery of embedded art.

From inside cultural fantasies perceptually constructed by mass-communication media, both leaders and followers dangerously toy with delusions that they are in control and know precisely what they are doing. Little in human affairs is controlled, or for that matter controllable, except possibly the delusion of being in control. These involve murderous fantasies of national power, military superiority, moral righteousness, and ethnic or cultural omniscience. These notions are foolish and inherently false, usually propelled by greed disguised as patriotism, or political or religious conviction. These fantasies compare with the fantasies of virility that camouflage the sexual uncertainties and castration fears of *Playboy* magazine's troubled, immature readers. The playboy turns out to be a frightened, lonely, pathetic little boy, playing with himself.

Subliminal persuasion appears most effective on subjects in whom no prior, strong, well-structured opposition exists, when confrontation with well-established habits or ingrained ideological beliefs is avoided. However, when an image is emotionally reinforced by subliminal stimuli, an unconscious ideological perspective can be added. Behavior and values initiated by subliminal stimuli appear similar to effects of posthypnotic suggestion. As in hypnosis, it may be impossible for some individuals to resist instructions not consciously experienced, regardless of how absurd they might appear under conscious, detached critical analysis.

Unconsciously induced behaviors closely parallel neurotic-compulsive responses. Posthypnotically suggested subjects will compulsively do bizarre things which they then attempt to rationalize, explain, or justify as normal. Those who perceive themselves as most in control almost invariably turn out to be the least, the most suggestible. Culturally, citizens of both the U.S. and U.S.S.R. (especially the roughly 50% of Soviets who are Russian) appear to have a built-in, traditional, compulsive *need to control*, a need exploited in both cultural systems. Control fantasies make these two nations extremely dangerous to each other.

In one of numerous similar experiments by this author, a student was given a posthypnotic suggestion to open a window and shout several obscene phrases at people on the street below several minutes after awakening from a trance. He was also told not to consciously recall the instructions. He performed precisely as instructed, closed the window, and took his seat in class. The student was then asked why he had acted so curiously. For fifteen minutes, quite sincerely, or at least so it appeared, he tried to convince the class first that he wished only to alert people on the street below to the dangerous traffic, then that he was venting his anger at someone he strongly disliked; finally he gave an elaborate rationalization about his experiments with reactions to obscenity for a paper he planned to write.

The student had demonstrated a profound aspect of human behavioral conditioning. He was not overtly lying, as far as anyone present could determine. With emotional conviction, he attempted to justify behavior that, by any outside criteria, would be considered bizarre. He seemed compelled to convince the audience that his behavior had been normal, defending it as if it were an ideological position, with allusions to freedom, obligations to society, and altruism.

Assuming the absence of emotionalized counter positions, subliminal stimuli can suggest both an action and an emotional or ideological component to justify the action. Food ads are excellent examples. Virtually everyone has met someone with an obsessive, ideological allegiance to a product brand—a particular soft drink, alcoholic beverage, cookie or cracker, et cetera. Ideological commitment can be generated around Coca-Cola as readily as around a political candidate. Such emotional commitment is rarely a product of conscious, critical evaluation, but generally derives from subliminal conditioning.

Drive-Related Behavior

Behaviors usually considered drive-related include such physiological needs as hunger, thirst, sex, comfort, and maternity.

Drives have been extended to include social need systems such as territoriality, greed, social acceptance, security, and aggression, which derive from survival needs, if not immediate physiological needs. Drive systems are perceived as generated from within, rather than from without. However, *within* and *without*, as far as mind-body processes are concerned, are impossible to delineate. Endless argument persists over what should be considered human drives.

Drive systems appear extremely vulnerable to management by subliminal stimuli. Subliminals can trigger a behavioral reaction to consciously acknowledged hunger. Food ads such as the Betty Crocker "Moister" (fig. 6) are especially sales-effective on a hungry woman—whether her hunger is gustatory, sexual, or involving some other drive system, as all of them interconnect within the brain. Packaging and point-of-sale advertising that utilize subliminal stimuli more powerfully affect the hungry shopper. It is wise, as many have discovered, to avoid food stores when hungry. The food basket fills up with high-calorie, high-sodium, expensive, heavily advertised foods.

The McDonald's Chicken McNugget cut-out coupon ad (fig. 14) requires little explanation. The "Buy One, Get One Free!" coupon appeared in newspapers throughout the country. The coupon ad was reprinted in the *Village Voice* under the title, "Pecker Order," with the question "what part of the hen is this?"

Unsettling contradictions lie between an individual's perception of what appeared in the ads (you think you know what you perceived) and denials of the validity of your perception from high-credibility corporations. In response to a query on the McDonald's McNugget ad, a spokesman replied, "There is no direct or implied relationship between our product promotions and sexuality." He went on to detail their twenty-nine-year history as a wholesome, "profamily" company. Doubters end up feeling guilty for having inquired.

In a TV commercial for Milky Way candy bars, two teenagers rest after a long, hard bicycle ride. Seductive music, not consciously perceived, is heard in the background. The two children voraciously eat their Milky Ways as they chat amiably. The dialogue ends when the girl asks, "Hey hot shot, aren't you coming?"

Perceptual Threshold

Neurophysiologists have long known that only a small fraction of any given perception registers consciously. Look out the window for thirty seconds. Close your eyes. Attempt to recreate all of the information perceived. An enormous quantity of data was visually peceived, but only small fragments are consciously available. With training, individuals can learn to increase conscious awareness of the total percept. This author was once trained to enter a room, exit after sixty seconds, then list 100 items perceived in the room. It is a technique almost anyone can be taught; unfortunately, the ability erodes rapidly when training stops.

Conscious awareness will never remotely approach the total information available from even a single perception. This line between conscious information and that recorded unconsciously (subliminally, subconsciously, nonconsciously, etc.) has been termed the *perceptual threshold*. Several writers have concluded that as little as $1/1000$ of a total percept recorded by the brain appears consciously available (*see* Dixon, *Subliminal Perception*, pp. 1–10). It is not quite that simple. The threshold constantly changes in response to physiological tension, prior cultural conditioning, incoming stimuli content, attitudes, and a variety of other factors. To make the problem more difficult, this imaginary line between conscious and unconscious varies from individual to individual. The threshold is also affected by cultural indoctrination. Some national cultures appear far more repressed, with generally higher thresholds, than others. The content of repressions can vary from culture to culture.

Perceptual engineers—artists, writers, poets, musicians, composers, and audiovisual technologists—constantly explore new ways in which perceptual thresholds can be managed among audiences or readerships. If an audience easily perceives the erect penis embedded in the Tanqueray gin ad (fig. 5), the ad is a waste of money and likely to provoke angry responses from readers. The embedded genital sells gin only if not consciously perceived. The artist had to anticipate correctly the level of cultural repression among potential readers to design the embed. It may seem surprising that, in the supposedly sexually liberated U.S. a genital embed is met with repression. Once again, media demonstrates that very little in the world is what it appears to be, especially cultural values that involve sexual fantasies.

A reader who can relax and scan details—abilities not encouraged in U.S. culture—can easily find the embedded Tanqueray genital. Similar ads were shown by this author to remote Inuit tribesmen in the Canadian arctic. In contrast to their civilized, educated (culturally propagandized) Anglo neighbors, they consciously perceived the genitalia immediately. They considered the ads outrageously humorous, thought it especially funny that anyone would want to publish pictures of genitalia. Several joked that the embedded penis was part of some strange Anglo fertility ritual. Subliminal embeds appear culture-bound. They evoke side-splitting hilarity in one culture and are invisibly repressed in another.

One of the most important discoveries about subliminal phenomena was that the more subliminal, the lower the threshold, and the greater the effects upon perception and behavior (*see* Dixon, *Subliminal Perception*, pp. 283–84). It is difficult for North Americans to comprehend that something invisible, empirically unknowable, can affect behavior. Allusions to DNA particles, viruses, ions, and atomic particles sometimes do not help.

On this printed page, the black ink offers visual contrast against the white background. If you kept thinning the black pigment, at some point there would be nothing visible on the paper—at conscious or unconscious levels. The closer the ink could be brought to the white color of the paper, without the letters disappearing completely, the more effective it becomes as a subliminal perceptual stimulus. The paper could then be overprinted a second time with clearly visible pictorial images or words. The white background would appear empty, yet the words would actually be there very lightly printed. Similarly, with audible volume levels, the lighter, less detectable the sound, the more effective it is as a subliminal behavioral influence.

Subliminally embedded paper stock has been available to printers for many years. Paper manufacturers learned long ago to texture, delicately emboss, or weave words such as *SEX* into paper stock. These embedded *SEX*es are not part of the watermark. This expensive paper is generally used for calling card stock or for sales or promotional brochures. Virtually any high-quality business card or sales brochure, held up to a light for ten seconds or so and viewed in a relaxed manner, will reveal a mosaic complex of the word *SEX*.

The Paper Is the Massage, Not the Message

In 1983, Osman-Kord, Ltd., a Southern California paper company, developed a process whereby made-to-order subliminal commands, strategy reinforcement messages, and other persuasive imagery could be very lightly inked on paper stock. The embeds are completely unavailable to conscious perception, regardless of examination techniques applied. Individuals who know the embedded message can sometimes pick out portions through normal perception. But, without such knowledge, there is no way to detect the subliminal content. This technique is superior to the simplistic *SEX* embeds, much cheaper, and extremely flexible. Many individuals had learned to detect the *SEX* embeds. But now the message remains unavailable to conscious perception, avoiding any threat to media credibility and integrity.

This subvisual enhancement process was tested by Dr. Sidney Weinstein's Neuro-Communication Research Laboratory in Danbury, Connecticut. Using a double-blind and three measurements—brain wave EEG evaluations, test subject ratings, and actual purchasing behavior—roughly 100 subjects were studied. Three paper stocks were embedded respectively with the words *BUY, SEX*, and *NO*. Ads for candy and books were then printed on the embedded paper stocks, as well as on control paper without embedding.

Weinstein's experiment indicated that embedded messages were "significantly influential" in stimulating purchasing behavior, modifying brain response measures of interest and arousal, and in influencing how the subjects rated the products advertised. And there was no way to prove anything was embedded in the paper. The *Wall Street Journal* hired the Georgia State Crime Laboratory and The Georgia Institute of Technology to test and examine the subvisually enhanced paper. They found nothing, yet the paper appeared to affect behavior. The Arizona State University Advanced Optics and Lunar Laboratories also examined the enhanced paper with computer image-enhancement techniques. They found nothing. Roughly 15,000 people, in various experiments, failed consciously to perceive embedded words and pictures in the paper. Potential users of the paper, however, were wary. They feared looking foolish if it turned out nothing was embedded in the paper. *Seeing is believing* is a deeply integrated cultural myth in Western civilizaton.

In another study, Dr. Bruce Ledford at Alabama's Auburn University used subvisually enhanced paper in research on self-esteem, an important factor underlying academic achievement (*see* Ledford, *Effects of Preconscious Cues*). The Rosenberg Self-Esteem Scale, a standard measurement test, was printed in two versions— one upon plain paper, the other upon paper subvisually enhanced with "I Love You!" and large hearts. Self-esteem test scores on the subvisually enhanced version increased an average of 34.7% in an underachiever group of students. Average students improved 13.1%.

Ledford's research demonstrated that human perception, especially at the subtle unconscious level, is far more involved in decision-making and value judgments than anyone had suspected. This perceptual sensitivity becomes extremely important as people nonverbally communicate mutual expectations during interpersonal relationships.

Another technique of subliminal paper enhancement utilizes dot-screen tints, in which microscopic dots 0.125 mm in diameter, 130 lines per square inch, 8 dots per millimeter, are computer-produced on transparent sheets. Positive images (words or pictures) are inked or printed on the transparent dot screen, then stripped away. The images are now negative rather than positive, made up of the areas where dots were removed. The dot screen is then transferred to an engraving. The printed page appears white but is not. The dots can be perceived through a 90-power microscope. This technique could have been used on the page you are now reading.

Heavier dot screens are used extensively in ad art for figure-ground differentiation and are available in most graphic art supply houses. In conventional ads, dot stripping provides an illusion of depth in the two-dimensional reproduction. The stripped-in dot layers usually appear in one or more color separations. These larger engraving dots can be viewed with a strong magnifying glass. The depth illusion enters perception unconsciously; consciously, the picture remains two-dimensional. Dot deletions or additions are also often used to embed *SEX*es. The technique manufactures reality illusions perceptually more real than reality itself. Expensive color reproduction in ads is only utilized because it more effectively controls purchasing behaviors than simplistic black and white.

A Sacramento, California audio-video recording engineer, William Nickloff, has developed ingenious, undetectable subliminal embedding. He utilizes argon-ion laser scanners on color separations through a Chromacom electronic image processing system. Nickloff designed unique dot patterns for commercial illustrations that modified conscious perception. Once the theory of subliminal communication is understood, technological innovations appear unlimited.

Verbal Behavior

The words we hear, speak, and write are stimuli for both thoughts and actions. They also provide rationalizations, explanations, definitions, and/or justifications for perceptions. Individuals seem to enjoy the fantasy that they say what they mean and are in control of language and behavior. "Tell it like it is!" we insist. But the language of commercial mass media is a highly developed tool of exploitive persuasion.

If we wished to turn out hard-nosed, demanding, critical consumers of language and media, we could. Numerous analytical methods are available to anyone who can read and write, and the subtle, devious, and exploitive aspects of language are not difficult to expose. But U.S. education does just the opposite; it inculcates passive acquiescence to the status quo and those who control and sustain it. Media truths become *the* truths: "Trust us, we wouldn't lie to you!"

Perhaps the most perplexing problem in language is *meaning*— not what someone *said*, but what they *meant*. *Meaning* offers a fundamental dilemma in human perception. No two individuals ever attribute precisely the same meanings contextually to the same words. Meaning variations appear in terms of *more or less* or *similarities and differences*, rather than simplistically as *either/or*. Meanings expressed by speakers or writers may also be inconsistent with those interpreted by the audience. And, of course, there exist unconscious meanings for words that may or may not be similar to those at the conscious level.

This author once participated, with two other writers, in preparing a speech for then President Dwight Eisenhower. Though a gifted administrator, Eisenhower was incapable of adequately constructing simple English sentences. His public speeches were written by numerous ghosts, among them the skilled verbal craftsman Emmet John Hughes. Even Eisenhower's famous phrase, "the military-industrial complex," is credited to Dr. Malcolm Moos, then president of the University of Minnesota, and presidential aide Bryce N. Harlow.

The speech in question, however, was presented in support of a local Republican senator during a brief Eisenhower visit to California. For thirty-six sleepless hours, three writers turned out draft after draft, reviewed by a White House deputy press secretary who offered terse comments like, "Much too specific!" "Ease up on factual references!" and "Take it back and fuzz it up!" "Fuzz it up," we discovered eventually, meant avoid all clear, factual statements about anything more specific than the time of day—and be careful about time references because of the four U.S. time zones. The speech was endlessly discussed for likely audience reactions, belief and attitude reinforcements, and implied meanings.

The final draft was a masterpiece. The verbiage was polished, eloquent, elegant, and inspired. There was only one problem. Would anyone take the empty rhetoric seriously? The speech read smoothly but said absolutely nothing about anything. This was precisely what it was intended to say. During audience interviews after the oration, most expressed satisfaction with the great man's words. "Ike really gave it to them!" "He has my vote!" "I like the way he thinks!" "Great speech!"

The audience had been given a verbal Rorschach inkblot—into which they could project whatever they wished to hear and interpret. Each perceived the speech in terms of their individual expectations, values, anxieties, and loyalties.

The Floating Cultural Crap Game

There are no fixed, immutable, time-universal definitions for any word or phrase in any language. Glossaries and dictionaries are continuously revised as meanings, definitions, and conscious and unconscious usage change from day to day. Surprisingly, this acknowledged fact of ever-changing, evolving language is rarely emphasized in school systems or researched in universities. Languages are learned as permanent systems of logical syntax with durable definitions and meanings.

At best, languages are floating cultural crap games of ambiguities, contradictions, paradox, and vague uncertainty, crudely organized around both conscious and unconscious perceptions of meaning. Meanings vary between speakers, writers, and audiences. The phrase, "I know exactly what you mean!" is questionable in any language. The phrase usually means exactly the opposite. Superficially, mathematics was thought to be the only objective language, until the development of quantum mechanics made even that objectivity questionable (*see* Russell). For any language system to be a reliable, objective, and precise instrument of human communication, lasting and specific agreements on definition would be required. These are basic reasons that extensive research efforts in the U.S. and U.S.S.R. over the past thirty-five years failed to develop computer-generated language translations. Contextual variations in meaning are infinite and constantly changing.

Nonetheless, fantasies of verbal objectivity and uniformity of meaning are constructed to sustain illusions of credibility, integrity, and authority. Such fantasies are accepted, apparently, because humans desperately need to believe in the permanence, predictability, and consistency of language. This psychological need appears common, and is imposed upon all known language systems. Absolute truth of verbal meaning is easily the most dangerous myth humans have created. Linguistic truths must always remain tentative assumptions, regardless of human cravings for eternal validity.

Guesses, or intuitive conclusions, can be strongly influenced by subliminal stimuli. These engineered guesses appear to function outside conscious awareness, though humans attempt consciously to rationalize their guesses. When someone *guesses* verbally that a product, person, or idea is superior or inferior to other options— totally outside any factual reference or structure—the guess is likely a product of subliminal indocrination. Guesses usually involve a preference. Once the preference is stated, factual verification and support are accumulated to justify or back up the guess, although individuals often invert their perception of the sequence involved. They convince themselves that logic and *cause* have resulted in a clear, specific, factually defensible *effect* or conclusion. Verbalized guesses are often the result of a collective aggregate of subliminal stimuli perceived from both media and the cultural environment. Little more than fantasized projections, these guesses appear retained in memory for extended periods. Collectively, guesses provide a durable cultural orientation. A predisposition to believe can be overturned only by extensive reindoctrination, an overwhelming barrage of indisputable factual data, or by some trauma related to the predisposition.

The cumulative effect of these guesses, as they reflect in behavior, can be described as *culture*. Culture, in this sense, has little to do with popular definitions. Derived from media, environmental influences, education, language, and interpersonal relationships, these guesses range from preferences for a food or beverage to evaluations of individuals, groups, and even nations. Can you really trust the U.S.S.R., the U.S., or Burger King? Such questions are nonsense, of course, as are all stereotypical designations.

Susceptibility to subliminal stimuli usually depends upon individual or group stress, anxiety, or intense concern. This probably evolved quite normally as a survival mechanism, and there may be no complete defense, nor would a complete defense be desirable. Perhaps the best we can hope for is some level of defensive ability to maintain a degree of autonomy against the pressures of media persuasion. The art, science, and craft of manipulation will certainly become more intense, more skillful, more sophisticated in the future.

Vulnerability can be reduced through a decrease in tension or stress, especially the stress media-engineered to merchandise products, people, and ideas. You can defuse anxiety-provoking media, but you have to learn how. Anyone with a relaxed, contemplative view of the world will perceive from a more reflective, analytical, detached perspective. Conscious concern with factual data, critical evaluations of intuitive guesses, and constant alertness to the human motives behind communciation would reduce the level of vulnerability.

Perhaps the most effective defense against media manipulation comes from knowledge about culture, language, media technology, and perception. People in high-technology cultures have been, in effect, trained in the opposite direction—to visual illiteracy, ignorance of language, and docile preferences for superficiality over substance. Most individuals cannot discriminate between a photograph, a manipulated photograph, and a painting; between reality-oriented perceptions and fantasies. They cannot even distinguish *real* ice cubes in an ad from fantasy ice cubes.

Adaptation Levels or Judgmental Values

Experiments in adaptation level (AL), or judgmental value manipulation, began over a century ago in psychology and sociology (*see* Peirce and Jastrow). AL studies recorded judgmental evaluations on scales ranging from *good* to *bad*, *weak* to *strong*, *beautiful* to *ugly*, et cetera. The early AL experimenters contributed to the development of public-opinion and attitude research widely used today in the media engineering of public consent. Public-opinion surveys are regularly utilized before, during, and after ad and public-relations campaigns, public policy decisions, elections, and merchandising efforts. Many experiments with AL scales (*see* Dixon, *Subliminal Perception*, pp. 31–38) have involved tests with subliminal stimuli. For example, perceptual judgments of hot and cold, electrical shock intensities, relative sizes, weights, and loudness were easily modified with subliminal stimuli.

Individuals and groups were asked to make perceptual judgments on numerical scales. They were then exposed to subliminal stimuli that portrayed the value as *more* or *less, stronger* or *weaker, heavier* or *lighter* in the direction opposed to the first judgment. Significant changes in the initial judgments occurred in virtually every experiment.

The implications of these obscure, academic experiments are awesome. These were perhaps the first scientifically measurable demonstrations that humans and their value systems could be easily manipulated. Humans could be media-engineered to become virtually anything anyone was willing to spend enough time and money to accomplish. If simplistic judgmental values could be altered by subliminal stimuli, certainly more complex judgments were vulnerable. It is a short step from judgments of size, loudness, and weight to those of truth, morality, validity, and significance. AL investigation should have provided a fertile ground for exciting research. It did not. Published research in the area was never publicly extended into meaningful areas of life experience—a typical trait of so much behavioral-science research. AL experiments virtually disappeared from university research and scientific journals. The commercial application of AL theory, however, continued in the mass media.

Advertising is the omnipresent background to U.S. culture. Ads enter perception unconsciously and once in the memory system compete for permanent storage. The cost of selling is a concealed portion of every item purchased by retail consumers, a hidden tax. According to a recent standard marketing text (Kurtz and Brone), the cost of U.S. selling (i.e., marketing) ranges from 40% to 60% of each consumer dollar. The cost of selling *exceeds* the costs of production—labor, raw materials, and manufacture.

U.S. culture institutionalizes and legitimizes the way selling manipulates, but conceals the mechanics of what is really going on. Consumers are incessantly admonished that they make the decisions, propagandized ad nauseam that they think for themselves. A critic might reasonably question why it is necessary to spend so much money, creative talent, time, and effort in the management of purchasing behavior if consumers really think for themselves. But anyone who questions the paradox will likely be written off as a subversive radical.

Few serious studies have ever been produced on the social effects of perceptual submersion in ad media. The subject is ignored in favor of heavy propagandizing for the communications industry, supported by the ad industry.

In studies of human behavior, anyone who seeks something new, untouched, and undiscovered is probably wasting his or her time. Human preoccupations have been endlessly described, measured, evaluated, and probed from every conceivable direction. One productive technique for discovering something new, unobvious, of major significance to survival, is not to search for something new. Search instead for something that has been around a long time, is taken for granted, so obvious as to have remained unseen, undiscovered, repressed, or hidden from public view intentionally or otherwise. Every society has such hidden, tacitly forbidden intellectual treasures that await discovery and illumination. Find out what is not discussed, not studied, not critically examined. Ignore what lies on the surface, what everyone else perceives, argues over, and finds threatening. Societies conceal their exposed nerve endings, which, when examined, become fearsome and painful. But, as mentioned earlier, "No pain, no gain!"

Purchasing Behavior

Scientists avoid subjects unlikely to compensate them for time and effort or that may evoke punishments. Scientists, like everyone else, pursue a society's rewards. Purchasing behavior is a major area of research concentration in this country, consuming hundreds of millions of dollars annually. Sophisticated computer systems correlate this data in hundreds of ways to provide insights into why, how, and which people purchase and consume various products and brands. Purchasing is the most exhaustively researched area of behavior in the Western world.

Priorities in the U.S. appear grotesquely inverted. The National Institute of Mental Health reported that "over a six month period during 1984, 18.7% of U.S. adults [29.4 million people, almost two out of every ten] suffered at least one psychiatric disorder. Only one-fifth of those with disorders sought treatment. Most consulted physicians rather than mental health specialists." The U.S. has evolved a culture that makes individuals mentally ill in large numbers. Drug and alcohol addiction statistics are included, of course.

To appreciate the economic and social magnitude of this hidden dimension of U.S. culture, during 1983 the top twelve U.S. food advertisers invested over $3.5 billion advertising their products— 3% to 11% of total sales income. Roughly 10% of the total ad investment was used for research on purchasing behavior.

Media ads have two simple, measurable objectives—to increase the number of consumers and to increase the quantities they consume. Success or failure is usually measured against these two criteria. Addictive substances such as alcohol, tobacco, and drug products are manipulated into purchasing behaviors. But these products induce a variety of medical and psychiatric pathologies. The well over $1 billion invested in alcoholic-beverage ads during 1986 (roughly half on beer) directly involved alcohol-related pathologies. The half-billion-dollar 1986 investment in tobacco ads correlated with tobacco-related pathologies, including cancer, emphysema, and circulatory and coronary diseases.

Psychopathology

A substantial body of medical research concludes that subliminal stimuli are responsible for most, if not all, psychosomatic illnesses. These illnesses originate in the mind or in mental or emotional conflict (*see* Dixon, *Preconscious Processing*, pp. 177–78). Psychosomatic illnesses include paranoia, phobias, and other stress syndromes, many of which eventually develop into a variety of physiological breakdowns. Both conscious and unconscious stimuli initiate interaction between mental and bodily processes. Repressed or unconscious information gleaned from ads usually involves sex or death taboos—socially unacceptable ideas. Such subliminally perceived ideas may sell brands and products, but they also conflict with current value systems. Their content often includes appeals to latent homosexuality, ethical dilemmas, bizarre fantasies, and suggestions of self-castration or self-destruction.

Such content can be destabilizing or worse for some individuals, evoking anxiety, anger, fear, resentment, revulsion, or even lust at some level of the conscious-unconscious continuum. Powerful emotional reactions can be induced in large audiences without their conscious awareness.

The physiological effects of subliminal stimuli are less intense when transmitted through media than, say, through interpersonal relations or environmental stimuli. Because of their widespread use in advertising, however, they occur very frequently. Unnoticed at a conscious level, the effects appear cumulative—eventually integrating into the general cultural system. Hysterical fear reactions were initiated by movies such as *The Exorcist* and *The Texas Chainsaw Massacre*. Their producers publicly admitted both films contained violent and frightening subliminal stimuli (*see* Key, *Media Sexploitation*, pp. 98–116). Such experiences repeated frequently, year after year, decade after decade, eventually provoke physiological changes in viewers.

Most individuals under subliminal stimulation consciously feel only brief discomfort, if anything. Few are aware of any specific threat or damage to their well-being. Over an extended period of years, however, the constant bombardment of subliminal stimuli can lead to permanent changes in organ systems and their complex processes. The constant overstimulation of physiological defense mechanisms could eventually modify or exhaust those systems. Such changes can initiate serious structural revision in the mind-body physiological interrelationship, varying in intensity and significance among individuals.

Moreover, subliminal stimuli have been demonstrated to affect physiological functions and behaviors even after a single, isolated exposure. The unconscious memory system appears to retain emotionalized information indefinitely. Subliminally induced memories feed back into behavior in many ways which are at present poorly understood. Purchasing manipulation is, of course, only one of these behaviors.

Both immediate and delayed responses to subliminal stimuli can activate various autonomic physiological systems within the body. Experimentally shown to respond to subliminal stimuli are the adrenal-neural-cortical systems. These interrelated organ systems initiate mind-body defenses against threats of injury. The two adrenal glands, for example, located near the kidneys, produce several important hormones, especially epinephrine and norepinephrine. The nervous system connects every glandular organ and bodily system to the brain.

When an individual confronts danger, epinephrine secretions heighten an individual's fear response and increase mental alertness to danger (flight reactions). Norepinephrine secretions help prepare an individual for action, particularly aggressive action (fight reactions). Both *flight* and *fight* reactions can be triggered by subliminal stimuli (*see* Dixon, *Subliminal Perception*, pp. 205–28, and

Preconscious Processing, pp. 124–26, 177–78; *see also* Brown, "Conceptions of Perceptual Defense").

Subliminal stimuli effects on the adrenal-neural-cortical systems—which interconnect organ, brain, and nervous systems—can also modify homeostatic functions, the body's way of regulating and controlling autonomic systems. These include the regulation of heart rate, blood flow distribution and pressure, sweating or body temperature, and respiration or breathing, which increases blood oxygen levels. Though the generalized response to subliminal stimuli of these autonomic systems can be measured, the systems are extraordinarily complex, interrelated, subtle, and only partially understood.

Media Damage Invisible and Cumulative

Subliminal stimuli can make an individual instantly more alert and more sensitive to additional stimulation (priming) due to changes in brain-activating systems.

1. Blood flow can be shunted to the muscles and brain from the peripheral blood vessels and digestive organs.
2. Heart rate can be increased to supply oxygen for muscles and the brain and to evacuate bodily wastes.
3. Blood coagulability can increase to counter threatened bleeding.
4. Peripheral blood veins can constrict to shunt blood to muscles and lessen blood loss in case of wounds.
5. Sweating can dissipate heat generated by muscle activity and the body becomes slippery.
6. Pupils can dilate to improve vision in the dark or make an individual's appearance frightening or sexually stimulating.
7. Increased blood sugar can decrease blood volume.
8. Increased respiration can alter oxygen–carbon dioxide exchanges.
9. Stomach and intestinal changes can precipitate bowel or urinary evacuation.
10. Finally, subliminal stimulation of adrenal medullary secre-

tions (brain and body glandular outputs) can trigger adreno-corticotrophic-pituitary hormones, which stimulate other major defense systems.

Every portion of the human brain connects to every other portion of the brain and body via billions of microscopic neuron networks. Nothing within the mind-body interrelationship exists in isolation. Endocrine, neuro-anatomic, and neurophysiological systems all interconnect. Emotionalized stimuli can influence an individual's resistance to illness, affecting the immune system and increasing susceptibility to infection. Subliminal stimuli can energize cerebral processes that underlie whole systems of emotionally charged ideas. These mind-body interreactions can also be initiated by hypnosis, suggesting a similarity of effects upon physiology and behavior for both hypnotic and subliminal phenomena.

Specific pathologies have been linked to subliminal techniques in ad media. Eating and nutritional disorders—such as bulimia, pica, anorexia nervosa, and obesity—afflict some 15 million people in the U.S. A large proportion of food advertising employs subliminal techniques, such as those demonstrated in the illustrations. Yet there has never been a serious attempt to study the relationship between food advertising and food-related pathology—a testament to the political influence of advertisers.

A 1986 National Health and Nutrition Survey indicated the average adult male carries twenty to thirty pounds more fat than he should, the average adult female an extra fifteen to twenty-five pounds. The U.S. population became substantially fatter while the media talked more and more about health food, exercise, and dieting. Twenty-five to 30% of people in the U.S. are overweight—the nation's major health problem. According to Metropolitan Life Insurance tables, 11 million people in the U.S. are severely obese, exceeding desirable weights by 40% or more. Obese individuals have three times the normal incidence of high blood pressure and diabetes, increased heart disease levels, shorter life spans, and extremely high risk levels for respiratory disorders, arthritis, and certain cancer types. Obese women have five times the normal risk for uterine-lining cancers and increased risk for colon, rectum, and breast cancers. Obese people have more osteoarthritis because of weight overloads on joints, more accidents and injuries as they are less able to protect themselves, more respiratory and digestive difficulties, and even more trouble sleeping.

Similar dangers from media apply to other consumption-related pathologies, such as alcohol, tobacco, and pharmaceutical drug abuse and addiction. Illegal addictive substances—marijuana, cocaine, heroin, and the so-called designer drugs—are also hyped and romanticized by subliminal stimuli in news, drama, and popular music. Drug usage is widely celebrated in U.S. media. Indiscriminately attacking drug usage in a society where drugs are widely legitimized ensures popularity of drugs among the emotionally immature of any age. Considering the vast amounts invested in media research annually, it is remarkable that media effects on public health remain completely unexplored.

3 | THE UNDERSIDE OF CONSCIOUSNESS

The most dangerous delusion of all is that there is one reality.

Paul Watzlawick, *How Real Is Real?*

There are no dangerous thoughts. Thinking itself is dangerous!

Hannah Arendt, *The Life of the Mind*

The natural role of Twentieth Century man is anxiety!

Norman Mailer, *The Naked and the Dead*

The following is an attempt to synthesize current views of the human brain, perceptual systems, and their physiology. These views, however, constantly change as new insights, technologies, discoveries, and cultural influences evolve. How and why perception appears to function as it does must be viewed from the perspective of this particular moment in history. This analysis tries to avoid any single theoretical bias such as Freudian, behaviorist, Gestalt, et cetera. The evolution of psychologies has been more involved with culture than with science, adapting to what societies desired to believe or disbelieve about themselves in any respective era. Today's conventional wisdom was yesterday's wild-eyed radical vision, which will become tomorrow's antiquated, obsolete, trite, time-tattered nonsense.

Psychological theories demonstrate a peculiar adaptability to prevailing socioeconomic-political-religious-cultural dogma. The U.S.S.R.'s political culture propagated the theories of Trofim Lysenko, an agronomist whose notions of environmental influences over heredity were extended into theories of human behavior. Similarly, the U.S. techno-entrepreneurial culture once made a near religion out of the behaviorism of B. F. Skinner, who simplified psychology into a verbal, logical, mechanical-man system of inputs and outputs from an engineer's little black box. Both Lysenko and Skinner have passed into history. Each told the societies of their time what they wanted to hear. This conformity to prevailing culture has evoked accusations that social scientists are both antisocial and unscientific, propagandists for the culture usually defined as the best of all possible worlds.

How and why the human brain functions as it appears to function is still a mystery. Various sciences have described the brain's anatomical structures in exhaustive detail, at least those portions perceivable. The neurological, circulatory, electrical, hormonal, chemical, intercellular processes and their supportive structures have been microscopically measured, surgically modified, charted, and experimentally manipulated. Yet clear, precise knowledge of brain function continues to defy high technology. The most accurate statement anyone can make about the human brain is simply that nobody knows how or why the organ works as it appears to. Neurophysiologists may be the closest to finding out. They report, nevertheless, that they know virtually nothing about how the brain stores, synthesizes, and correlates perceived information. There are only theories—literally hundreds of them.

Study of the human brain involves a paradox—studying a system by use of the system under study. The dilemma is fundamentally one of language—the uniquely human tool that enables us to study, explain, and rationalize our world. It is easy to explain the world with words, very difficult to relate words to realities. Descriptions of brain physiology (how it works) must be reported in a linear, sequentially perceived, definition-oriented verbal or mathematical language—one item at a time, one system at a time, one process and action at a time. Language is symbolic—a remote and simplistic referent for incredibly complex, interrelated, multiple-process realities—all operating concurrently at microsecond speeds through billions of microscopic neuron networks. However anyone attempts to linguistically describe the operation of the brain, their verbal description could never adequately describe the complex reality. Even if the complexity were understood, the understanding would have to be expressed in language far removed from the actual reality. Words and numbers are not the things they represent but only distant, approximate, symbolic representations. Linguistic fallibility undermined so-called behaviorist psychology, rendering it little more than a pseudoscience. Behaviorism attempted to exclude unconscious processes and has often dominated U.S. psychology. Author Arthur Koestler described behaviorism as "a monumental triviality marked by innate naïveté and intellectual bankruptcy."

The largest electronic computer theoretically possible still remains, by comparison with the human brain, a child's toy. The human brain's complexities promise to remain in the foreseeable future mankind's most impenetrable enigma. Nevertheless, new psychological theories continue to be formulated and published every year. *It is important to constantly keep in mind that theories are not truths.* No completely validated theory of human mentation has appeared. Theories are, at best, conjectural, speculative, circumstantial, projective, and often little more than wishful thinking.

In the pragmatic world of technology, often misrepresented as science, few have succeeded by emphasizing what they did not know. Theories easily become intermixed with perceptual truths. Many psychologists, notably the simplistic progeny of writers such as B. F. Skinner, Wilhelm Wundt, Edward Thorndyke, James Cattell, Abraham Flexner, and John Dewey maintained they did not utilize theories, only empirical facts derived from human and animal experimentation. These behaviorists developed elaborate semantic stratagems to avoid theories. They literally created theories about not using theories.

When recognized as such, theories are simply tentative ways to understand something, and they can be useful, especially when they are all that is available. Albert Einstein once commented, "It is the theory which decides what we can observe."

A theory can be useful only in a particular time, place, and situation. Some theories have been more useful than others. One thing appears certain: The human brain has nothing, even remotely, to do with electronic computers—mechanisms whose simplistic repetitive operations must be directed and controlled by humans. Current cognitive theory models the brain along the lines of a high-speed computer (*see* Kihlstrom, "The Cognitive Unconscious"). Curiously, Norbert Weiner's pioneering book *The Human Use of Human Beings: Cybernetics and Society* (1954) conceptualized modern computers on a comparison with the brain. Today, theorists conceptualize the brain based on comparison with computers. Over the past thirty-five years, mechanistic theories of brain function traveled full circle, changing with what societies wished to believe.

Unintelligent Intelligence

It is fascinating to observe the latest commercial computer fantasy promoted by corporations in the interest of profit. Recent fantasies about artificial intelligence and languages provide an example. What is retained more or less permanently in any human brain might be designated *intelligence*. Of course, if the memory content is repressed, unavailable to conscious awareness, the memory would not help during an intelligence test. A vast literature argues endlessly over just how intelligence should be defined. What occurs in the most sophisticated computers, though, is hardly comparable to human *intelligence*. Intellectual games played over notions of artificial intelligence—such as those in the delightful book

Gödel, Escher, Bach, by Douglas Hofstadter—are entertaining distractions. Construction of an artificial language to communicate with aliens from outer space, however, borders on the ludicrous. Human language, utilized as a manipulative tool, often makes it difficult to communicate over the backyard fence with a neighbor, let alone between antagonists such as the U.S. and U.S.S.R. Intelligence is hardly a quality attributable to machines. A dumb machine simply does what it is told and cannot, even under the most optimistic rationalizations, think for itself. As this book hopes to point out, this quality may be rare even among humans.

Studies of human mentation have focused upon *perception*—how the multitude of sensory devices input information into the brain—and *abstraction*—how the information eventually emerges as behavior and language. Thought processes themselves can be considered behavior, with the senses feeding data into the brain at microsecond speeds. Chemical and hormonal processes also appear involved. Billions of cells within the brain communicate with billions of sensory neurons throughout the body. Perception can be generally considered *instantaneous* and *total*. That minute portion of perception, however, which becomes consciously apparent operates very selectively and much more slowly.

As readers sit comfortably in a warm, well-lighted room near a fireplace where logs burn slowly, their eyes follow these sequential, printed lines of word symbols. They concentrate on the meanings and feelings of the words, sentences, and paragraphs. Consciously, the reader is aware of only the words printed on each page, perceived by the eye mechanism, and transmitted into the brain, where associations and ideas initiate at both conscious and unconscious levels. But there is much more going on in the brain than that of which the reader is consciously aware. The distant sounds of street traffic, radio or TV receivers, wind or weather outside the room, temperature, humidity, ionization, et cetera, all register in the brain. There is the pressure of the reader's body upon the chair, clothing upon the body, gastric sounds and feelings of food inside the stomach, flavors and pressures of chewing gum in the mouth, an ankle itch, a slight throb from an old knee bruise, dryness on the lips, the odor of burning wood, and soft, crackling fire sounds.

This information, all at the same instant, continuously flows from the senses to the brain. Consciously, you are aware only of the printed page. Unconsciously, all the data is perceived and processed, some of it stored for future reference. Everyone in the world has vast quantities of information in their brains that never becomes consciously available.

Definitions Include and Exclude

In addition to peripheral perceptions, the brain interprets and defines each word on the page. Definitions include information at the conscious perceptual level and exclude material at the unconscious level. Mind, culture, and language are intimately interrelated and interdependent. Most individuals have the illusion that they control perception. At best, this control involves only a small portion of the process. Each culture and language categorizes and defines perceptual experience differently—controls what will be consciously perceived as significant, unconsciously stored, or dumped as irrelevant. The process also involves an individual's past experiences and emotional needs. Somewhere during the early growth process, humans learn what *not* to perceive consciously, to alter and restrict their perceptions, to perceptually defend themselves against taboo or undesirable feelings, drives, and anxiety-provoking memories.

Cultural taboos and the unconscious perceptual systems become, therefore, fundamental to the total perceptual process. What humans think they think about what they think—were people capable of this kind of abstract evaluation—is only a fraction of the total going on. Perceptual defenses appear one of the ways the brain focuses, channels, concentrates attention upon a very limited portion of the vast aggregate of information that flows each instant in, out, and through the brain.

Perceptual defenses can be described as mechanisms that subordinate information into the unconscious. Individuals have no conscious control over perceptual defenses, which operate automatically. Significant information deleted from conscious awareness is apparently stored by the brain indefinitely, and feeds back into behaviors. The most important of these behaviors, in the context of this book, is purchasing behavior. Purchasing behavior, however, is unconsciously a part of ideological, political, and other social behaviors. Very little in the world of perception is isolated from the rest of what is going on in life.

Perceptual defenses operate continuously to limit conscious perception and enable us to focus on what we are doing at any particular moment. The perceptual defense process allows humans a simplified, linear, verbal definition-oriented, culturally biased illusion of reality—a slowed-down, detail-stripped, fantasy abstraction of the world, consciously perceived as the reality of the moment.

Individuals consciously perceive that eyes, ears, or other sensory inputs take in some data and ignore others. This perception is illusionary. The senses operate merely as servomechanisms—indiscriminately transmitting prodigious quantities of data into the cerebrum. The editing process occurs in the brain's cerebral cortex, the outer layer. How it all actually works is unknown, perhaps unknowable.

Eight perceptual defenses have been described, ways in which we hide information from ourselves to avoid anxiety, depression, confusion, and perceptual overload. These include *repression, isolation, regression, fantasy formation, sublimation, denial, projection,* and *introjection* (*see* Lidz, pp. 256–61). These may be different aspects of the same perceptual process. To a significant degree, in any case, they control our daily lives, thoughts, actions, and destinies. What is left out (excluded from conscious awareness) can be far more significant to survival than what appears in consciousness.

Differences among human cultures, as far as perceptions are concerned, appear a matter of degree and bias, not a difference in kind. Perceptual defenses appear universal and are largely responsible for human vulnerability to manipulation. Any cultural system is both a way of knowing and a way of not knowing.

Perceptual defenses inhibit and distort reality, and no one is ever completely exempt. These defenses modify our views of self, motives, and human relationships. Manipulation of perceptual defenses can create serious adjustment and survival problems. For example, if one world leader argues that everything he says is truth and everything his opponent says is propaganda, such nonsense— if taken seriously—sets the scene for dangerous confrontations.

The questionable nature of any such statement disappears as audiences defend against doubting the credibility of a trusted leader loyally serving their nation. Some degree of self-deception, however, appears socially necessary. Voltaire commented that anyone compelled to look into the mirror of truth would instantly become insane. Self-deception via perceptual defenses, nevertheless, is risky business in a world where life and death—and the often thin line between them—have become fragile, momentary, and tentative. Self-deception has evolved as a basic ingredient of world cultural systems—a dangerous ingredient capable of initiating the final miscalculation.

In a TV ad for Downy fabric softener, a thirty-second drama opens in a child's bedroom. In a cheery voice an actress says, "Hi! I got something to show you!" The camera cuts to her genital area, where a bottle of Downy is held with its handle pointed at her genital. No picture of her face appears, only her genital area and the Downy bottle. Innocent viewers, if they consciously made the obvious linkage (most unlikely in U.S. culture), would conclude the linkage was accidental or in a critic's dirty mind. Perceptual defenses protect individuals from threatening associations.

The Hidden Dimensions

Repression, often considered the central mechanism of perceptual defense, involves a banishment from awareness of memories, perceptions, or feelings considered threatening, traumatic, or taboo. Events or information become consciously hidden from individuals. The information still remains in the memory, however, and continues as a potential ingredient in motivations and behaviors. Individuals repress, as do groups and national cultures. Repression is entirely automatic, consciously undetected, and uncontrollable. Repressed information surfaces in behaviors. The complex process is poorly understood. *Repression* can be compared to hypnotically induced amnesia, where subjects are directed to forget specific information, then instructed to forget they have forgotten.

Repression should not be viewed as an either/or phenomenon. Some types of information appear more or less permanently hidden; memories from the first four or five years of life illustrate this. Repressed information surfaces in symbolic dream responses, rationalizations, disguised motives, and in projective behaviors where, for example, the behavior of a hero fantasy projects into our own. The two major repressed areas surround reproduction (sex) and death—*love* and *death*, the beginning and end of life. Perceptual experiences appear most powerful when they involve these two sensitive, taboo-laden polarities of human existence. Subliminal suggestions of sex and death are ruthlessly exploited by the U.S. mass-communication industry.

A frequent aspect of repression, *reaction formation*, usually describes a tendency to repress unacceptable impulses or wishes and to manifest consciously their opposites. Austere puritanism, for example, may be a reaction formation against forbidden—though attractive—hedonistic feelings. *Undoing* or *correcting* often involves ritual behaviors such as prayer, penitence, or ceremonies that are fantasized to magically undo a forbidden wish, desire, feeling, or act. Undoing can either be consciously experienced or, more frequently, repressed so individuals are unaware of the game they are playing with themselves.

Let's say someone commits what they or significant others perceive as a vicious, forbidden, unpardonably cruel act. At that time, the individual constructs justifications for the act, ways responsibility can be redirected to another person or group. Humans have an extraordinary ability to project blame for their acts—real or imagined—onto others. Current German rationalizations for World War II atrocities are as ingenious as American justifications for the nuclear attacks upon Japan. Such social perceptual constructions can be treated as reaction formations. As time goes on, the actual circumstances will be consciously modified, repressed, or even denied to avoid self-condemnation. On the other hand, some individuals or groups may pursue lifelong careers of atonement for real and imagined events that evoked guilt.

The evolving perceptual construct has little or nothing to do with the original event that initiated the whole process. The greater the perceived guilt, at both conscious and unconscious levels, the more dogmatic, elaborate, and self-aggrandizing become the rationalizations. The mechanism appears common to every human being and every society. It may be an indispensable survival technique. National histories are often constructed around undoing a reaction formation of repressed unpleasantness that would evoke anxiety if consciously deliberated.

Repression techniques are utilized by the mass-communication media, both in advertising and in the selling of so-called news information in support of advertising. The *Time* Gaddafi cover (fig. 9) is one example. If consciously available information is repressed, it functions as subliminal stimulus. The best strategy is to take nothing for granted! Consider nothing irrelevant! Commercial media content is usually arranged to increase tension and involvement. One example of perceptual overload is the rock music concert where multisensory demands assault audiences. Perceptual overload is also apparent in the design of gambling casinos. Perceptual distractions—noise, flashing lights, people, and provocatively dressed waitresses—instantly somnambulize gamblers, evoking behavioral conformity and high levels of suggestibility. The modern gambling casino has been architecturally engineered and decorated into a behavioral money-milking machine. Like the rock concert, nothing in the casino design exists by accident or oversight. As in ad media, every detail has been exhaustively studied and constructed for maximal investment return.

Casinos are media-hyped as recreational and fun. Las Vegas casinos advertise gambling as "America's greatest relaxation!" A walk through any casino, however, reveals people pumping mechanistically away on slot machines and tensely hunched over gaming tables. Grim, expressionless faces appear robotlike in their uniformity. Recreation, relaxation, or fun is not apparent. The gamblers appear hypnotically turned in upon themselves, into private fantasies of striking it rich, of momentarily living as the fantasied rich and famous. The biggest irony, of course, is that there is actually no *gambling* going on in casinos. The outcome of a gamble is indeterminate; in casinos, the outcome is always certain. The casinos win! Always! The self-styled gamblers play only to lose.

Safely Isolated

Isolation is a perceptual defense through which humans can know something consciously but avoid associations that invoke anxieties, guilt, depression, or other threatening feelings. Isolation of linkages occurs with both individuals and groups, and can be a product of culture engineered by journalists, ads, or public-relations strategies. Isolation is not a conscious process whereby individuals or groups decide they will not associate one idea with another. It is far more subtle and insidious. Isolation can develop out of a cultural system's vested interest in preventing certain conscious connections. It can also be indoctrinated into individuals through training programs. Isolation blocks or redirects what might be considered reasonable, logical, conscious idea linkages.

Perceptual rigidity and *conformity* are priming conditions for subliminal indoctrination. Rigid conformists or zealots appear the most vulnerable, because they are already willing to accept the compartmentalization of ideas and relationships. What has been left out of fixed verbal definitions often becomes the most significant part of the definition. Terrorists are easily converted into freedom fighters through simple definition games for those whose worldview demands simplistic, rigid categorization.

Culturally induced isolation often develops to legitimize acts or ideas that might be offensive or questionable if perceived via normal association. Ads provide extraordinary examples. Few people consciously notice the deluge of ad media in which society is immersed. Ads are simply accepted, taken for granted as an aspect of environment. Physicians and public health officals rarely profess to see any threat to the public welfare in ads. Indeed, ads are commonly joked about and considered ineffective, a point often made by media apologists. Yet business and government know much about ad media's ability to move products, ideas, and people.

U.S. audiences are frequently surveyed about the perceived causes of alcohol and drug addiction. The long list of believed causes usually includes family break-up, peer pressure, heredity, parental failures, and boredom. Ads are rarely mentioned. The legitimization of ads is no accident. Hundreds of billions of dollars were invested over the years in the advertising of advertising. One of the most powerful forces in society, ads appear on the surface innocuous, insignificant, and benign.

From early childhood, the population has been culturally indoctrinated to accept alcohol, tobacco, and pharmaceutical products as solutions to problems of emotional adjustment. The cultural groundwork is laid by ads. Later in life the early conditioning often explodes into addictive, self-destructive behaviors for increasing proportions of the population. Adult cigarette smokers have decreased in number by roughly one-third over the past thirty years, especially among the economic, educational, and occupational groups most able to defend themselves against media persuasion. The ban on TV cigarette ads helped, but ad budgets switched to print, billboard, and movie ads.

Tobacco smoking decreased, but only after three decades of increasing publicity about health damage from smoking. As each new public health revelation appeared, cigarette marketers increased ad budgets. Now the attrition of addicted smokers has slowed to a trickle. As illustrated in my four books on subliminal advertising, the industry heavily utilized subliminal techniques to sell and justify cigarette consumption. Anyone who has quit smoking became acutely aware of ad power during their withdrawal period. Ads sustained millions of smokers in their self-destructive behavior. Smoking, however, is becoming restricted largely to lower socioeconomic groups. In the past, most of the great movie heroes smoked—John Wayne, Humphrey Bogart, Robert Taylor, Gary Cooper, et cetera, and so did the characters they portrayed. The cigarette was symbolic of sophistication, manhood, courage, success, wealth, and even honesty. Today, on the other hand, when a writer introduces someone who smokes, that character is invariably a loser. In the movie *Fatal Attraction*, cigarette smoking symbolized Glenn Close's character's emotional instability.

Another unsettling example of *isolation* involves the selection and training of nuclear missile launch crews. These young officers have been carefully selected, trained, and rigorously disciplined to avoid conscious linkages between their duties and the fate of millions of human beings in target populations. Initial selection as suitable candidates was based on strict psychological test criteria. The average combat-experienced officer usually does not qualify for missile training. In personal combat, an ability to make quick conscious linkages is vital to survival. The missile-launch crewperson must have a potential for being disciplined into a dehumanized, narrowly focused, task-oriented professional. Candidates receive rigorous conditioning never to dwell consciously upon the human consequences of their work. Technologically indoctrinated, they are taught to view themselves as merely mechanics, engineers, and administrators. They must be capable of discarding personal considerations. Their ultimate act will incinerate millions of humans and condemn millions more to lingering, excruciatingly painful deaths. Indeed, the outcome of their act is certain to vaporize the past, present, and future of civilization. The vast majority of their victims will be those who have never lived, and who never will. The monstrous consequences are, perhaps, beyond human comprehension. This helps facilitate isolation and repression. Very few people can do this kind of work.

Through relentless, disciplined psychological conditioning, the air force trains missile crews into fantasy technological obsessions, totally removed from human realities. Trainees are never permitted to ask why. Blind obedience is the overpowering central objective. Missile crews are under constant surveillance, testing, and evaluation for psychological "weakness." High rates of mental disorders prevail among the crews, for which they are usually transferred into lower-pressure assignments. The Strategic Air Command's definitions for mental disorder are curious. In the real world, only a seriously ill psychopath could launch a nuclear missile. *Insanity* must be reconditioned to appear as *sanity*, and vice versa. Any slight indication that a launch crew member might not fulfill the mission when ordered results in career termination. Somewhere in their brains, nevertheless, crew members continue to know exactly what they are doing. Madness, for some, is one reasonable way out of the paradox.

Testimony at both the Nuremberg war-crimes trials and at the Tel Aviv trial of Adolf Eichmann verified that the Nazis faced a similar problem in the selection and training of SS extermination-camp officers and enlisted personnel. Rigorous, disciplined dedication to technology, fanatic patriotism, religious zeal, and other obsessive preoccupations were utilized in carefully planned selection and training programs. Reality perceptions were reconstructed. The camp work was isolated from human, ethical, and legal considerations. Not everyone qualified as mass executioners. Combat veterans were usually excluded. SS personnel were viewed as a select elite, dedicated patriots, men and women able to make a heroic sacrifice for their nation.

After victory, few Allied investigators understood what had occurred from a Nazi perspective. SS men and women were viewed with horror by the Allied nations, as a hand-picked group of psychotic, sadistic monsters. This was convenient scapegoating, blaming a few for the sins of the many. The SS were not perceived as psychopaths within Nazi Germany. They reflected the highest ideals of the Third Reich. Most societies define *psychopath* as an unstable, unreliable, irresponsible, mentally ill individual preoccupied with his or her own delusions. SS volunteers were considered the most desirable of all German citizenry. Superbly trained, they *isolated* daily acts from all human considerations. They served and obeyed, extraordinary technicians who nobly performed for the greater good, for survival of their way of life, their freedoms, and their faith in the Nazi leadership.

Isolation, as a perceptual defense, plays an important role in the world today. It is not always easy to determine whether information has been isolated, repressed, or both. Isolation separates emotion from thoughts or ideas by suppressing linkages and conscious recognition of consequences. When reaction formation, undoing, and isolation combine, public prayers for peace and goodwill may conceal unconscious desires for war as an outlet for aggression, personal indulgence, power acquisition, profit, or combinations of all of these.

Both the U.S. and U.S.S.R. military leadership have now murderously destroyed civilian airliners, Korean and Iranian, and slaughtered hundreds of innocent men, women, and children. Both nations gave identical, ludicrous justifications—the tragedies were the fault of the civilian airliners. That such rationalizations were found acceptable demonstrated the lack of conscience and power of repressive isolation that dominates what passes for world morality. Professional moralists in both nations said little except to exploit the propaganda advantages. Each ignored their own terrorism while condemning that of the other side.

Hiding Behind Numbers

Quantification is another kind of isolation technique. Numbers inhibit the conscious use of information, and are often perceived as incontestable fact. Quantification (among nonmathematicians, at least) also implies *objectivity*—another mythological belief structure. Quantification, statistical or mathematical, can be used to isolate information from reality-oriented perceptions, verbal descriptions, and counterreferences. Numbers offer a superb technique to depersonalize and dehumanize people. In Nazi death camps, detailed numerical records neatly concealed and legitimized the horrors inflicted upon humans. The U.S. military's daily body count in Vietnam—enemy bodies, of course; ours were "casualties"—concealed the slaughter for many Americans.

The preoccupation with numbers in both the U.S. and U.S.S.R. is often an exercise in hiding things. Both societies have deeply instilled cultural fantasies that numbers do not lie. Perhaps numbers do not lie, but mathematicians and statisticians frequently lie, manipulate, and deceive. They are paid handsomely to do so. Numbers can misrepresent reality as easily, if not more so, than words. Both languages—verbal and mathematical—are useful tools only with conscious awareness of their limitations and frailties. Symbols can never be the things they symbolize.

Numerical objectivity is a fallacy. Like verbal language, numerical designations must be abstracted by humans. They are subjected to varying interpretations by both initiator and receiver. Numbers constitute merely another language with built-in paradoxes, confusion, contradictions, and hidden agendas.

So-called scientific facts—like so much of perceived reality—are rarely what they appear to be. The moment a scientific fact is cited in support of an argument, it no longer has anything to do with either science or facts. While scientific methods of inquiry, examination, and discovery have produced useful explorations into the unknown, science becomes psychological silly putty when used to hype an industry, cause, ideology, product, person, group, or nation. *Unquestionable scientific facts attributable to high-credibility sources* impose an end to critical thought. Especially in high-technology cultures, science is accepted as a mythological, godlike creation presumed omniscient, omnipresent, and omnipotent.

Real scientific advances usually stem from the discovery of errors in human perceptual judgments, judgments once considered scientific themselves. Scientific advances are new perceptual formulations that correct prior errors or omissions. The process continues infinitely, and always with considerable uncertainty. People with something to sell indiscriminately lump technology into science. Technology is a machine, a gadget, a profitable process or invention easily perceived, profitably produced, and usefully applied. All this has nothing remotely to do with scientific exploration. The illusion of scientific truth provides the ultimate attribution, replacing scriptural confirmations of validity. Scientific truth, accepted without question or reservation, isolates an individual from constantly changing reality perceptions. Science must always be viewed as tentative. The discovery of "truth" terminates the scientific and intellectual process.

Regression: Marching Forward into the Past

Regression is perhaps the most easily observable of the perceptual defenses. It functions throughout life as a recurring part of development. When people become obsessive in their regressions, however, they retreat from reality-oriented perceptions. This occurs, for example, when individuals or groups strive excessively for independence, then fall back to a point when they felt secure, protected, where others assumed responsibility for their lives. Regression occurs collectively in nations that seek the fantasied solutions of the past for the threatening dilemmas of the present.

The Old West, celebrations of military victories, and the proverbial "good old days" are U.S. examples. The "good old days" of Norman Rockwell and Garrison Keillor are nostalgic fantasies of a world that never was except in today's imagination. Such idealized fantasies provide a cover-up for unpleasant realities of the moment. Many desperately need to believe such a world existed, where security was realized in simplistic moral platitudes, where fear and anxiety were absent, where family and friends were reliable and trustworthy. The worse contemporary realities are perceived to have become, the more intense this regressive search for security.

Regression begins early in life and can be considered a major adaptation technique to the instabilities always present in perceived realities. Regression can become so thoroughly established during childhood that such dependent tendencies appear normal and natural. Regression may also take the opposite turn. Dependency may be rejected for a fantasized worship of independence, autonomy, and a lack of social rules and responsibilities. Whichever way regression turns, it depends upon a rejection of perceived reality in favor of a simplified fantasy of "the way we were."

Individual or group failure to overcome regression and deal with reality adjustments can evolve into major psychopathology. The mass-communication industry has developed the regression mechanism into a multibillion-dollar annual bonanza. Years after the "Bonanza" TV series was canceled, tourists still search Nevada for the site of the original Ponderosa ranch. The ranch, or anything resembling it, never existed outside of Hollywood. The actual Old West was a nightmare of filth, disease, discomfort, privation, greed, injustice, and criminality, coupled with imminent threats of violent death.

The fantasy prevails as a substitute for a reality that would hardly be saleable either to audiences or to advertisers. The media fantasies constructed around various wars—Vietnam, Korea, the two world wars, the Mexican war, Civil War, War of Independence, et cetera—become glorified versions of a grim, complex, brutal, and morally indefensible reality. Populations constantly indoctrinated with such fantasies lose the ability to distinguish between illusion and reality. Regression fantasies can threaten adjustment and survival. Someone who attempts to resolve complex problems in day-to-day life with the techniques utilized in violence fantasies by actors such as Sylvester Stallone, Clint Eastwood, Charles Bronson, and John Wayne may soon find themselves either in prison or in a mental hospital.

So-called traditional values exist in all known cultural systems. Looking backward into history, however, as a nation or individual walks forward into a dangerous and unknowable future, avoids reality. Even researched by a professional historian, the past is a fantasy construct. The "good old days" adapts idealized perceptions of the past to perceived needs of the present—a fantasy adapted to a fantasy. The Old West, of course, looked back to the Old East for basic value systems. The Old East, in turn, looked back to Western Europe. Every era creates a mythology about its predecessors, with values that seem unattainable in the contemporary period.

The principal problem with history, of course, is that only a small portion of what actually happened can ever be known. Knowledge is always biased, subjective. What is known, for the most part, is what certain individuals or groups wanted known. Histories are highly selective, as are the biases that lie consciously and unconsciously behind human perception. The biases behind history can be far more intriguing and insightful than historical "facts." It appears to be a basic human need to perceive the past as a justification for the future. Histories are vital to individual and group identities, the basic building blocks of culture. Usually, they are handed down from generation to generation verbally. Written histories are still a new invention, representing only the past two thousand years or so. Where histories have not existed, they were invented.

The psychological need to project present uncertainties upon a fantasy of a stable past may constitute the most significant perceptual vulnerability in the human heritage. In the U.S., of course, the past is created by the mass-communication industry in the pursuit of profit, power, or both. U.S. history, like most national histories, tells people what they want to hear about themselves. "Objective history" is as much a mythological creation as "objective" anything else. Inherent biases in human perception will never disappear. A mathematical science of history is as inconceivable as an international history of the world, a history acceptable to all cultures.

Regression technique is rampant in alcoholic-beverage advertising. Portrayed by an actor with whom the target audience can identify, the drinker is surrounded by friends and family who are accepting, forgiving, and undemanding. They accept the heavy drinker as he or she perceives himself or herself—lovable, dependent, friendly, and good-humored, a joyful companion. Seagram's 7 Crown whiskey sponsored a series of magazine ads that portrayed large numbers of people at parties. There was always one person in the crowd who stood out, surrounded by warm, supportive, accepting friends, who fitted into the group as jovial, warm, sincere, a person who could take a drink or leave it. This special individual was even shown as not drinking, but supportive of others drinking, and happy. Real life, of course, is never like this for incipient alcoholics. They are usually a painful embarrassment to friends, family, and employers, quite the opposite of their fantasy selves.

Fantasy Formation:
Mythology Versus Reality

Mythology is generally associated with ancient history, and modern peoples view themselves as liberated from such primitive notions. We perceive ourselves as hard-nosed pragmatic realists, far removed from the superstitions of yesteryear—as did the ancient Greeks and all the societies that existed between us and them.

Nonetheless, we are all involved in *fantasy formation*, a subordination of reality in favor of a fantasy world, peopled by fantasy people, in fantasy relationships and situations. This unconscious process provides a supportive structure for escapes from mature reality orientation. When combined with elements of regression to a past with imagined glories, security, justice, honesty, and so on, fantasy formation can become obsessional.

Rooted firmly in reality, creative fantasy can be an asset. Retrenchment into magic and wishful thinking, however—coupled with a search for fantasized sensual gratification—can plunge individuals and groups into serious psycho- or sociopathology. Constantly reinforced by high-credibility media, fantasies can become the perceived reality of a society. The absurdity of the deliberately generated fear of capitalism in the U.S.S.R. is equaled only by the fear of communism in the U.S. Such fear results from a manipulation of the latent paranoiac tendencies in most populations. Frequently, when fantasy dominates reality, anyone who questions the fantasy will be defensively considered subversive, insane, or even criminal. Romanticization of justice can impede the pursuit of justice. Fantasy substitutions for reality in any area of life can become tragic, even lethal.

Profitably manipulated by communications industries, the mechanisms of fantasy formation have become instruments of power, status, and privilege. Fantasy formations via stereotypes of Jews, women, communists, blacks, homosexuals, and heretics (virtually anyone not like "us") were the fundamental victims of the Holy Inquisition, the Third Reich, and many world dictatorships. Political or ideological prisoners are subjected to punishments and tortures far more barbaric than those inflicted upon murderers, thieves, rapists, and other criminals.

Fantasies about ghosts, goblins, witches, and heretics are as far removed from reality as are the fantasies of ethnic, political, cultural, psychological, or social stereotypes. Decisions based upon one nation's fantasies of another nation's fantasies, acted out as realities, provide little hope for survival.

Sublimation: Push-ups, Jogging, and Cold Showers

Sublimation is not, strictly speaking, an unconscious perceptual defense, though it can become compulsive, obsessional, and involve unconscious motivations. Sublimation is a normal, essential aspect of human growth, development, and socialization. Taboo or consciously unacceptable drives and wishes are sublimated, channeled into more socially acceptable or constructive pursuits. In self-destructive behaviors, such as with the compulsive workaholic or in other obsessional avoidance strategies, sublimation can evolve into a nightmare.

Sublimation involves the replacement of libidinal, aggressive, or otherwise unacceptable energies with counter-energies or drives. Athletic competition, scholarship, or compulsive work can substitute for anger, sexual preoccupation, or ego sensitivities. Sublimation can occur in response to unconscious motivations but is in itself a consciously determined behavior. It is often unclear, however, where repression and sublimation begin or end. The threshold between conscious and unconscious perception is a delicate, constantly moving barrier.

Excessive drives for achievement, power, money, or control over others involve sublimation. Religious idealism or fanaticism often stem from individual or group attempts to deal with powerful but unacceptable emotions, wishes, fantasy projections, and feelings.

Denial: It Did Not Occur

Denial is used by individuals, groups, and even nations to defend themselves against disturbing feelings, contradictions, thoughts, or events. An unpleasant situation is simply rendered nonexistent. Responsibility or blame is projected neatly upon someone else. Repression and denial are often interrelated and undistinguishable. Denial is far subtler than simple lies or misrepresentations. Lies are usually discovered and exposed. Denial is an unconscious mechanism that permits anyone to escape conscious awareness. Denial can even develop into a powerful conviction. It is often involved in religious fervor, irreconcilable marital conflicts, chauvinistic nationalism, and political or national idealism, and is a frequent aspect of *blind faith*.

Denial gets us off the hook when we are confronted with unpleasant, verifiable facts or contradictory information. For example, there is virtually nothing constructive or complimentary anyone in the U.S. can publicly say about the U.S.S.R.'s communist government, and vice versa. After some seventy years of antagonistic confrontation, the two populations have been exhaustively conditioned to dehumanize each other. Consciously and unconsciously, each society is indoctrinated to deny any but the most negative view of the other. Anyone thinking autonomously would have become suspicious about the consistency in each side's negative view of the other. (Consistency is another constructed illusion in human affairs.) About the only thing consistent about human beings is their inconsistency.

Culturally reinforced denial becomes what each side perceives as normal, reasonable assumptions about the other. Each denies the validity, justifications, idealism, convictions, legitimacy, humane motives, and integrity of the other. If children behaved that way, they would be punished and sent to bed without dinner. To be sustained over a long time, denial must have some perceived factual justification, which can be created or simply selected out of context. If you wish to dislike someone, a reason can always be discovered. High-credibility sources must constantly reinforce denial. This defense mechanism is rarely powerful enough to self-perpetuate when opposed by a respected majority.

Reaction formation may accompany denial, turning an unacceptable feeling into its opposite. Feelings of jealousy or hatred, for example, may be denied, undone, and converted into apparent trust and love. The conversion process is completely unconscious and serves as a cover for the unacceptable feelings, which persist at an unconscious level, though likely to surface sooner or later.

Marriage counselors frequently comment upon the mating of incompatible couples, a culturally integrated phenomenon in many Western cultures. Incompatibles attract each other like magnets— "across the crowded room," "love at first sight," "love walked in," "from the first moment on . . ." Mutual attraction between incompatibles is powerful, often irresistible. Each individual has converted underlying hostility and distrust into conscious, emotionally overpowering love or physical attraction.

Media love, as reflected in commercial drama, often depicts such relationships as ideal. They rarely follow up on "true love" two, five, ten, or twenty years later, after years of unhappiness, divorce, and tragedy. A priest employed as a marriage counselor commented, "Individuals are creatures of God, made in His own image. The mating process, however, appears to be operated by the devil. Media models persuade two totally incompatible individuals to share life experiences. Basing their lives upon media fantasies, especially those that emphasize sensual indulgence, the two are guaranteed to subject one another to the tortures of the damned. Heavenly bliss uncontrollably evolves into Dante's Inferno." Successful, profitable drama, perhaps, but vicious, mutually destructive human relationships.

Projection and Introjection: Whom to Blame?

Projection and *introjection* are extremely important perceptual defenses, both to individuals and to the mass-communication industry. These defenses are converted via media into large-scale public behaviors. Both are completely unconscious to the individuals affected. They appear, like the other perceptual defenses, natural, logical, reasonable, and supported by perceived facts, consensus, and respected sources. *Projective images* are universally false. They project stereotypical generalizations that can be either good or bad, rarely both (which might be more consistent with reality). Audiences, with the reinforcement of media, construct perceptually a fantasized image of the Libyans, North Koreans, Nicaraguans, Palestinians, Iranians, Russians, or whoever appears as the antagonist of the moment. Similar image constructs develop among peoples who are the targets of stereotyped projection. Mutually reinforcing stereotypes invariably involve generalized fantasies of good guy–bad guy—none of which ever have anything to do with reality. Projections unconsciously involve repression, denial, and fantasy formation.

Projective stereotypes unconsciously project powerful, simplified, reciprocally confirming abstractions. These fantasies can justify a wide range of dangerous, even homicidal behaviors. Projections conceal human diversity, complex motives, and factual information behind barriers of blinding bigotry and simplistic labels. Individuals are reduced perceptually to objects. The devastating process is shamefully manipulated by world leaders who often project their own ulterior motives on their adversaries. Simply, we blame them for what we have been trying to accomplish ourselves in the pursuit of profit and power. Projections appear in such assertions as "you cannot trust" the Soviets, Cubans, Arabs, Japanese, Germans, Chinese, Indians, people over or under thirty, et cetera. The process, once put into motion, is unconscious within both individuals and groups. As it gains media momentum, however, fewer and fewer individuals question or oppose the fantasies.

As long as projective gymnastics are a conscious aspect of strategy, calculated for effect, they simply misrepresent reality in order to influence opinion. This assumes the other side is informed about projection and consciously considers it rhetorical nonsense aimed to attract votes, sell products or persons, or please audiences. Serious dilemmas occur when projective strategies are believed by the easily influenced. Adolf Hitler told the world in his 1926 autobiography, *Mein Kampf,* exactly what he planned for Germany, Europe, Russia, communists, Jews, and the world. Leaders of the day refused to believe his insane projective fantasies, which appeared as mere cynical rhetoric designed only to win elections and power. Such rhetoric had been used throughout the world, and still is, as rabble-rousing inducements, simplistic answers to complex questions.

On the other hand, if projective lies, exaggerations, and manipulations are perceived as truth, the perception could be terminal for all involved. When U.S.-baiters in Moscow, or their counterparts in Washington, hurl violent, projective rhetoric, the world can only hold its breath in the hope that they are lying in the pursuit of some momentary objective; and, of course, in the hope the other side will assess the insults as theatrical ploys designed only for propaganda.

Projection is unconsciously accepted as truth by those who do not understand the strategy. This may constitute the world's most dangerous manipulative practice. Survival in such conflicts as the 1962 Cuban missile crisis depended upon each side's ability to assess correctly the other's projective lies, exaggerations, and manipulations. Had anyone really considered the projective rhetoric valid—and had the Soviets been capable of a strategic nuclear response—the planet Earth might well have ceased to exist.

Moving from the dramatic to the banal, every heavily advertised brand in the economy has been exhaustively market-researched for strength and weaknesses against its competitors. Brand ads usually emphasize as strengths those qualities perceived as weaknesses among competitors. As most brands in a product market are manufactured by similar machinery, raw materials, technology, and labor, brands are usually quite similar. The realities are similar. The perceived realities manipulated by ads, however, appear vastly different. Differences are cosmetic rather than substantial. Perceived variations in quality or value are projectively managed through inducement of unconscious projection among consumers. Thus Subaru is "The kind of car Mercedes might have built if they were a little more frugal and a lot more inventive." (Trust us, we wouldn't lie to you.) An ad for Merit cigarettes proclaims, "Almost every low tar cigarette claims great taste and less tar. But try a few and those claims quickly go up in smoke. With Merit, there's a real difference. It's called Enriched Flavor. Only Merit has it." (Tobacco smoke actually suppresses and anesthetizes taste and enriched flavor.) Stay Trim diet gum's promoters advise, "By the time your diet pill starts working it may be too late." (If you believe this, it is.) Gordon's gin comes from "England—known for its playboys. And its gin." (Keeps playboys playing with themselves.) And Noxzema promises "finally, a cleanser that won't clash with your complexion." (Incredible; does the president know?)

Jealousy in marital relations is also often a manifestation of projection. One mate projects his or her infidelities, real or fantasized, on the other. Projection is a complex perceptual defense that plays a part in a broad range of psychopathologies, as well as in day-to-day relationships. The process can be compared to efforts at ridding the body of irritation, discomfort, tension, or frustration. Projection can also involve unconscious desires to be free from an unacceptable wish, desire, or feeling.

In media, whether in entertainment or the structuring of news and information, writers weave projective characterizations into their stories. These are characters into which the audience will project or identify. Projective characterizations can be either positive or negative, but usually reflect archetypal values.

For example, the character of J. R. Ewing in *Dallas* was designed by the writer, director, and actor around unconscious projective identifications of older, lower-middle-income males who could hate J. R. for those qualities of malice, greed, and lust they deny in themselves, or like him for acting in ways they would like to but do not dare. *All in the Family*'s Archie Bunker provided audiences with projective identification of the bigot as a nice guy. Prejudiced individuals, constantly under pressure in a society where open discrimination has become unpopular, could project into Archie their own frustrations and dilemmas. The TV show was widely acclaimed for opposing prejudice, which it did for audience segments who enjoyed making fun of a not-too-bright bigot. The large national audiences that supported the series over many years contained, however, large audience segments with a strong appeal to projective intolerance. In effect, Archie Bunker told each segment what they wanted to hear. Once again, very little in media communication is what it appears to be on the surface.

Marshall McLuhan described projections as "Narcissus Narcosis." As we perceive endless hours of media involvement, we unconsciously project and identify with heroes against villains. Audiences identify with characters in ads, dramatic programs, and news in a simplistic, stereotypical good guy–bad guy context. They vicariously become the characters in the drama, projecting into roles in a way that narcotizes, anesthetizes, and numbs them against reality intrusions. Rambo transforms from a funny-book hero into a potential solution for real world complexities. From the investor's perspective, the only intolerable characterizations in commercial drama, ads, or news are those that go unnoticed. Love or hate him, but he'll be out of work if audiences ignore him!

The design and staging of rock groups provide another example of projective identification. Images are engineered by sophisticated music investment corporations to be instantly revolting to parents and evoke panic about their children's welfare. For the immature audiences, the group must project their defiance of parental supervision and moral restrictions and offer an affront to authority figures of all types. The engineering of rock music and the groups who play it focuses on the instabilities inherent in the ages of their fans. Heavy metal rock groups, for example, are designed to project a fantasy of Satan as savior for neurosis-prone, lower-working-class teenagers. Heavy metal has made enormous profits for record companies but has promoted suicide and antisocial violence as an answer to adolescent problems.

It's My Fault

Introjection parallels projection; it is the unconscious turning in upon oneself of responsibility for evil thoughts, unacceptable feelings, distrust or contempt for others. The introjective process is typified in the reflections, "It is not his fault, he is not bad. I am!" Or, "They are not hostile to me. They don't like me because I am hostile to them. It is me who is worthless!" People may blame themselves or project into themselves someone else's negative traits. Self-condemnation may be perceived as a way to preserve a needed love or identification figure.

For example, when projection engineering succeeds through · rock music and the fan becomes estranged from loved authority figures, introjection may develop as a compensatory behavior. Immature, manipulated rebels eventually blame themselves for their rebellion. Even among those individuals who have been rocked into alcohol and drug abuse, the musicians, music, and promoters are rarely blamed. Damaged fans invariably blame themselves. The result is a tragic loss of self-esteem.

Much of the mass-communication industry depends on the exploitation and manipulation of human weakness. The one consistent theme permeating virtually all advertising is consumer inferiority. By unconscious comparison, the consumer has to be a loser, deficient, and ordinary. Ad models are always glamorous and desirable. The idealization works like the unobtainable carrot being dangled in front of a jackass. That carrot can dangle just out of reach throughout a lifetime of consumer behavior.

When individuals are persuaded to view themselves as inferior, they can be directed into the purchase of any product or brand that promises fulfillment and human completeness. Consumption will supposedly bring ever-elusive perfection. Advertiser promises, of course, remain eternally unfulfilled, and the individual gradually submerges into a fantasy of consumption as an end in itself. Ad-dependent consumers become increasingly dissatisfied. Failure to attain the ideal proposed by ads is devastating to self-esteem. The mechanism, however, is self-perpetuating. Consumers are propelled from one new product to another, then another, then another, as life continues on the treadmill of consumerism. They consume, therefore they exist.

Part Two

LANGUAGE
AND
CULTURE

THE TOOLS OF INDOCTRI- NABILITY

4 | MEDIA— THE BRAINWASHING LAUNDROMAT

Whoever undertakes to set himself up as a judge of *truth* and *knowledge* is shipwrecked by the laughter of the gods.

Albert Einstein, *The Evolution of Physics*

Everyman's world picture is and always remains a construct of his mind and cannot be proved to have any other existence.

Irwin Schrödinger, *Mind and Matter*

We build this world, for the most part, unaware— simply because we do not know how we do it.

Ernst von Glasersfeld, *Introduction to Radical Constructivism*

In a small though very important volume published in 1973, Nobel Laureate Konrad Lorenz outlined *Civilized Man's Eight Deadly Sins*: those eight areas of imminent disaster created and sustained by so-called modern civilizations. Each of these eight areas has the potential to end our biological and social heritage within the next century or less—possibly much less. Lorenz's list of sins is ominous and familiar—nuclear energy and weapons, overpopulation, environmental devastation, atrophy of feelings, abuse of inventive and innovative energies, genetic decay, destruction of traditions, and human indoctrinability.

It is the last of these that makes all the others possible. If humans can be indoctrinated to mindlessly pursue their self-destruction— as they have especially been in high-technology cultures—the process may be reversible. We must at least hope that self-annihilation is not inevitable. But it is clear that technologies of indoctrination are well known throughout the world. In the U.S., the commercial mass media—that is, the ad and public-relations industries—indoctrinate and control culture and, through culture, the perceptual constructions of the general population.

A political-economic-cultural propaganda exists in even the simplest ad—much more powerful as implication than as overt statement. In the U.S.S.R. and other communist bloc nations, political ideology is propagandized overtly, which may actually render the media far less effective. Propaganda that looks and sounds like propaganda must fail. Soviet information technicians hard-sell their political and philosophical system with the same fervor that their Madison Avenue counterparts bring to the hyping of underarm deodorants.

Indoctrinability, however, is never apparent to the indoctrinated. The indoctrinated includes *all of them*, of course, and, far more difficult to admit, *all of us*. With its linguistic pretensions to superiority, the human species is by far the most vulnerable to persuasion, indoctrination, propaganda, brainwashing, programming, conditioning, or whatever label anyone may wish to use. In laboratory experiments, monkeys must be rewarded for compliance, usually with a cracker. Humans have been taught to comply when rewarded only with a picture of a cracker, embedded with subliminal *SEX*es. The people most vulnerable to indoctrination are those in media-managed, high-technology societies. The U.S. population, subjected to roughly $150 billion in ad investment during 1989, is the most exhaustively propagandized society ever to exist.

Remarkably, virtually everyone in developed countries desperately tries to believe they are immune to indoctrination. They think they think for themselves and readily know the difference between truth and falsity, fantasy and reality, superstition and science, fact and fiction. Technologically sophisticated cultures are conditioned to accept belief systems, behaviors, and values that would have been rejected out of hand by their stone-age predecessors. Primitives would instantly sense the obvious threats to survival and adjustment, or simple nonsense, inherent in many of the treasured beliefs of modern society. Many readers of this book cannot distinguish a real broken bottle from a painted fake or a real ice cube from a fantasy ice cube. Can they be taken seriously with their pretensions to knowledge about what is going on in Washington, Moscow, or their own living rooms?

The perceived "free, educated, intelligent, civilized" populations of the world now provide the greatest danger to world survival. They are, generally, unaware of the extent to which they are manipulated, managed, and conditioned by media, governments, leaders, and institutions that serve the vested interests of their political-social-economic systems. Vested interests and ruling elites appear a constant throughout the known evolution of human societies—perhaps the only constant in social organizations.

The issue of *how humans think they think* is central to the continuation of civilization as we have come to know it. Unfortunately, the issue usually provokes outrage, anger, irritation, defensiveness, or boredom. Those individuals most vulnerable and victimized by human indoctrination systems will be the most defensive about their particular indoctrination.

The question of "objective reality" appears fundamental to human survival in this and the next century. It appears impossible to know for certain what goes on around us at any given moment. We are an integral part of the reality we perceive. No known way has been discovered whereby humans can detach themselves from their perceptions and their myriad of inherent biases. Self-help with unconscious perceptions is absurd, impossible. The realities

95

perceived are products of unconscious socioeconomic-political conditioning. Over time, these perceptions aggregate into cultural perspectives.

For well over 2,000 years, scholars and scientists have questioned whether there *is* a reality outside, independent from the mind. It has been difficult, especially for so-called civilized men and women, to accept that human perception and experience exist only in the brain. This includes religions, ideologies, knowledge, and everything perceived over a lifetime.

The perceivable environment appears largely an invention, one often manipulated in the interest of those who profit from human perceptual conditioning. Among the earth's species, only humans appear to self-manufacture their thinking, knowledge, cognitive perceptions, and consequently their actions. Few, however, consciously acknowledge that they do this themselves, have it done for them, or both. Humans have traditionally projected justifications for behaviors onto some fantasized "objective reality."

The questionable nature of what we accept as *objective reality* or *truth* remains carefully repressed, hidden from awareness, yet ever-present under the surface of consciousness. This underlying threat to perceptual validity drives us into stronger, ever more violent defenses of illusions and rationalizations. Repression does not occur accidentally or casually. Humans unconsciously repress to avoid anxiety or unwanted confrontations with reality. Ideologues, the most repressed of all, perceive their world as a simple, symmetrical, logical place that avoids complexity, contradiction, inconsistency, or paradox, and have an abiding fear of being unable to cope with undefined or uncertain reality.

The ideologues' ignorance occurs not because they do not know. Many adamantly *do not want to know how* they manufacture their reality, who controls the manufacturing process, and the concealed or invisible objectives, agendas, and mechanisms of the game. Most of us take the world pretty much for granted. It was here long before humans evolved. It is tacitly assumed the world will be here long after they leave. The daily vexations of life are, for most, an all-consuming preoccupation.

Since Plato, arguments have raged over how humans achieve their knowledge of reality, and how reliable and accurate that knowledge can be. One common thread through well over 2,000 years of recorded science and philosophy is that *truth* must relate to some idea of objective reality. In order to be considered *truth*, a proposition must be verifiable and related to a verbally definable objective reality in the world around us. Mankind's most noble preoccupation has been the search for *truth*. Each time *truth* was discovered, however, tragic mischief ensued.

Is Objective Reality Real?

In *The Critique of Pure Reason*, Immanuel Kant in 1783 argued that the human mind does not evolve laws from objective reality, but imposes these laws upon reality, conforming it to preconceptions, motives, self-interests, biases, and cultural conditioning. Though Kant's *Critique* is still read, his questioning of perceived reality is usually skipped over. The notion is subversive, threatening, certainly incompatible with the conventional wisdoms of a high-technology society.

So-called modern men and women are well indoctrinated—especially many of those considered scientists, scholars, experts, and authority figures—and highly disciplined in cultural conformity. They rarely question the notion that verbal truth must always match perceived reality—an impossibility. Any suggestion that perceived realities are a variable product, manufactured by human perceptual bias, immediately threatens the way in which humans have been conditioned to interpret their world.

These questions, at first, appear complicated, remote from immediate concerns, and completely impractical. They are easily ignored, even though the nature of perceived realities is a fundamental aspect of decision-making each day in business, government, family relationships, military strategy, and almost every other area of human endeavor. Many convince themselves they cannot understand the questions and have no reason to care about the answers.

It has been fascinating, often amusing, to observe individuals attempt to cope with the exposé of subliminal advertising. The problem has never been that they cannot perceive the embedded obscenities; almost everyone perceives them quite easily. But they do not want to deal consciously with the embeds, and will often

seek any avenue of escape possible. The idea of subliminal indoctrination evokes fear among many. This author has been accused
of hypnotizing audiences and readers, putting dirty ideas into their
heads, playing projective games with Rorschach inkblots, forcing
people to see pornographic images that were not really there.
Anyone who doubts the power of repression can simply try to
explain the illustrations in this book to their friends, neighbors,
and family.

Fortified against any assault upon the world as we have been
indoctrinated to perceive it, humans often channel such threats
into the wastebasket of repression. The power of individual or
group repression should never be taken lightly. Over many tragic
centuries, humans have defended themselves, even with violence,
against disturbing insights into the mechanics of *how they know
they know.*

To an average, practical, hard-nosed individual, this probably
seems at first glance to be philosophical nonsense—conjecture, meaningless speculation, even boring pedantry, just another vain exercise
in how many angels can dance on the head of a pin. Nothing could
be further from the truth! A continuation of human life and what
passes for civilization will be predicated upon an ability to untangle
the above dilemma. Our belief about *how we think we think* is the
basis for most of the world's assumptions about itself. Many of
these assumptions point toward self-destruction.

The human brain creates, or constructs, its own perception of
reality in relation to its indoctrinated preconceptions, engineered
motives, self-interests, and cultural backgrounds. We actually manufacture these ideas, concepts, and percepts—or have them manufactured for us by the media. For example, humans invent their
friends and enemies, loves and hates, success and failure, truths
and fallacies. Ideas such as freedom, democracy, justice, security,
along with a dictionary of similar verbal concepts, continue to
guide our decisions—at least consciously; such verbal concepts,
however, mean vastly different things to different individuals. Contradictions often render the concepts meaningless. For example,
socialist nations define these generalizations far differently than
does the capitalist world, the Latin world differently from the
Anglo, the Christian differently from the Moslem, the Catholic

98

differently from the Protestant. One nation's terrorists are another nation's freedom fighters.

Economist Thorstein Veblen considered "occupational psychosis," a society's means of perceived economic sustenance, to be the basic conditioning source for behavior and value judgments. For example, a simple bridge over a canyon will be perceived far differently by truckdrivers, pedestrians, city planners, bankers, engineers, bicyclists, or housewives. Economic bias is an extremely important aspect of perception, though the phenomenon is certainly far more complex—operating at both conscious and unconscious levels.

In the U.S., U.S.S.R., and other technologically advanced societies, the major instrument for the manufacture of reality perceptions is the mass communication industry. In the U.S. these media are controlled to reflect the reality perceptions of corporate executives and ideologically compatible institutions. Their collective self-interests become culturally integrated, blindly or unconsciously accepted by audiences as reality perceptions—in effect, *truths.*

This does not include the superficial day-to-day events, polemics, ups and downs, conflicts, successes or failures within the system; rather it is the basic, underlying belief structures, things known to be *true* at conscious, if not unconscious, levels of perception. Belief structures usually go unnoticed by individuals who hold them. Assumptions or expectations are taken for granted, accepted without question, considered immutable facts of life. To assault or question these suppositions, whose most tenacious grip on an individual exists at unconscious levels, is usually considered a subversive act, or even worse if the assault is taken seriously by others. Jean Piaget, the French child psychologist, noted, "Intelligence or knowledge organizes the world by organizing itself."

A useful analogy might be drawn from U.S. news information, organized to sell ads, which patronizingly tells readers about themselves rather than about world events. Such "news" highlights the reader's infinite wisdom, nobility, kindness, freedom, pleasure, good taste—all the positive self-image values. Negative information, at this perceptual level, would evoke conscious rejection by audiences.

Glorified, romanticized pseudo-information about celebrities, for example, endlessly confirms the one-dimensional stereotypical objects with whom audiences identify. People, in any reality-oriented sense, will never make it in *People* magazine. *People* creates and sustains celebrity fictions designed to sell the magazine and its ads. From the teenybopper fan magazines to network TV interviews with the rich and famous, the celebrity-milking industry serves as ads for ads.

Advertising and its supportive "news" information work similarly. The audience is the basic subject matter covertly embedded in each sentence, each picture, each scenario. Credibility rests not upon verifiable factual perceptions, but upon audience identifications and projections. Media fantasies of reality, manufactured in the interest of advertisers, reflect the emotional needs of the audience—what they wish to hear about themselves is *included*; that which would offend fantasy projections is *excluded*.

Media audiences, conditioned through many decades of constant reinforcement of wishful thinking about themselves, lose their ability to discriminate between perceptual fantasies and realities. Periodically, events occur that cannot be swept under the perceptual rug and force themselves upon audience attention. Objectionable information, in conflict with popular perceptions of reality, may be considered for short periods. But really bad news will eventually be repressed and will disappear from public attention.

Journalist I. F. Stone made a long, successful career out of exposing deceptions, deceits, and lies by politicians. Stone simplified the problem: "Every government is run by liars, and nothing they say should be believed." The problem is that he left off half the equation. No lie ever works unless someone is willing to believe it. People often prefer lies over truths if they uphold cherished self-images. This condition is at least partially a product of long-term immersion in the ad-media massage.

No one gets away with an overt lie or misrepresentation if the audience really wants to know what actually occurred. Victims participate in the crimes of the victimizers. For a con to work effectively, those being conned must be participants in the game. Alert, critical, questioning audiences cannot be conned. They must first be persuaded to trust, believe, have faith, and accept the "objective truths" of their manipulators.

Perceptual bias also plays an important role in manipulation.

The selection of one single sensory stimulus relegates the other senses to the status of unconscious, subliminal inputs into the brain. Sight, for example, is an overpowering sensory experience. If something looks good, the sensitivities of the many other sensory inputs into the brain turn off consciously, even though they remain active subliminally.

In one experiment, two dozen students camped out in a weekend retreat at a Canadian monastery. During the three days, the group was continuously blindfolded. Blindfolds were padded so light could not enter perception. Most of the students learned to cook, dress, wash, and care for themselves without dependence upon sight. The experience was powerful and revealing. For the first time in their lives, they realized the unused sensory potential that exists within every human. Two students, sightless since birth, were included in the group to serve as guides.

By the second day, the students knew—they were uncertain just how they could know—when an animal entered the room. Many accurately distinguished whether the animal was a cat or a dog. Most could walk rapidly through a nearby apple orchard without bumping into trees or one another. A few even ran through the orchard. The students also later reported they somehow understood the deeper feelings of others much more clearly than ever before. Many found it easier to *trust*, or—in several incidents— to *distrust* the motives, sincerity, and honesty of others. Several students dropped out during the second day. The discovery of an entire range of sensory potentials—most of which became available in a nonverbal, feeling, intuitive awareness—was emotionally overwhelming.

In his autobiography, Jacques Lusseyran reported his World War II experiences as a leader of a French underground network, *Défense de la France*, which successfully fought Nazi occupation forces. Lusseyran lost his sight in an accident when he was eight years old. As a young scholar, he organized a Resistance cell that later joined with the larger network. Lusseyran's unique role was to interrogate new recruits. Unsighted, he was able to perceive the candidates through voices, smells, and audible movements, and he weeded out traitors, weaklings, and emotional unsuitables with uncanny accuracy. Lusseyran used the term "moral odor" to describe his unsighted perceptions of sighted individuals. "They were not at all," he explained, "as they were said to be. They never suspected I could read their voices like a book." Finally captured, he spent fifteen months as a prisoner in Buchenwald. He was among the thirty out of 2,000 in his original transport to survive. Lusseyran eventually became a professor at Cleveland's Western Reserve University. It is extremely difficult, if not impossible, to lie successfully to an unsighted individual. This is one of the reasons the sighted often feel uncomfortable around the blind without understanding why.

While truth remains an evasive, ephemeral product of perception, a remote approximation or at best a well-intentioned evaluation of multilevel realities, calculated lies are comparatively easy to discover unless vested interests anesthetize perceptual agility. In a heavily documented article in the respected *Columbia Journalism Review*, *Newsday*'s managing editor Anthony Marro recorded a shattering list of overt lies told by recent presidents and their administrations. A few of the lies might have been vaguely justified by national defense considerations. Marro demonstrated that the Reagan White House developed lies into institutionalized tools of public administration. President Reagan's appearance and his actor's skill with nonverbal communication powerfully concealed the often shallow substance and content in his rhetoric. Misinformation became a major policy. Worse, the Reagan lies were motivated by politics—not national security. President Reagan lied to the world at a level unprecedented in recent history, a significant achievement considering the awesome misinformation policies of former presidents Lyndon Johnson and Richard Nixon.

Reagan overtly, calculatedly, looking his audience straight in the eye, lied on a grand scale about a balanced budget, the Grenada invasion, food stamps and welfare recipients, El Salvador, Nicaragua, Central America, the Middle East, civil rights, commitments to the handicapped and retired, environmental protection, social security disability laws, the attack on Libya, military expenditures, the federal deficit, and the Strategic Defense Initiative (Star Wars). A sizable pyramid of lies and deceptions surrounded the secret Iranian arms shipments and the illegal funding of Contra terrorists in Nicaragua, an affair that became a damaging embarrassment to the U.S. and its allies. Anyone remotely in touch with reality could have anticipated this logical consequence of ad flimflam operating at the highest level of public trust and confidence. Unfortunately, this is not the only recent example of manipulation and deceit in governmental information policies. Considering the culturally institutionalized nature of public manipulation, it will probably not be the last.

These lies do not include statements reflecting an honest difference of opinion, interpretation, or emphasis. These lies were specific, known, misstatements of recorded, verifiable, factual data. The misinformation mechanism is well known to politicians. The president can lie like a used-car salesman before eighty million people on national television; subsequent exposure of the misinformation appears in scattered, piecemeal, uncoordinated form over succeeding days, weeks, or months. The follow-up stories appear inconspicuously in the *Washington Post, New York Times, Wall Street Journal, Atlantic Monthly,* and other publications. Journalist James Nathan Miller tells in the *Atlantic* of the twelve hours of research to expose as a lie only one sentence of a Reagan speech. Compounding the problem of time and expertise, editors across the nation are reluctant to buck the fantasies of their readers unless the stories reach major magnitude.

Marro cited President Reagan's excuse for the lies, announced through his public-relations staff, that "It didn't matter whether some of his [the President's] stories were literally true—his numerous misstatements of fact, his confusion about detail, and his repeated anecdotes about supposed welfare cheats no one was able to confirm, for example—because they contained *a larger truth.*" According to Bill Kovach, a *New York Times* editor, "We've been dealing with an administration that freely states—and stated early—that literal truth was not a concern." David Wise wrote in his unsettling book *The Politics of Lying,* "The chief criterion in government is not truth, but the opposite, developing lies that will be plausible enough to be accepted as truth, lies that will be believed."

The importance of all this is not merely the existence of liars in high places. Most people already knew this, at some level of knowing. What is important, especially in today's dangerous world, is that populations accept lying as a normal aspect of government policy. Liars, as mentioned earlier, cannot succeed unless they find people willing to cooperate—enthusiastic victims conned into believing they will also benefit from the lies.

Self-Flattery—
The Foundation Stone

Audience self-flattery, both overt and, more often, implied, is the foundation stone of effective commercial communication. Above all else, audiences must be told what they wish to hear about themselves. The phenomenon is not unique to any single culture. Negative information will often be ignored, repressed, or otherwise perceptually defended against.

The average U.S. newspaper is today over 95% ads. Unconscious perception does not discriminate between so-called news and advertising information. Most readers do not draw a clear distinction between the two, nor could they. Information is simply information at unconscious perceptual levels stored in a vast memory system not compartmentalized as good and bad, true and false, fantasy and reality. Value judgments appear a function of conscious deliberation. Audiences are not conditioned consciously to accept news as truth and advertising as lies. The idea might be worth exploring, however, as it could resolve several major public health and sanity questions. Unfortunately, the world of perceived realities is not that simple.

The residue of information accumulated at the unconscious level provides the basic cultural program or bias upon which other conscious perceptual systems or structures are organized. Through this information residue, individuals and groups define who they are and where they are going, and derive hierarchies of basic values. This analogy must, of course, be multiplied by all the other media perceptual exposures each day, week, month, year, and decade. Each medium manufactures or produces a residual orientation, quite invisible to the individuals, groups, and nations involved. The orientation is omnipresent and provides a cultural screen through which topical current events, entertainments, amusements, and momentary distractions filter.

In a seminar on culture and technology, a question was introduced as to what an alien from outer space would perceive about U.S. culture after a brief visit. The group made a list of the obvious: massive alcohol and drug abuse, indifference to the plight of others, mindless sensory indulgence, family disintegration, criminality and needless violence—the list of horrors filled several pages. These were subjects about which most sensitive, socially concerned and informed individuals would be consciously aware, since they appear regularly in information media and are widely discussed and debated. The seminar finally concluded the alien would likely draw a grim picture of the U.S., perhaps concluding the place was hopeless.

These were observations, however, by people who spent their lives in U.S. culture. The alien, at least for a while, would have greater objectivity. Would the alien perceive the same world experienced by the seminar members? What was left out of the scenario were those things individuals in the U.S. rarely question. The single thing most obvious to the alien would be our inability to perceive consciously our own complicity, involvement, and profits derived from the long list of social ills. For example, there exists a prodigious legal investment in crime, sickness, poverty, and drug addiction from which many individuals and institutions benefit.

Another obvious thing to an alien observer would be the contradictions. These might include the continually reiterated beliefs in freedom, democracy, and equality contrasted against the ready willingness to control and exploit other peoples, or stated beliefs in peace and goodwill contrasted against the maintenance of excessive military power. The belief in equality of opportunity contrasts against the actual suppression of minority or deviant groups. The stated dedication to the common welfare contrasts against a willingness to sacrifice almost anything or anybody to the preservation of privileged status, private property, and greed.

Contradictions are usually invisible and repressed by those within mainstream culture—the beneficiaries of the system—but available and obvious to the cultural outsider—the alien from outer space, or those from poor white, black, Hispanic, or Indian ghettos. The alien's conclusion might well be that, indeed, the earth is hopeless. On the other hand, the alien might conclude that if humans could be taught to perceive *around* their cultural repressions, nationalisms, biases, and vested interests—and especially around their fantasies of objective truth—they might eventually resolve their dilemmas.

The work of knowing or perceiving what appears to be going on in the world cannot ever produce a true and unbiased picture. *Unbiased truth* is a fictional conception. In modern science, even theoretical mathematicians and physicists frequently question whether they have actually discovered a law of nature or if their education, theories, and experimental techniques have molded the appearance of nature into a structure that seems to justify a law.

The point is apparent in experimental research with rat behavior. Are psychologists training the rats or are the rats—with native cunning—training the psychologists to reward them? Few rat psychologists find this possibility humorous, demonstrating anew the power of repression and cultural conditioning to invalidate questions that threaten treasured perceptions.

Marshall McLuhan admonished students to constantly question every assumption they could dredge from their memories. The moment something appeared logical, reasonable, sound, clear, and obvious, McLuhan demanded another very careful look. Perception often functions to flatter the self. This is the moment of greatest danger, when human vulnerability reaches its highest point.

Perception of Language Abstractions

Realities are described by words, pictures, or numbers. All of these abstract symbols are even further removed from reality than is sensory perception. An individual first perceives, then conjures up symbols to describe the perception. Whatever may be said or written about reality is only a symbolic representation. Symbols never become the actual perceived reality they attempt to describe.

What human perception has, so far, been able to understand about reality separates out at least three levels of perception. So far, each level appears unique in the perceptual limitations it imposes upon observers. Different perceptual techniques are required in each. The levels do not overlap, nor can they be perceived concurrently. The three levels are *macro*, *micro*, and *submicro*.

The *macro* level includes what can be readily perceived via the senses—taste, smell, touch, sound, sight, and the myriad subdivisions of each. Simply illustrated, a slice of chocolate cake can be seen, weighed, measured, smelled, tasted, and the texture felt. Without too much difficulty or confusion, one can collect considerable macro data about the cake slice. A finger can even be pointed at one unique slice to differentiate it from another. The macro level appears disarmingly simple, obvious, and straightforward. Beware! *Macro* perception is where reality abstracts into commonsense, everyday language. It is also the level of perception where most quandaries, misevaluations, misperceptions, and disasters of a thousand varieties occur.

The *micro* level, the first step toward a deeper comprehension of reality, can be perceived with instruments that extend human sensory abilities, such as microscopes, thermometers, micrometers, spectrographs, carbon-dating techniques, and a rich assortment of mechanical and electronic instrumentations. These gadgets can extend perception down to the molecular level of reality. Precision observations and quantitative measurements of reality become possible at the *micro* level that could never be attained at the macro level.

These two levels of reality perception make the cake slice a perceptual event of staggering complexity, ranging from the molecular and cellular components up to the smooth, soft, moist texture of the icing and crumb. There is still, however, much more to know (perceive) about our slice of chocolate cake—the *submicro* level. Submicroscopic reality—the atomic nuclei, electrons, protons, neutrons, photons, ions, and the other minute particles, many yet to be discovered—cannot be perceived directly by the human senses. At the *micro* level, an individual can visually perceive cellular structures, even molecules, with an electron microscope. No one can ever directly perceive an atomic structure. The electrons and other particles orbiting the nuclei travel at the speed of light and would have to be stopped to accommodate perception. The submicro level of perception is only available to humans via mathematical abstractions—a language incomprehensible to most nonmathematicians.

There conceivably could exist other levels of perception not yet available to scrutiny, but these three basic dimensions are useful in exploring perceivable reality, the so-called real world. Difficulties begin when someone casually observes the cake slice, or a picture of the slice, and then glibly states, "I know all about that slice of chocolate cake!" As long as we are concerned only with a single cake slice, in a single situation, no really great problem appears. We can use the symbol *slice* and point at the specific *cake slice* with a reasonable expectation that our verbal description will be understood. If, on the other hand, we utilize the symbol *cake slice* to describe all the millions of different slices in the world, we have moved our language symbol far away from any simple reality.

When the word symbols *slice of chocolate cake* are replaced by the symbols *Russians, Moslems, blacks, Chinese, Jews, Hispanics*, or any other abstract symbol, perception moves into an area of perceptual complexity with a lethal potential.

These three levels of perceptual reality—*macro, micro*, and *submicro*—are inherent in all physical and biological reality known to human experience. For anyone to assume they know all, or even a lot, about any individual or group is as absurd as would be a conviction they know all, or even a lot, about the Russians, Moslems, Americans, or the Shoshone Indians. These are, of course, arbitrary verbal categories, merely convenient for illustration. Verbal categorization must always remain arbitrary and tentative. There could be six, sixteen, or sixty verbally definable levels of perceivable reality. Humans may perceive enough about any subject to achieve a particular objective; they should be humbled, however, by the realization that there will always be more they do not know about any subject than the shallow superficialities of what they think they know.

As a practical matter, however, most of us live—often precariously—only at the *macro* level, a few live at the macro and micro levels, and a minute few at *macro, micro*, and *submicro* levels of perception. These three levels, it is important to remember, cannot be perceptually experienced simultaneously. Reality, of course, exists concurrently. But humans must perceive reality levels one at a time.

Human survival and adjustment would be well served if individuals were educated in their perceptual and linguistic limitations. Any pretense to objective truth or knowledge at merely the *macro* level of human perception is at worst a lie, at best a naïve misrepresentation. The simple statement that you cannot trust Panama, communists, Republicans, Rotarians, anarchists, or Lions Club members, though often taken quite seriously, can be subject matter only for a logic of the absurd. The relationship between language and the objects or people language seeks to describe is universally subjective. In spite of this, most of us have been carefully indoctrinated to accept language at face value, to trust implicitly superficial *macro* perceptions.

Perceptual instruments, techniques, and mathematical reasoning assist human observers to achieve some degree of perceptual distance. But what passes for science at the moment continues to discover, quite unobjectively, what it is rewarded for having discovered. Much like art, science is usually whatever you can get away with at any particular moment in history. And you can get away with a lot if you understand the game. Any society that wishes to survive would be wise to carefully challenge its politicians, public and corporate administrators, generals, scientists, engineers, and others who present themselves as experts, authorities, seers, or gurus. Nobel prize-winning physicist Werner Heisenberg's perceptual principle remains a warning to the gullible: "No perceptual judgment can ever be made with complete certainty."

The *macro* level of perception is where perceivable reality translates into words and pictures. It is the level at which most people live their lives. *Macro* wars are fought, policies evolved, and definitions made that control, threaten, and destroy human life. But any attempt to define word or picture symbols must arbitrarily both include and exclude information. Not unusually, what has been excluded becomes more significant to understanding and meaning than what has been included.

Objectivity Isn't Dead— It Never Existed

Scientific attempts to define things objectively with words from dead languages, such as Latin, never worked. Though the languages were dead, individuals using them were not. Such pseudo-languages do more to control and inhibit discovery and exploration than to objectify language. They are also effective ways to conceal information from lay audiences. Latin, of course, has rapidly disappeared as a defensible scientific language. It has been replaced by Madison Avenue hard-sell, group-think vocabularies that are even further removed from perceivable realities. The rhetorical game of labeling pharmaceutical, electronic, and biological products with unconsciously meaningful symbolic word associations has more to do with magic and myth than with science. Notice the clever sales labeling of prescription and nonprescription drug products. Such magic labels as Cephalexin, Zovirax, Enalapril, Luride, and Theo-Dur evoke feelings of strength and wholesomeness without the vaguest hint of which sicknesses they treat. Science and what science produces have become mere commercial entities designed to be hyped in the marketplace.

The elaborate multisyllabic jargons that developed in the social and behavioral sciences were similar attempts to escape the perceptual bias trap inherent in verbal language. Unfortunately, they ended up in an even worse trap—incomprehensibility. In such areas as psychology, sociology, and anthropology, pedantic attempts to coin words with specific scientific meanings, words not subject to human perceptual bias, produced a meaningless pseudoscientific babble. The moment specific definitions were accepted they began to shift and change through new interpretations. Making word definitions is much like planting trees in quicksand. The jargon became confusing, fictional, and obsolete before the ink dried on the latest glossary.

Contextual variations in meaning—what words *mean* in various contexts or arrangements—have an infinite number of possibilities; there are far too many variations to fit into even the largest computer. The meaning dilemma applies to all language systems. First, there is what the writer intended, seemingly simple enough. Then there is the question of what various individuals and audiences, at various times and places, perceive the writer to have meant—not so simple.

In addition to contextual variations in meaning, individual word meanings, idioms, and colloquial expressions proliferate in every language from day to day, and disappear at roughly the same rate.

Computer translation designers assumed that in specialized areas with limited vocabularies, everyone more or less understands everyone else. They had the computer translate articles from scientific specialties, such as neurosurgery, in a crude style. Constant and uneven changes in each language and culture, however, prevented the production of any intelligible translation without exhaustive editing by someone both bilingual and skilled in the specialization involved.

Again, variations in meaning were the impediments. The expensive effort in several nations failed to produce a usable language translation system. The most complex entity humans have evolved is language. Nevertheless, most humans simply take language for granted, at face value—often to their eventual regret.

One additional factor must be included in any attempt to describe the process of reality perception—time. Perception must involve a time continuum. The earlier slice of chocolate cake— the real slice, not the pictorial version in figure 6—endured continuous change throughout its existence. It is not the same cake slice today that it was a day, week, or month ago. Any valid perceptual evaluation of the cake slice should include a valid time reference. In other words, any meaningful reference to the cake slice should include time, place, perspective, associations at both conscious and unconscious levels, and information about observer biases. Chocolate-addicted individuals are known to perceive chocolate cake differently than the nonaddicted. Hungry individuals will perceive the cake slice quite differently from others who have just eaten. Nevertheless, regardless of how detailed the verbal or pictorial description becomes, the word symbols can never approximate the complex multilevel perceivable reality.

Our perception of the cake slice may never involve life-or-death questions. But what about such perceptual realities as capitalism, socialism, love, hate, freedom, slavery, loyalty, environment, or people? Such subjective verbal and pictorial concepts—high-order abstractions—can be described only by other words. The mounting pile of descriptive definitions takes us further and further away from verifiable reality. Individuals continue to stumble about in a dense verbal, intellectual fog, attempting to confirm increasingly vague or ephemeral perceptual fantasies based upon fantasies, based upon fantasies, et cetera.

Uncommon Common Sense

From Euclid to Descartes, through Newton to Einstein, traditional modes of thought were based upon three-dimensional space perceptions: height, width, and depth, coupled with movements of time. This simplistic way of thinking is often called "common sense." For most societies of our day, common sense provides the basic scientific and social reality constructions. *Common sense* usually appears constant, reliable, simple, and noncontradictory—a model of linear cause-and-effect relationships. Yet the real world—outside the limitations of human perception—appears to be not at all like our fantasies of a neat, orderly, logical, predictable, and describable perception.

New words, phrases, verbal concepts, and meanings—collectively utilized to express *common sense*—constantly enter the language via the work of skilled word merchants. Language innovation is not a product of the general population. H. L. Mencken, in his exhaustive *The American Language*, called these innovators "the writing men." Curiously, women—though this may be changing in the technologically advanced nations—have so far played a minor role in the creation of new language. Coiners of language include novelists, storytellers, dramatists, lyricists, playwrights, journalists, and most importantly ad copywriters. Word merchants' phrases usually enter the language inconspicuously. The writer is anonymous or soon forgotten; the words remain indefinitely.

The $150 billion ad expenditure in 1989—only one year's investment—introduced scores of new words, phrases, and meanings into the language. Some of these quickly disappeared; others will persist indefinitely. Anyone who sponsors new language inputs in effect controls language definitions and meanings. Most importantly, the way *meaning* itself is defined is controllable at both conscious and unconscious levels of audience perception. Most of the gifted word and phrase makers in the U.S. work, in one way or another, for the ad industry. Entertainment industries are heavily integrated with corporate ad and promotion interests. Ad media can exploit a writer's work, or they can ignore it when their vested interests are threatened. The ad industry has a powerful investment in language, in how it is utilized, and in controlled interpretations of meaning. Ad media provide a language-culture machine for society.

The frailty and vulnerability of human perception and language has been widely recognized by philosophers, mathematicians, and scientists at least since the Greek sophists. In the U.S. today, quite unlike many other nations or cultures, the relationship between words and the perceptual realities they propose to describe is ignored. People have been conditioned to accept mindlessly word or picture symbols as realities—even when they lack any conceivable relationship to perceivable reality. Ads supply the model for language. Ad lingo conveys nothing verifiable or specific. Everything is sustained in the realm of fantasy projection, identification between vaguely eroticized products, consumed by people presented as stereotypical images. Questions about perceptual bias and *meaning* versus *reality* rarely appear. Critical evaluations of *meaning* in the *macro-micro-submicro* perceptual levels are either attacked as subversive or, worse, ignored as pedantic.

Over 2,000 years ago, Plato advised the rulers of his *Republic* to seek control of the popular idiom as the first strategy of political and economic domination. Human populations can be unconsciously (subliminally) conditioned to any desired design. With currently available technology, this requires merely an expenditure of enough time, money, and human resources. Each year, U.S. audiences observe individuals who literally *buy*—through ad media—elections, public support, consumer expenditures, and national as well as international public policies. The heaviest ad appropriation usually wins; not always, of course, but often enough to make such investment a cost-effective technique for the engineering of public consent. Then, most frighteningly, everyone pretends that they thought out their behavior all on their own and were not bought and sold by clever manipulators.

Advertising provides a near perfect stimulus-response-reward system, even though the rewards are more symbolic than real. The eventual outcome, however, appears much closer to the nightmare of Dante's *Inferno* than to an idyllic utopia. At its present level of development, media technology could make the world and its peoples into virtually anything. The U.S. has cleverly persuaded itself, however, to use this technology to turn its culture into an enormous vending machine that exists because it consumes.

Those who understand the limitations of language and perceptions can accept responsibility for their own reality definitions. They can avoid or reduce vulnerability to manipulation. They can achieve autonomy as individuals. And they can truly realize their vast potential for growth, dignity, and achievement. The trouble is that most would rather follow the herd, accept the ready-to-wear perceptions of leaders and media who pursue only their own selfish interests.

5 | HOW WE KNOW THAT WE KNOW THAT WE KNOW

To think is to differ!
Clarence Darrow, from the Scopes Trial transcripts

A civilization or individual who cannot burst through its current abstractions is doomed to sterility after a very limited period of progress. Almost any idea which jogs you out of your current abstractions may be better than nothing.
Alfred North Whitehead, *Process and Reality*

Common sense must be jarred into uncommon sense. A major service mathematics rendered humanity over the past century was to put "common sense" where it belongs, on the topmost shelf next to the dusty bottle labeled "Discarded Nonsense."
Eric T. Bell, *The Principle of General Relativity*

Human language usually appears so simple, logical, reasonable, and natural that most of us take it for granted. We rarely question how perceptions of the world process into language and how language affects behaviors; or the ways language determines how and what we think we think. In the mass-media managed societies, individuals are relentlessly harassed through the language of words and pictures. Every waking moment—and through dreams, every sleeping moment—has been targeted by the ad media. Most North Americans appear consciously unaware of media intrusions into their lives.

Western tourists in the U.S.S.R. are culture-shocked by a sudden awareness that something is missing. Soviets are not subjected to all-pervasive media demands on every waking moment. Do you wonder which society is the most relentlessly brainwashed? The question is academic. Both are deeply immersed in manipulative media that manufacture contemporary culture. Soviet media are simply less obvious.

U.S. education has moved away from the liberal arts ideals of thirty-five years ago, when the goal was an autonomous, spirited, critical, intellectual perspective. Education was considered a path to full, rich, more meaningful life experiences. Students were expected to comprehend relative modes of thought and evaluation, and the emphasis was on learning to think critically, rather than learning *what* to think. Students are now exhaustively propagandized, taught to fit into perceived contemporary realities, adapt, adjust, and accept conventional wisdoms of the moment. Great emphasis is placed on vocational fantasies about high-paid employment.

Business schools, with roughly 25% of U.S. undergraduate enrollments, legitimize business. They rationalize greed and profit as ends in themselves with a frankness that would have embarrassed Al Capone. Strangely, however, they provide little of the basic, intellectual education that might prepare an ambitious, creative entrepreneur. When entrepreneurial types find their way into business schools, they usually quit from boredom. Similarly, communication schools legitimize and romanticize the mass-communication industry. With endless courses of vague, fact-deficient generalities, they provide little education about language, thought, and behavior—the ultimate considerations in human communication. Young

116

people are indoctrinated for a place on the endless belts that carry them as marketing statistics in and out of countless shopping centers as they process through life. *I consume, therefore I exist*, or vice versa, becomes the philosophical premise upon which much of life is predicated.

Techniques for critical language analysis are available. They could provide the intellectual toughness to defend against verbal manipulation, to discriminate between fantasy and reality. But the language system to which most individuals are educated ensures they will become both victims and victimizers with little awareness that anything out of the ordinary is going on.

The Logic of Illogic

The language system we live with was actually designed by a Greek scholar around 350 B.C. Few people today know or care much about Aristotle. Unconsciously, however, the U.S. population remains victim to rules of thought he worked out over 2,000 years ago. His rules still govern the ways perceptions are described and assumptions are expressed, in words, pictures, and simple mathematics. The mathematics-based languages of science generally discarded Aristotelian logic almost a century ago. For the average citizen, however, the old language logic still provides an integrated, largely unconscious structure through which humans submit themselves to control and manipulation. Aristotle apparently thought he was merely describing the language system of his time. But over the centuries, his system was useful to those who controlled societies and came to be perceived as actual rules of thought—the way the brain thinks, the way language works, even the way God intended humans to reason.

Language structure exerts a powerful subliminal influence upon human life. For the individual, however, who is part of the language-cultural system, the whole thing appears natural and reasonable. Few question the system; few even know a system exists. From within the system, any critique does little but reconfirm the system's perfection, logic, reason, and truths.

A prolific scholar, Aristotle described the way language appeared to work in three fundamental laws of thought: *identity*, the *excluded middle*, and *contradiction*. His genius lay in an ability to describe a linguistic system that appeared neat, reliable, ordered, and verbally definable—a system that could be verified internally. Aristotle's system was later integrated from ancient Greek into most of the language cultures of the Western world. His three laws made logical sense. They established and legitimized—for over two millennia—the ways in which language, thought, and logic would be accepted and applied. Anyone who questioned, disputed, or contradicted the system was socially excluded, imprisoned, executed as a heretic or subversive, or all three. Aristotelian logic is still defended by those whose vested interests might be threatened by another language system more consistent with the progress experienced in the natural and physical sciences over the past century.

Scientist-mathematician-philosopher Alfred Korzybski was one who attempted to apply scientific principles to verbal language. His principal work, *Science and Sanity* (1933), is still one of the most important attempts to examine how Aristotelian structures had locked Western civilization into a primitive, restrictive, destructive system of language logic. He explored ways in which contemporary scientific notions could be expanded to include the social and linguistic sciences. Korzybski was bitterly denounced in the *Soviet Encyclopedia of Science*. Though initially given serious attention in the U.S., he was soon angrily censured by those with vested interest in the linguistic status quo. His attempt to evolve a sane, nonexploitive language system threatened those who depended upon myth, magic, and fraud.

S. I. Hayakawa, later a U.S. senator, was an early student of Korzybskian semantics. Numerous ad executives, however, became intrigued with non-Aristotelian logic. It offered them a perspective—a key, in effect—with which consumer perceptions could be more effectively manipulated. Pierre Martineau, *Chicago Tribune* ad director, was one of the earliest to utilize the new logic in marketing strategies. Korzybski hoped for a language system to protect individuals from language exploitation. The system became most useful to those doing the exploiting.

The three basic Aristotelian Laws are simple. They offer a psycholinguistic structure for logic and reason, and impose an illusion of order upon language and its applications. This assumes, of course, that everyone knows, understands, and accepts them. The trouble with rules, of course, is that once they are imposed and more or less accepted, clever people will exhaust every possibility to discover ways in which the laws can be manipulated, circumvented, and disregarded.

A history of laws would make for very dull reading. A history of how civilizations violated, circumvented, or adapted their laws for greed, power, and profit would be fascinating—though likely subversive. Today, Aristotelian laws prevail in the verbal definition-oriented sciences. Once people are persuaded or coerced into accepting the laws of a system, those who thoroughly understand them can manipulate trusting believers in any direction desired.

Judicial rules throughout the Western world provide excellent examples of Aristotelian logic. The search to determine guilt or innocence through words provides more-or-less gainful employment for armies of legal professionals. The U.S. has more statute laws than the rest of the world put together. One might conclude that all dilemmas were resolved by this mountain of verbal prohibitions and definitions. Thousands, however, dedicate their lives to the discovery of exclusions, contradictions, loopholes, and errors. This proliferation of laws has often created more problems than were resolved. Attempts to reconcile human dilemmas only with words are doomed from the beginning. If humans do not really desire solutions to problems, a mountain of words will make little difference.

Aristotle's contribution to the study of language was truly extraordinary for his time. Left alone, his logic would have undergone a natural evolution, along with science, technology, and civilization. Unfortunately, his ideas served the structures of power and profit too well. They were assimilated by scholastic philosophy during the Middle Ages and ultimately enforced as church doctrine by the Inquisition. Even after the Reformation, Aristotelian laws survived and continued to dominate Western thought and language.

Science and technology finally broke free of Aristotle in the early twentieth century, primarily through mathematics. A handful of sophisticated mathematicians and physicists skilled in the new areas of relativity and quantum mechanics rapidly moved science out of the dark ages where creative insights into perceptions had been theologically suppressed. Once the logic of Aristotle, the geometry of Euclid, and the physics of Newton were set aside, scientific progress could no longer be restrained. The verbal-pictorial-oriented sciences, however, remained entrapped in Aristotelian logic.

Euclidean geometry, for example, became a typical victim of progress. Euclid's proofs, like Aristotle's, were constructed from human language—verbal, mathematical, and algebraic—and depended upon verbal/pictorial language, with pitfalls, fallacies, and hidden structural weaknesses.

Every word or picture has both a *meaning* and *definition*, though the two are rarely congruent. The more frequently used, the more varied, complex, and contradictory meaning becomes. Definitions are constantly changing. Actual word or picture symbol usage is also guided more by unconscious than conscious associations. Euclid's definitions, as he initially appeared to intend them—his axioms, postulates, definitions of point, straight line, circle, triangle, et cetera—began to erode, modify, expand, constantly evolving first in subtle, then in major ways. After 2,100 years, non-Euclidean geometry appeared in 1823 and continues to develop. Euclidean geometry became only a historical footnote read briefly during one's early mathematical education. Newtonian physics similarly disappeared in the face of relativity and quantum theories. Euclid and Newton fell, not painlessly but quickly.

Aristotle's laws, on the other hand, have hung on tenaciously and continue to rule broad areas of popular thought, legal doctrine, and the so-called social and behavioral sciences. They persist like an intellectual vise clamped tightly around the minds of millions. These laws govern the ways humans both *know* and *don't know*—repress information that is not verbally definable in any relationship with reality.

The best way to use and misuse any language system is to approach it from the outside, from a counter-system. This strategy has not been overlooked by the media industries, especially those involved with mass communication—advertising and public relations. Anyone skilled in the use of Aristotelian logic, and its non-Aristotelian counterlogic, can easily manipulate value systems, beliefs, attitudes, opinions, and behaviors. In this light, let's examine Aristotle's three laws one by one.

The Logic of Identification

The law of identity is often summarized by the phrase, "Whatever is, is!" For over 2,000 years, the concept has been directly responsible for a disaster of confusion and endless human quandaries. Words are never the things they describe. Maps are not the territories or perceptual realities they represent. A picture is not what is described in the picture. Interpretations and verbal descriptions of reality are only interpretations and descriptions, not reality. Aristotle believed words or symbols were identifiable with people and things. Non-Aristotelians demonstrated that words and symbols were merely vague, approximate abstractions—having little to do with actual perceivable realities. Recall the earlier consideration of *macro*, *micro*, and *submicro* levels of perception.

The fallacy of *identification* can be demonstrated by any of the subjects portrayed in the illustrations. The Seagram's Crown Royal broken bottle (fig. 15) would have us perceive and identify the broken bottle with the real thing. Most do! Studies of the ad revealed that nearly everyone considered the picture an actual broken bottle. It is not! Take an empty liquor bottle and break it upon a hard surface. The resulting pattern of shattered bottle parts and glass splinters will look *nothing* like what is portrayed in the ad. The ad bottle is an expensive painting. Several artists, who do comparable work for advertisers, estimated the painting to be worth $40,000 to $50,000. A photograph of a broken bottle could have been made for around $100 but would not have sold the product. Photographs and paintings are perceived from a specific point, stopped in space and time, time-stopped at a particular instant. Reality, and our perceptions of reality, exist in a constant state of process and change.

Even at this remarkable fee, the artist may have been underpaid considering the amount of whiskey the ad must have sold over the years it was frequently published. It first appeared in 1971 and was still in use in 1987. An estimated $12 million of marketing capital was invested to purchase media space for the broken bottle. The ad appeared repeatedly in every national magazine in the

U.S., and was translated into other languages and published internationally. The $12 million painting of a broken whiskey bottle was able to sell several hundred million dollars worth of alcoholic beverages.

A second type of identification proposed in the ad involves the caption, "Have you ever seen a grown man cry?" The logical Aristotelian identification would be that the "grown man" was crying over the broken bottle and wasted alcohol. But the statement is illogical. Only a pathetic alcoholic would cry over the broken bottle, assuming *cry* refers to tears rather than a cry of pain. Virtually all the consumers who perceived the ad did, however, make the appropriate, predictable, Aristotelian identification—as they had been culturally conditioned to do—between pictures, words, and the reality supposedly represented. They perceived the ad much like unthinking robots operated by electronic computer programs. They did and thought precisely what they were supposed to do and think, according to conventional wisdom and Aristotle's law of identity.

Were anyone to question the broken bottle ad from a non-Aristotelian point of view, it would instantly be exposed as a lie expensively designed to entrap consumers in alcohol consumption—a fraud, a flimflam, a deception, a manipulation of consumer gullibility. The ad was designed to be mindlessly absorbed in the consumer's instantaneous perception. Like most ads, the broken bottle was not designed for conscious perception, which does not affect consumer behavior.

Alcohol spirit manufacturers invest roughly 6% of their gross receipts in ads, according to the Department of Commerce. This is an extremely high ad-investment level. At a cost of $12 million, this ad—in order to break even—would need to sell well over $200 million worth of Crown Royal at the wholesale level. Nobody breaks even and stays in business long, so this sales estimate is conservative.

Several years ago, I was interviewed on a religious TV program hosted by Pat Robertson. We looked at a copy of the broken bottle ad with an eye to discovering what made the ad work.

Study the ad carefully at this point. Look for anything that suggests devious intent. Remember, most ads are designed to be perceived in a second or two. Do you perceive or feel anything peculiar about the ad? Robertson discovered several embeds painted into the broken bottle, though he appeared to perceive the picture as an actual broken bottle. He pointed out the swan's head and neck (fig. 41), the bird (fig. 42), the screaming man (fig. 43), and the silhouette of a Roman soldier (fig. 44).

During the interview, additional embeds were demonstrated: the angel in the bottleneck (fig. 45), faces (fig. 46 and 47), and an ax or cutting instrument (fig. 48). Perhaps the ax broke the bottle to liberate the angel in the bottleneck. Ads do not have to be logical at the unconscious perceptual level. I turned the ad on its left side to simplify perception of the profile of a cartoon face embedded in the broken bottle (fig. 49)—the round black nose, forehead, an eye above the nose, the back of the head curving down to the neck. The ax (fig. 48) forms an elongated lower jaw below the open mouth.

Just below the profile's upper lip, a stub hangs down from the ground area. The stub appears to have been bitten off by the open mouth. The rest of it appears falling below the jaw, having just been castrated (fig. 50). "Have you ever seen a grown man cry?" Indeed! The caption takes on an entirely new dimension, but one unconsciously invisible under Aristotle's law of identity. Identification locks the viewer into a specific set of perceptual expectations. When you unthinkingly or uncritically identify words with words, words with pictures, or words and pictures with things or people, you have been victimized. The *law of identity* has served the power elite and its institutions for well over 2,000 years. Until ad technicians learned to think around Aristotle, they could not have worked out the successful flimflam.

"Have you ever seen a grown man cry?" is a poetic scam. The tears are not for the broken bottle, but for what was within the broken bottle—a castrated penis. Ad agency researchers well know that substantial quantities of alcohol are consumed as a means of sex or intimacy avoidance. Alcohol is one of the greatest enemies of sex man has invented—a few ounces in the blood destroys sexual ability, even if it engenders virile fantasies. Castration themes are frequently found in alcohol, tobacco, and drug ads. (*See* Key, *Clam-Plate Orgy*, figs. 5 to 19; Key, *Media Sexploitation*, figs. 35 to 37; and Key, *Subliminal Seduction*, figs. 16 and 17.)

Alcohol ads are not directed at mere drinkers. They are aimed at *heavy* and *very heavy* drinkers. Ads are tested against these special consumers before large media investments are justified. These "heavies" consume inordinate quantities of alcohol and also serve as leaders among drinkers for instilling brand preferences. Want to know a good Scotch? Ask someone who drinks a lot of it.

The Self-Destruct in Alcohol Ads

Death or self-destructive imagery is a frequent aspect of subliminal content. Advertisers of alcohol, tobacco, and drugs know that subliminal death imagery sells the brand and product. Ad effectiveness is an empirical, measurable quality. *Why* death sells is impossible to answer, except in theory; no one knows, as yet, how the brain functions. Death-oriented embeds are rarely found in food ads, though one could certainly argue that compulsive eating is a self-destructive syndrome. If death sold food at the subliminal level, ad agencies would certainly use it.

The so-called death wish, the unconscious compulsion to self-destruct, is a part of every human psyche. In the Seagram's ad, death is symbolized by self-castration. The death wish idea dates at least to Thomas Hobbes, a mid-sixteenth-century British philosopher. The theory was further developed around Thanatos, the personification of death from Greek mythology, by Sigmund Freud. Humans often exhibit a predisposition to destroy themselves, either actually or symbolically. The tendency is more pronounced in some individuals at certain periods of their lives, but appears common to all. Self-destructive behaviors—which include drug abuse and addiction—are visibly rampant phenomena, especially among young people. Suicide, of course, has reached epidemic proportions in the U.S. It is presently the second most frequent cause of death among teenagers (the first being accidents, many of which suggest suicide).

Millions of dollars are spent by major corporations to exploit consumers' self-destructive compulsions. Few families today have not been hurt by alcohol abuse and addiction. Alcohol kills at least half the victims involved in fatal auto accidents and suicides and is directly responsible for unmeasurable human suffering. It is a factor in most wife- and child-abuse cases, crime, unemployment and unemployability, and in an extensive range of medical pathologies. In spite of this, alcoholic-beverage ads totaled well over a billion dollars in 1987. This most profitable industry has ignored the public welfare in favor of financial gain. The alcohol ads illustrated are certainly immoral, and appear to be illegal, according to the unenforced U.S. Treasury (ATF) ruling (*see* Appendix). Legislators still find excuses to ignore the issue.

Conscious and unconscious identification erodes an individual's ability to discriminate between fantasy and reality. The fantasies become more real, more vivid, more lifelike, more desirable than reality. The reality of alcohol consumption is hidden carefully behind the fantasies—an emerald, a broken bottle, happy athletes joking over their light beer, the sophisticated sexualized model sipping liqueurs, all appear far more real than reality, which, as far as the alcoholic is concerned, can be pretty grim. Of course, there is no immediate need to think about it—until the drinker winds up in a treatment program. A major objective of advertising is to ensure that consumers never think about the black side, consciously at least.

When fantasies completely replace realities, when individuals make uncontrollable identifications between symbols and things or people, they can be clinically diagnosed as schizophrenic. Most of the U.S. population identifies the cleverly contrived illustrations in ads with the real thing. Few consumers even suspected the Seagram's broken bottle was not a real broken bottle, the Betty Crocker chocolate cake had nothing to do with cake, the hands pouring Chivas Regal were not real hands. Consumers appear incapable of discriminating between fantasy and reality. The problem of fantasy versus reality is far more significant than obscene imagery embedded in ads. Advertising and sales hype provide an educational system. In high-technology cultures, an individual learns far more about the world from ad media than from schools. Much of U.S. formal education, for example, has degenerated into training in perceptual repression, indoctrination into the way we wish the world were structured, rather than in a creative search for reality-oriented perceptual experiences.

Anyone who uncritically accepts symbols, words, or pictures as the "real thing" cannot avoid being led down the perceptual garden path. Likewise, anyone who unthinkingly patterns their values and identity upon verbal and pictorial symbols is being manipulated and exploited. Media operate in behalf of commercial objectives to establish perceptual structures for audiences to bring about un-challenged identifications between symbols and realities. *Real* and *natural* usually turn out to be fake—*unreal* and *unnatural*, simply a manipulation of symbols and those who take them seriously. Coca-Cola, a totally synthetic substance, is not *the real thing*. The cosmetic *natural look* requires more cosmetics than the cosmeticized look.

Identification works on the premise that words, symbols, and objects are directly comparable, that there is an appropriate specific word or picture for every reality, that word definitions held by others are identical to those held by ourselves. Each of these three assumptions about symbols is false, both on the street and in science.

Through identification, an individual unconsciously accepts that verbal or pictorial statements are accurate, concrete, all-inclusive representations of *truth*. The word or picture tells it all! Physicist Eric Bell once commented, "The wretched monosyllable 'all' caused mathematicians more trouble than all the rest of the dictionary." Nothing verbal, pictorial, or mathematical is ever *all*-inclusive. Verbal or pictorial statements cannot be more than abstract, remote, simplistic symbols that attempt to describe only a partially per-ceived reality. Both observers and what is observed exist in states of process and change that may consciously be imperceptible. Un-believably destructive and psychopathic behaviors have been imposed upon civilization from verbal, all-inclusive, dogmatic, absolute, and blind unreasoning acceptance of the word. A long, cruel, and bloody history evolved over the *true* meanings of words. The dev-astation promises insanely to continue.

Humans are often entrapped by symbols and perceived mean-ings. There appears no escape—at least no escape until the Ar-istotelian Laws are eventually repealed, when individuals decide they have had enough.

Where Dirty Words Hide

During a lecture, this author once introduced the law of identity by printing on the blackboard in large capital letters, "FUCK IT!" I then turned and smiled enigmatically while the class became increasingly disturbed. A few giggled and worked themselves toward amused hysteria. Some blushed, well-scrubbed faces glowing with embarrassed flushes. Others paled, their lips thinned, jaws tensed. Several arranged books as though anticipating a walk-out.

"What's the problem?" I finally asked pleasantly.

"That dirty word you wrote on the blackboard," someone eventually replied.

"Dirty word?" I touched one of the letters on the board and examined the chalk dust on my fingers. "You're putting me on," I said. "These are only chalk particles on the graphite surface of a blackboard. Dusty, perhaps, but there is nothing here that appears dirty. Why are most of you bright, literate people emotionally reacting over mere chalk embedded in a graphite surface?" I asked.

There was, of course, nothing wrong with the symbol on the blackboard. The "dirtiness" was in their heads, not in the phrase. *FUCK IT!* is only a symbol for a rather complex reality. There exist at least half a dozen possible interpretations that might have been made of the phrase, only a couple of which relate to the reproductive process. In any respect, the word symbol was only that—a symbol, albeit a complex symbol, a high-order abstraction only definable through other verbal abstractions.

Every atom, molecule, organism, personality, language, and society is a novelty—a constantly changing novelty. Language categorizations, or the perceptions that result from them, are fantasies and illusions of the first order. They may be useful from time to time, but they remain fantasies.

For example, the words *love* or *god* to one individual will mean something both similar to and different from what they mean to another. It is curious when people insist their definitions are "true," and compel others to validate their fantasies. The infinite possible meanings in such words can be fun—an aesthetic, stimulating experience, as the poets discovered. The inherent verbal uncertainties could provide an extraordinary incentive to expand and deepen knowledge of the world, people, and the languages humans use to communicate. It does not, as most well know, work this way.

There is, for example, a remote, abstract distance between the word labels *love* and *god* and any specific reality. Realities represented by words such as these can be described only through other verbal symbols. Meaning cannot be demonstrated by simply pointing at the reality represented, as in the abstraction *chocolate cake*. *Love* and *god* might be called high-order abstractions in comparison with low-order symbols such as *cake, chair, dish, book*, etc. High-order abstractions lead to devastating quandaries as humans endlessly attempt to verbally define them, in a delusionary search for permanence, security, and some guarantee in which to believe. High-order abstractions can be defined or explained only by other words—often additional high-order abstractions—resulting in fantasies built upon fantasies built upon fantasies, et cetera.

In a provocative attempt to satirize Aristotelian logic, a brilliant seventeenth-century Mexican nun, Sister Juana Inéz de la Cruz, wrote a philosophical treatise that proved, beyond any doubt, how many angels could dance on the head of a pin. Church authorities and the Inquisition suspected they were being ridiculed but found her impossible to refute by the rules of language. Who could attack someone who so fervently believed in angels? Though the book was humorous, the argument that is still with us is really not. Daily news stories argue over how much national security can dance on the head of an MX missile or inside the fantasied Strategic Defense Initiative. Such arguments in support of profit and power are silly but highly dangerous when taken seriously.

High-order abstractions can be productively utilized, but only when they can be confirmed and tentatively validated by reality-oriented perceptions. They can be responsible for deep philosophical and poetic insights—vital to the enrichment of life and thought. But wide areas of human vulnerability to exploitation surround the use, or misuse, of high-order abstractions. Consider how many words have been written to define variant meanings of *love* and *god* and how many people have been slaughtered over the definitions. The world might have been enriched by an acceptance of multiple interpretations, had anyone thought about it.

Verbal or pictorial descriptions have the same relationship to reality that an ad has to the product it invariably misrepresents. Conscious or unconscious motives will always stack the perceptual deck with both seen and unseen bias. The concept of *truth*, were it actually to exist, could never be described through words or pictures, not even through mathematics. *Truth* exists only in reality, outside the symbols that attempt to describe it. *Truth* would also have to be free from human perceptual intervention and influence—a paradoxical impossibility.

Times, Places, and Situations

Though words can never *be* things or people, the accuracy of language to describe reality could be improved. Individuals could be trained to index meanings to specific times, places, and situations, which would substantially reduce their vulnerability to manipulation. For example, consider the recent ad on the back cover of *Time* magazine (fig. 51), "Here's to more gin taste!" The illustration depicts a female hand toasting a phallic bottle of Gilbey's gin. "Here's" is an idiom signifying a toast or salutation usually directed at another human. Readers have a right to question whether reasonable behavior could include a discussion with a gin bottle, comparable to a conversation with a door, house, or frying pan. Such anthropomorphic projection, though widely utilized in expensive ad campaigns, in this case seriously toasts an inanimate gin bottle. Such fantasization should easily get the drinker a spot on a psychiatrist's couch. A simple analysis, such as that suggested above, might include the questions *when* someone might use such a phrase, *where*, and in *what* conceivable situation? The only reasonable answer would be never, nowhere, and only in the case of a blind drunk mumbling meaningless gibberish.

Similarly, "more gin taste" is another clever phrase that means absolutely nothing in terms of reality. As the glass in the ad is full of ice cubes, the temperature of the liquid is presumably low— roughly 40° Fahrenheit. Lowered temperatures sharply reduce the ability to distinguish flavor—if, indeed, flavor is what "taste" refers to. The words *taste* and *testes* associate at the unconscious level and have a phonetic similarity that often stimulates identification. Even at room temperatures, however, taste tests demonstrate that statistical majorities of people cannot determine the brand of gin they are drinking. Furthermore, when drinkers cannot smell, most cannot determine whether they are drinking gin, vodka, or whiskey.

Again—*when, in which place, in what situations?* Answer: Never! Nowhere! And only in conversation with a fool or someone also blind drunk! The ad copy line, of course, is meant to be read at the undiscriminating, unconscious level of perception, thus, taken for granted. Like most alcoholic beverage ads, it is also directed specifically toward *heavy* drinkers in debt to alcohol for helping them escape reality. Enough people identify with anthropomorphic verbal nonsense to make such ads profitable to everyone involved with their publication. The message succeeds because consumers do not pay critical, conscious attention; they shrug off the absurdity, and go about drinking as though they really thought for themselves.

The Gilbey's gin toast ad is, of course, a painting. The woman's hand, martini, olive, gin, glass, and the bottle are painted fantasies, having nothing to do with reality. In figure 51, several of the embedded *SEX*es have been inked in and numerous others can be discovered by perceptive readers. On the seemingly turbulent surface of the martini, at least five monsters have been airbrushed into the bubbles, grotesque faces floating, perhaps drowning, in the delusion. View the detail illustration (fig. 52) from different perspectives—left, right, upside down—for a preview of what may lie ahead in the lives of heavy drinkers. Repetitious use of the meaningless word *taste* in the bottom ad copy promises to drive away the alcoholic's goblins.

Another major problem stemming from the *identity* law occurs when the subject of a sentence is consciously or unconsciously identified with the predicate, usually via the verb *to be*. In the phrase, "Ronnie is a communist!" *is* implies a fixed entity, unchanging and inflexible. A reality evaluation is needed to explore *Ronnie* as to time, place, and situation. Ronnie, like all humans, has changed throughout his life. Change occurs biologically and psychologically at every moment in time. Ronnie is a different person at sixty than he was yesterday, last year, at twenty-five, forty, or will be at sixty-five. To have any validity, the sentence must specify at which particular age, where he lived at that time, and the conditions under which he lived.

Hypothetically, assume that Ronnie, whoever he may be, has lived since birth in numerous languages, cultures, and political-economic systems. He has been deeply involved with various sociopolitical struggles. Which of the infinitely many possible Ronnies are we trying to describe?

Another largely unconscious dimension of Ronnie is in identifications made with other Ronnies, known or imagined. Even though Ronnie is only a hypothetical person, merely an arrangement of syllables, most individuals could describe a Ronnie they carry around in their heads—a *Ronnie* quite different from *Algernon, Prince, John*, or *Buboobla*. Every name, even a nonsense name, has significance at both conscious and unconscious levels—as every ad copywriter well knows.

Similarly, *communist* is another meaningless term—though highly useful as a propaganda device among individuals trained not to think beyond stereotypical labels. Communists display an astonishing variability, and always have, even though you may never have heard about it—left-wing, right-wing, centrist, and countless degrees in between. There are currently over forty varieties of communist-socialist groups visible in the world and cer-, tainly a great many more invisible splinter groups. Some of these varieties—Yugoslavian and Chinese, at the moment—are socially acceptable to the capitalist world. Communists have always differed in various cultures, at different times, and under different situations.

Stereotyping *communists* is about as meaningless a preoccupation as stereotyping capitalists, Republicans, Jews, Catholics, or visitors at Disneyland. Such stereotypes may be meaningless, but they are often useful. Few politicians could survive if their mothers had not allowed them as children to play with stereotypes, if their unthinking followers could tell the difference between nonsense labels and the complex perceptual realities involved. Both the subject and predicate of our sentence—"Ronnie is a communist!"—proved to be verbal fictions. The most devastating misevaluations in language have grown out of an uncritical use of the verb *to be*. *I am, he is, we are, you are,* and *they are* imply permanence, a rigid, fixed connection between subject and predicate. *Ronnie* (the subject) was connected to *communist* (the predicate)—a verbal fiction uniting two verbal, stereotypical fictional concepts—a fiction of a fiction of a fiction, et cetera.

The little word *is* (a conjugation of *to be*) has its tragedies. *Is* marries and identifies things and people that are not really related. The marriage is an illusion of language structure and the invisible, unconscious human perceptual process. Though the problems of identity appear common to most language systems, those surrounding the verb *to be* may be of a lesser magnitude in some. Latin languages have two verb forms for *to be*—one denoting permanence, the other a transition verb for a *temporary* condition, time, or status. In Spanish, for example, *es muerto*—"he is dead"—describes a permanent condition (even in a Catholic country), while *está enfermo*—"he is sick"—denotes a temporary condition. In English, however, there is often neither conscious nor unconscious recognition of transitory conditions.

When something or somebody *is*, it *is* presumably forever, welding subject and predicate together. When a Chevrolet Nova ad tells us "It is the best of both worlds," the statement is nonsense in any relationship with perceivable reality. But it is carefully conceived nonsense designed to persuade naïve, uncritical individuals that something of significance has been communicated. The subject "It," of course, refers to all the Novas ever manufactured, even those considered lemons by their owners. *It* is also a frequent ad euphemism for sex. In the ad, the Nova has been manipulated to appear as a long, phallic, powerful symbol of authority.

The words "the best" are—at best—a meaningless adjectival description. The best for what, at which times, under what conditions, in comparison with whom or what? The phrase, "of both worlds" alludes, in this case, to the U.S. and Japan; the car is apparently a joint venture between General Motors and Toyota. Of course, by projection, "both worlds" may imply that one of the worlds is in outer space—the painted illustration of the Nova does suggest a space-ship design. A *nova*, of course, is a star that suddenly brightens, then in a short time dims. If you think about it, as few consumers ever learned to do, *novas* may not last very long. Ads depend on human gullibility and ignorance.

Nova's ad strategy was designed to counter growing resentment against imported cars. Imports have cost tens of thousands of U.S. workers their jobs, but the prejudice is ambivalent, as Japanese cars are generally considered cheaper, better quality, and more dependable than American cars. The negative U.S. auto image is especially strong among the lower socioeconomic consumers who are the major Nova market.

Again, the Nova ad copy—like the painted illustration—is unadulterated nonsense, designed to move trusting, uncritical readers into an unconscious identification between Nova and "the best."

Anyone who identifies the broken Crown Royal bottle (fig. 15) with an actual broken bottle has projected a fantasy. The bottle in the painting clearly has nothing to do with an actual broken bottle. Similarly the Gaddafi portrait on *Time* magazine's cover (fig. 9)—as well as other illustration content—has nothing to do with reality.

In summary, identifications work in two ways—between words and words (symbols matched with symbols) and between words and things or people (symbols matched with perceptions of reality). Both are far removed from any describable reality at a specific time, place, or situation. Such identifications ignore process and change in both perceivers and their perceptions. Regardless of what we allege something or someone *is*, the thing or person is never the words or pictures we use to describe our perceptions.

Animals and Things Are Not Human

Anthropomorphic identification of human qualities with objects or animals is an ancient technique of mind management to which millions are highly vulnerable, especially in ad-managed cultures. Anthropomorphism is often engineered to sell automobiles, for example, by suggesting in body design and ads that cars possess human, even superhuman attributes. Several Cadillac models, for example, had mammary-shaped spheres on both front and rear bumpers. No human female is so abundantly equipped. The masculine-designed Mustang competed with the feminine-designed Camaro in the early years of the two models. As time passed, however, gender became less distinguishable. Such manipulations are far less successful in European and Asian cultures, where people tend to perceive correctly that automobiles are only inanimate machines.

It is no random accident that most U.S. presidents have pet dogs in the White House, at considerable taxpayer expense for damaged rugs, furniture, and draperies. Consciously and unconsciously, the presence of a loving, obedient, trusting dog produces a positive image of the owner. The president must have a dog. Voters would reject a politician who preferred cats, pigs, boa constrictors, or chimpanzees.

Used-car pitchmen, comedians, and others who solicit the public trust long ago integrated animals into their acts. Who could not trust a man who loved animals? In reality, anyone who uses animals to enhance pretensions of honesty, kindness, and trustworthiness can only be a con artist, profitably exploiting the con in confidence. Asians make endless jokes about North Americans with their dogs and cats. In the real world, where most humans survive on the edge of starvation, the food and affection lavished upon pets in the U.S. would nourish millions. Perhaps everyone should be frequently reminded that both Genghis Khan and Ivan the Terrible were animal lovers.

The Logic of
Excluded Middles

The *law of the excluded middle* was one of Aristotle's more imaginative ideas. It can be briefly explained as "Everything must either be or not be." Thought must be verbal; individuals can *feel*, but not *think* without words. If verbal thought can be restricted to either one idea, thing, or proposition, or to another idea, thing, or proposition, the world becomes a neat, definable, orderly place in which to live. The real world, where many things occur chaotically at the same time, is not like this. Those who know and obey this law can fantasize that they know precisely at any given moment where everything either *is* or *is not*. The fantasy that there are only two sides to every question makes truth easily attainable. The world will never be such a simplistic place. When objects or people are perceived as *either* this *or* that, *neither* this *nor* that, they project into simplistic two-valued reality illusions.

This illusion, consciously and unconsciously structured by millions throughout the world, represents one of the truly great political, social, judicial, and economic con games of all time. No reality perceived by humans has ever been so simple as to possess only two sides. The two sides are perceptually constructed, imagined, made up. In reality, there can be as many sides as there are people involved—or many more.

Perceived values might, were we educated in a more reasonable, reality-oriented system, be more accurately assessed on a broad, flexible scale between any two polarities—good-bad, weak-strong, beautiful-ugly, moral-immoral, etc. Evaluation would involve qualities of *more or less*, rather than *either/or*. Whenever people are engineered into an acceptance of a two-valued system, they have been set up to accept black-and-white stereotypical nonsense. They have lost autonomy and control over their perceptions. Perception can then be narrowly channeled in virtually any desired direction; *truth* can be logically, often eternally, ascertained.

Perceived reality, as expressed verbally, pictorially, or mathematically, has an infinite range of possible values, meanings, orientations, and potentialities. The "two sides to every question" is a fiction that flatters the human need to perceive the world in a balanced, symmetrical, proportionate, simplistic illusion. With language, almost anything is possible. Why not three sides, twenty-seven, or even sixty-nine?

Verbal splits, divisions that cannot be made in the reality world, further enforce the law of the excluded middle. Examples include *mind* and *body*, *thinking* and *feeling*, *emotion* and *intellect*, and *conscious* and *unconscious*.

There appear abundant economic justifications for verbal splitting. In medicine, for example, there exists an entire dictionary of specialties. Medicine has become a depersonalized production line such as those in automobile plants where workers assume limited responsibility. Such systems were developed to optimize returns on invested capital. In medicine, they optimize returns on the physicians' investment in education and office equipment. They also reduce work to repetitive, simplistic tasks. Physicians can always pass the buck to another specialist. The victims, of course, are the patients—both in physical well-being and in their pocketbooks.

Mind and *body* are totally integrated. No bodily function operates independently. *Thought* and *feeling* are likewise inseparable, as are *emotion* and *intellect*. No one can be certain where *consciousness* begins and ends. *Conscious* and *unconscious* are completely integrated, interdependent processes. These functions operate all at the same time. In the reality of the human body, these complex processes are nonverbal.

Verbal concepts are fictional descriptions of perceived reality that may not exist in any actual physical or biological way. Verbal descriptions are useful from time to time as tentative, theoretical concepts or conjectures. As individuals become more skilled in understanding their abstraction processes, earlier perceptions often turn out to have been repressed and restricted. New discoveries both in science and everyday life rely upon the availability of new reality perceptions, perceptions previously unavailable. Virtually nothing in the human environment is genuinely new. Something may be labeled "new" as a marketing or ad ploy, but upon close examination the pseudo-new usually turns out to be the same old stuff, redesigned for perceptual hype.

Scholarship, science, and even business unfortunately train individuals to follow in the footsteps of those who have gone before. Entrepreneurs usually know that following someone's footsteps leads to the same places where others have already arrived. Few, if any, discoveries result from conformity. Societies, nevertheless, typically punish or restrict nonconformity. The nonconformist in science, scholarship, art, business, or any other form of human activity threatens the security of conformists—usually in the majority. Like discoverers, discoveries are rarely welcomed. They scare hell out of everyone with a vested interest.

Sacred Profanity

Titian's masterpiece *Sacred and Profane Love* portrays two women seated at a well—the one fully and most properly clothed being "sacred," the other, a voluptuous nude, presumably "profane." The longer a viewer considers "sacred," the more profane she becomes. The more reflection given "profane," the more sacred she becomes. The viewer finally realizes that the two women are the same individual painted twice. Both sacred and profane appear as inherent qualities in all women, the two polarities inextricably interrelated. A similar verbal paradox appears in all two-valued assumptions. "Normal" behavior, or "normal" anything, upon close scrutiny often becomes perversely abnormal. The world's *absolute truths* are inevitably unmasked as the lies of scoundrels, fools, or both. Whenever morals ("truths") triumph, many evil things occur. As far as perception can precariously navigate reality, and verbally, pictorially, or even mathematically symbolize it at any given moment, the only certainty remains uncertainty.

Uncertainties can be fun. Disaster is not ensured when "eternal truths" are questioned or doubted. The present collection of absolute truths that dominate world decisions, policies, and perspectives appear certain to destroy civilization eventually. The present collection of absolute truths were enforced during 1986, the International Year of Peace, by $900 billion in global military expenditures. This massive waste of vital resources, capital, and people is detailed in Ruth Leger Sivard's annual *World Military and Social Expenditures*. No disaster of greater magnitude is imaginable in a world where two-thirds of the population go to bed hungry every night while they are being saved from or by someone's eternal truth.

In a brief summary of Aristotle's law of the excluded middle, British psychiatrist R. D. Laing outlined the ultimate in human folly for a world narcotized by self-indulgence, unyielding greed, and flagrant hypocrisy.

As long as we cannot up-level our "thinking" beyond Us and Them, the goodies and baddies, it will go on and on. The only possible end will be when all the goodies have killed all the baddies, and all the baddies all the goodies, which does not seem so difficult or unlikely since to Us, we are the goodies and they are the baddies, while to Them, we are the baddies and they are the goodies.

Millions of people have died this century and millions more are going to, including, we have every reason to expect, many of Us and our children, because we cannot break this knot.

It seems a comparatively simple knot, but it is tied very, very tight— around the throat, as it were—of the whole human species.

But don't believe me because I say so, look in the mirror and see for yourself. (Laing, *The Politics of the Family*, p. 49)

The Logic of Contradiction

The *law of contradiction* was Aristotle's tidiest contribution to logic and thought. By outlawing contradictions, he dismissed, ignored, and camouflaged the annoying problems inherent in verbal, pictorial, or mathematical language systems. The *law of contradiction*—often summarized as, "Nothing can both be and not be"—cleaned up difficulties stemming from the contradictions, inconsistencies, and paradoxes that are rampant throughout the world. Future generations could ignore loose ends that did not fit into an orderly, consistent language system.

Over the centuries, Aristotelian laws evolved into actual commandments over thought and reason. Had Shakespeare's Hamlet known he could have both *been* and *not been*, at the same time, he might have lived a much happier, more well-adjusted life. But, as Shakespeare well knew, great literature and drama are rarely written about well-adjusted lives.

After Aristotle, humans could verbally inventory and explain the complete world in which they lived—the world they thought, and thought that they thought, they perceived, categorized, defined, and isolated. Human confidence in what was believed to be perceived allowed construction of a logic through which most mysteries, uncertainties, and contradictions vanished. A word or phrase could always be invented, constructed, defined, or redefined to create an illusion of knowledge. The human ego even stretched into the heavens. God was verbally defined by dozens of religions and hundreds of sects, each in their own interest.

In troubled family relationships, for example, therapists finally conceded that anything that affects one influences all. Though husbands and wives blame each other individually, they are mutually involved and supportive of each other's dilemmas. The perception that individuals are independent and isolated from one another constitutes an incredibly destructive illusion of reality. The illusion, nevertheless, has political, ideological, and commercial potentials for those who profit from such illusions.

The world of perceived reality, counter to Aristotelian laws, is interconnected; everything in it is influenced by everything else in that world. *Nothing exists in isolation.* Isolation or exclusivity is only a perceptual illusion—often a dreadful illusion. Poet Carl Sandburg was once asked to identify the most evil word in the English language. Without hesitation he replied, "Exclusive!"

Inside the body, for example, all physiological systems interconnect through the brain, circulatory, and neurological networks. All these *known*, *unknown*, and *unknowable* systems operate continuously, inextricably coordinated with one another. What *appears* to be going on is often a matter of mere biased, superficial speculation.

Verbal descriptions, only definable by other verbal descriptions, permit humans to convince themselves they know *all* about something about which they know absolutely nothing. Such pseudosciences as economics, psychology, sociology, and anthropology— generalized as social sciences—are crammed with verbalistic nonsense. Judicial verbalization also floats similarly within dense clouds of human fantasy. The social sciences are rarely scientific and are quite often antisocial.

For example, the University of Kansas Medical School produced an educational film on tuberculosis for a refresher course for physicians, many of whom had labored years in tuberculosis sanatoriums. Researchers placed transparent plugs in rabbit ears, then introduced tubercle bacilli into tissue beneath the plug. Through time-lapse photography, they documented the bacteria in the ear tissue—how the growth involved cell, neuron, circulatory, and blood-chemistry interactions; how these complex interactions were affected by the rabbit's fear, sexual stimulation, hunger, thirst, and the introduction of various drugs.

The film upset and confused many older physicians who had spent their lives with only verbal definitions of tuberculosis treatment and cure. Their training and practice had been based on simplistic verbal descriptions, far removed from the perceivable interrelated reality of the disease. Even the *submicro* level of perceivable medical reality is now available to those physicians who have mastered higher mathematics, already a consideration in the treatment of cancer and other pathologies.

The subvisually enhanced paper discussed earlier provides another illustration of the law of contradiction in a business situation. After development of the embedding process, the paper company discovered it was virtually impossible to convince controllers in large corporations that monthly invoices subliminally embedded with "Pay now! Imperative! Most Important! Cannot Wait! Vital! Give Precedence!"could increase cash flow. The paper, however, had to be sold to corporation controllers. Controllers, especially among the larger companies, are probably the most ultraconservative executives in business. Their job is to administer cash flow— money in, money out. They are employed to rigidly evaluate—in terms of strict, traditional, empirical, Aristotelian, conscious, visible criteria—the numbers that describe the day-to-day financial status of complex organizations. Even the mention of *subliminal* or *the unconscious* will likely evoke anger, disbelief, and incredulity from such officers. They are perceptually very special people—which probably accounts for their becoming controllers. Most dismissed the idea of subvisually enhanced paper as complete nonsense. Sales managers, on the other hand, were immediately excited about any idea that might influence purchasing behavior. The controllers could not perceive around Aristotle's law of contradiction. They were biased to believe *nothing could both be and not be*. Either the subliminal embeds in the paper were there or they were not there.

The paper company then developed a version of the embedded paper that concealed the subliminal message when viewed from a 90° angle but which was visible by turning the paper to 15°. The embedded message was both there and not there. *Being* and *not being* is a perceptual issue. The verb *to be* is one of the most complex verb forms in any of the world's languages. *To be* literally means "to exist," and existence is a perceptual issue. The demonstration paper illustrated that a message could both *be* and *not be*—at the same time. Most of the controllers appeared finally convinced.

Consistency appears a fatal flaw in every iron-clad system, theorem, or law of language—whether linguistic, pictorial, or mathematical. Spanish philosopher Miguel de Unamuno wrote, "If one never contradicts himself, it is certain he knows nothing." Inconsistency is a natural human condition, certainly for language systems. An illusion of consistency, however, can easily be constructed—either in relationships between persons and persons or between persons and things. Ad and public-relations technicians construct and sustain illusions of consistency—at least until some-

1

2

3

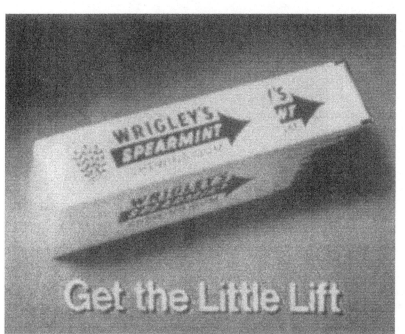

4

5

6

7

8

9

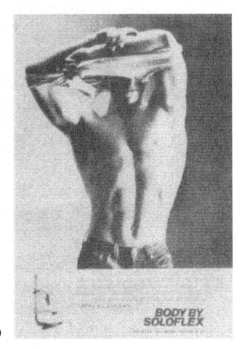

10

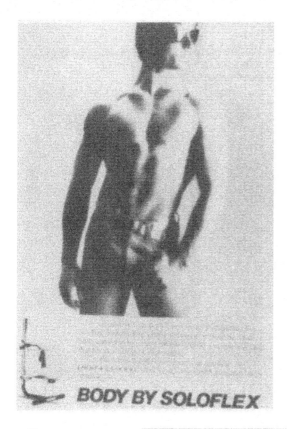

BODY BY SOLOFLEX

11

"No pain, no gain."

BODY BY SOLOFLEX

12

13

14

15

16

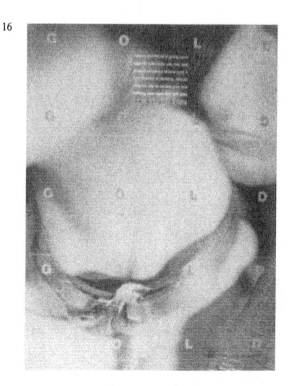

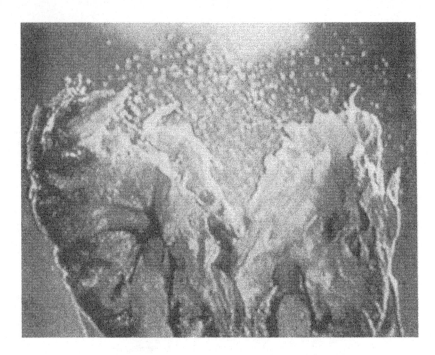

17

18

19

20

21

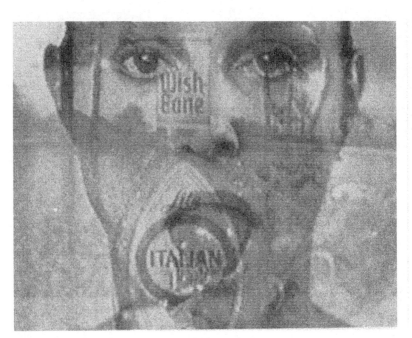

22

23

24

25

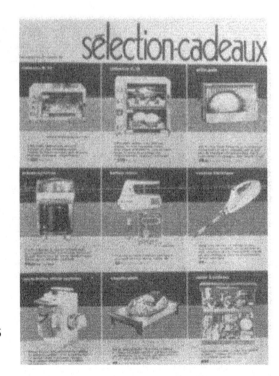

26

27

28

29

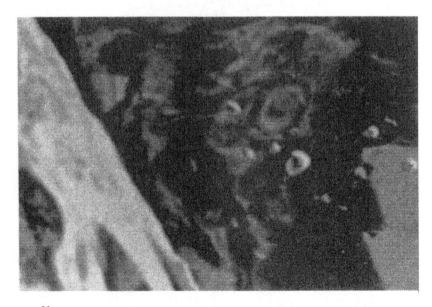

30

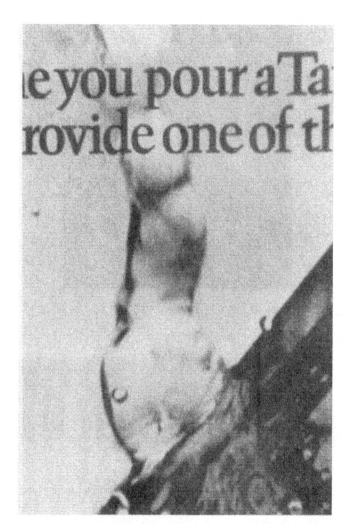

32

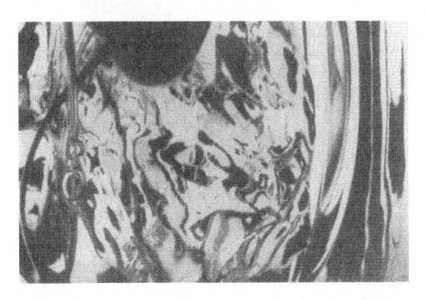

33

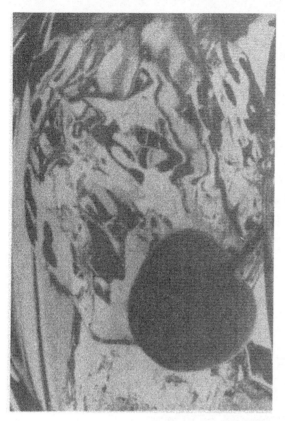

34

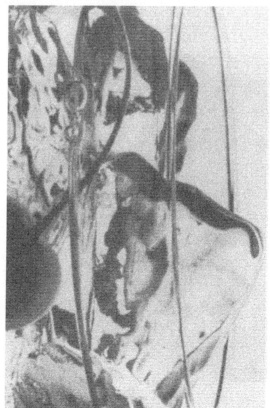

35

36

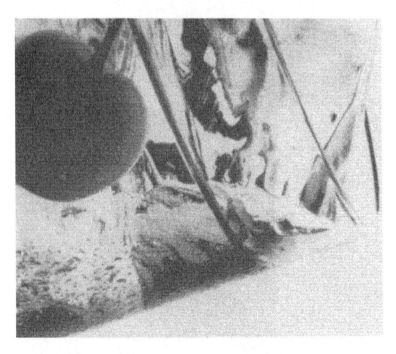

37

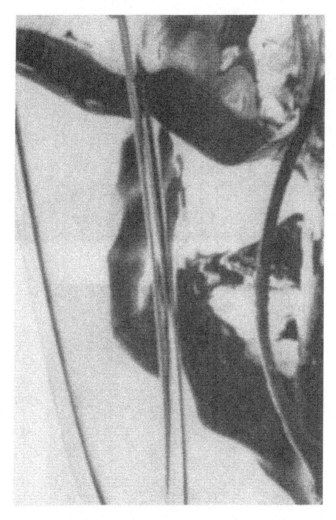

39

40

41

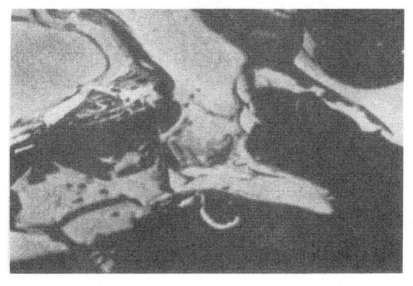

42

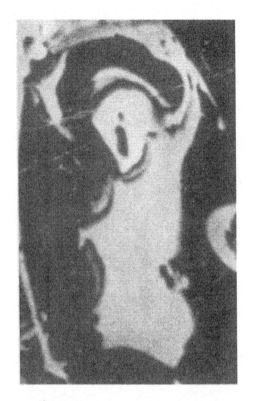

43

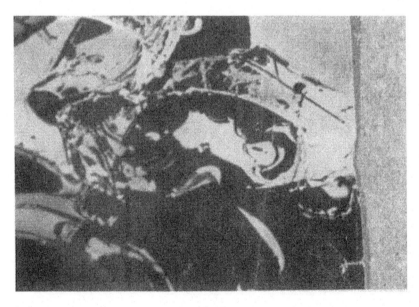

44

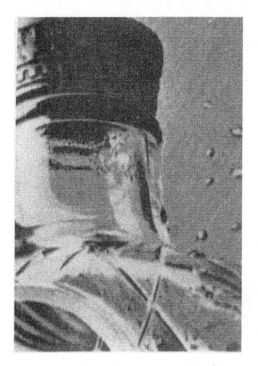

45

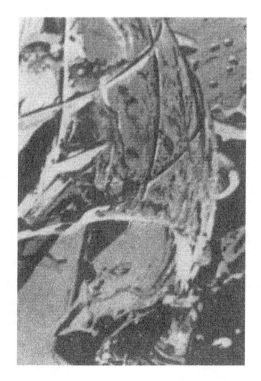

46

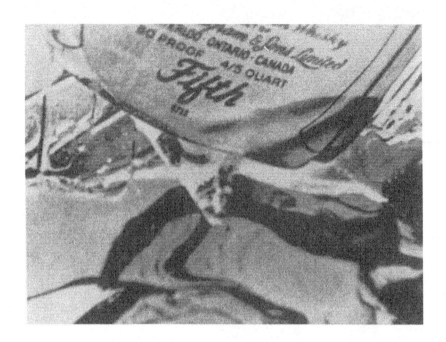

47

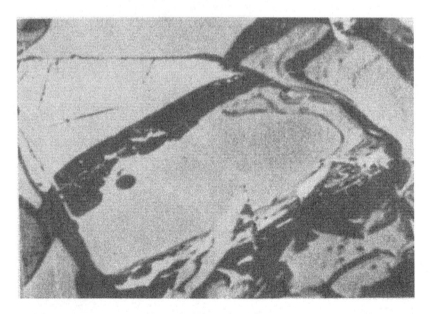

48

49

50

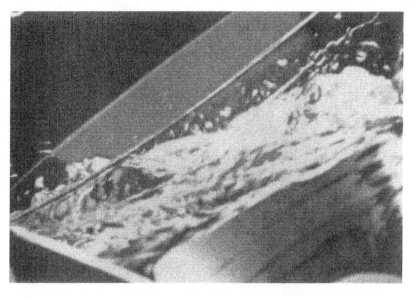

52

53

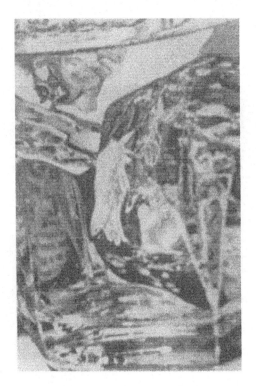

54

55

56

57

58

59

one takes a careful, critical look. Consistency is a constructed role individuals play in various occupational situations. Politicians and corporate executives often become very adept at the role. Consistent reconciliations of inconsistency are perceptually constructed. They may look good on paper, but they are inherently fake.

To disagree with, or disobey, the language structure heretically violates the conventional wisdoms. Paradox, inconsistency, and contradiction are normal expectations in scientific logic and reasoning. When one does not find them, extreme caution should be the rule. Can anyone actually *be* what they have consciously and unconsciously molded themselves into an appearance of being? Actually, the more consistently honest someone appears, the more carefully the silverware should be guarded. Images are stereotypes, lies, cosmetic concealments, and misrepresentations. Images usually conceal their opposite characteristics. When contradictions do not appear, they have been deleted or camouflaged. Intelligence analysts search for consistency constructed to fulfill normal expectations, then distrust it completely. Personnel investigators usually question too-perfect résumés.

Verbal, pictorial, or mathematical statements *can* be both true and false. Truth and falsity are perceptual conclusions and constructions. They are products of the ways humans feel, see, hear, think, smell, and believe they know, or are manipulated to believe they know. Humans usually impose perceptual evaluations upon reality for practical reasons. Motives, of course, can be altruistic, self-serving, or varying degrees of both. The first question in language behavior analysis should be "What is the speaker really trying to do?"

Truth in Advertising

The law of contradiction plays an important role in the mass-communication media. Audiences have been taught to accept information at face value from high-credibility sources. They rarely probe beneath the surface. They should! High-credibility sources are readily purchased by any ad or public-relations flack. Unnamed "high government officials," "four out of five doctors," "reliable sources," "confidential informants," "recent surveys," or similar ghostly attributions are frequently a setup for false, self-serving misinformation.

Public-relations manipulation—much of which is presented as news information—can be true in a simplistic, linear sense, even provable in court. On the other hand, such statements can also be false when considered in context, or in relation to other concealed information. Ad copy is often a technical masterpiece of deception that can be true at one level, but—upon closer examination—also false. A maze of federal agencies supposedly regulates ads for false and deceptive statements. The Federal Trade Commission is the most important, with a large staff of attorneys who act against only the most blatant offenders. Among ad copywriters, FTC regulations are considered a joke. Any experienced writer can verbalize around any law that could be written—simply through a knowledge of Aristotelian logic. Ad writers also make angels dance on the head of a pin. Anyone who gets caught at the game is usually considered inept.

The Food and Drug Administration supposedly controls ads for food, drugs, cosmetics, medical devices, and hazardous products. The Federal Communication Commission indirectly controls broadcast ads through its licensing power but as a practical matter serves the industry, rarely the consumer. The Postal Service supposedly regulates direct mail ads. The Treasury Department's Division of Alcohol, Tobacco, and Firearms has broad, usually unenforced powers to regulate deceptive alcohol and tobacco ads, including the recent ruling that prohibits subliminal ads for alcoholic beverages (see Appendix). The Grain Division of the Agricultural Department supposedly regulates truth in seed ads. The Securities and Exchange Commission ineffectually regulates the ads for securities. Finally, the Civil Aeronautics Board pretends to regulate air-carrier ads.

These federal agencies, with similar state regulatory groups, presumably protect the consumer against deceptive ads. In fact, they serve to legitimize ads. They provide consumers with the illusion that they are secure from manipulation, that they think for themselves, are protected from false and deceptive information. U.S. consumers have been taught to believe that anything published or broadcast must be true. Anything that passes muster with all these publicly funded agencies must be legitimate. Institutional ads by the National Association of Advertising Agencies—the advertising of advertising—publicize the fantasy that ads are validated by regulatory agencies.

The ads published as illustrations in my four books—all very successful ads—are false, deceptive, and misleading. Subliminal ads, for example, have been declared "contrary to the public interest," "clearly intended to be deceptive," by the FTC, FCC, and ATF. Subliminals are also prohibited by the voluntary advertising and broadcasting codes of the industries. No federal agency has ever brought a case against an advertiser over subliminals.

Round and Round the Paradox

In a world long dominated and ruled by Aristotelian laws, paradox is a difficult contradiction to demonstrate. End and beginning, cause and effect, merge into one within a paradox. They become a circular, mutually reinforcing unity. This unity has been symbolized at least since ancient Greece by the Ouroborus—the snake that bites its tail. A paradox reveals the fragile nature of contradiction and consistency in verbal formulations.

There exists an assortment of mathematically derived paradoxes, perceptual constructions that do not fit, are logical to a point where they become totally illogical. Unfortunately, mathematical paradox relates to an unimaginable world for nonmathematicians. The two distinct languages—ours and the mathematicians'—are so different that even the best attempts at translation fail. Kurt Gödel, a German mathematician, used mathematical reasoning to explore mathematical reasoning. The attempt was not unlike using the Aristotelian system to comprehend inconsistencies within the Aristotelian system. Attempts to analyze a system by itself lead nowhere unless a perspective outside the system can be discovered. This is like trying to prove ads false when by conventional logic they can be proven true.

Gödel translated an ancient paradox—the Epimenides or *liar* paradox—into mathematical terms. Simply stated verbally, the paradox reads, Epimenides was a Cretan who made one immortal statement, "All Cretans are liars!" Translated into mathematical terms, Gödel's paradox read, "All consistent axiomatic formulations of number theory include undecidable propositions." Paradox demonstrates that every language system includes inherent, unprovable statements.

Another paradox is: "The following sentence is false. The preceding sentence is true." Such *strange loops*, as they are called in mathematics and logic, involve rules that change themselves directly or indirectly. The preceding paradox appears unsolvable within Aristotelian laws of logic. Once outside the system, however, in a non-Aristotelian world, the verbal definitions of *true* and *false* can be expanded to include situations where *false* is sometimes *true* and vice versa. Or, in response to unresolvable inconsistency, the logical sequence can be inverted: "The preceding sentence is true." There is no preceding sentence, so the sentence must be false. Therefore, "the following sentence is false" is actually true—achieving verbal consistency. Either sentence, of course, could be both *true* and *false*.

Contradictions, inconsistencies, and paradoxes can be productively confronted, tasted, enjoyed, and played with endlessly. They are the source of new insights, innovations, inventions, and creative problem-solving. They appear at the roots of human intelligence. Innovation usually upsets the status quo, and especially people whose investments depend upon the status quo. Aristotle's *law of contradiction* compels us to sweep all those lovely contradictions under the intellectual rug that divides formality from informality, flexibility from inflexibility, creative play from serious obsession.

Paradox often unconsciously affects our daily lives. We rarely suspect we have been entrapped by an Aristotelian law of language and thought. Language creates paradox when it talks about itself. This is one of the reasons so many writers who try to explain communication communicate so poorly. When you discuss "what she said, about what you said, about what she said, about what you said," et cetera, you are into paradox. Marital competitions often evolve into paradox. The Ouroborus bites its tail in every conflict where effect feeds back on its own cause. For example, when she blames his impotence, and he blames her frigidity, and she blames his impotence and he blames her frigidity, ad infinitum. Edward Albee's grim play *Who's Afraid of Virginia Woolf?* cruelly demonstrates the disasters of paradox. Once established, paradox leads into the circle with no beginning or end, beyond cause and effect, self-perpetuating until disaster or death, via unmeasurable unhappiness.

The popular television personalities who huckster themselves as religious prophets—Jimmy Swaggart, Oral Roberts, Jerry Falwell, or Pat Robertson—all of whom claim regular talks with God— should ask Him during their next conversation if He can make a stone so heavy He cannot lift it.

No system can explain or verify its validity, or lack of validity, unless it utilizes concepts outside the system. These concepts must be developed from larger, more flexible systems. Unfortunately, this larger system inevitably becomes subject to incompleteness. It also is a perceptual product, like its predecessor. An even more comprehensive system must then be evolved, ad infinitum. This is, or should be, the process of scholarship, science, and human growth—a never-ending succession of language systems constructed to verify one another. The search for *truth* should never cease, especially when someone perceives he or she has found it.

Unpredictable Predictions

When Aristotelian laws of thought reign unquestioned, a curious conceptualization of *reliability* and *predictability* magically appears. Three non-Aristotelian axioms should be considered basic requirements for literacy.

First: Today's science acknowledges that everything in the perceivable biological and physical world (people and things) exists in a state of process and change. Nothing in the perceivable world is static and permanent. Like the people and things observed, the observers are also in a state of process and change.

Second: Everything in the perceivable world affects everything else. Nothing exists in isolation.

Third: Perceived reality is, for better or worse, simply a perception. Human perception can never be considered free from varying degrees of subjectivity. Nothing can seriously be considered as objective perception of an objective reality. Perceivers can never be removed from their perceptions.

Perceptions of the world are both conscious and unconscious constructions. Perceptual constructions are put together to be per-

145

ceived and acted upon. They are built to serve motives, objectives, or sometimes just for fun. As for the certainty, truth, or validity of these perceived realities, physicist Werner Heisenberg concluded, "All information between humans can only be exchanged within a field of tolerance for uncertainty. Every judgement, especially those judgements of science, stands upon the edge of error." Perceived reality constructions in the area of U.S.-Soviet relations are particularly dangerous, especially since one wonders how well peceptual processes are understood by each side. These processes are not publicly acknowledged to exist.

Even when the language-logic structure is intellectually understood, it is quite another matter to utilize this knowledge in everyday life. Language is deeply ingrained in human personality, culture, conscious and unconscious memories, thought, and even dreams. Any modification of the system will require time, patience, determination, and, for most individuals, a new type of rigorous self-discipline.

Every assumption about the past, present, and future must be doubted, questioned, and tested repeatedly for accuracy in its relationship to perceived realities. Value systems must be critically appraised for validity. Conclusions must be reviewed and repeatedly questioned. Relationships with objects, individuals, and groups must be reappraised in relation to time and perceivable fact structures.

Psychologist Prescott Lecky utilized a concept of *self-reflexiveness* to describe the new learning process. With practice, individuals can develop the ability to view themselves, as they view themselves, while viewing themselves, et cetera. The objective is to move perception farther away from the first, immediate level to a more abstract perspective. It is a way to become more aware of perceptual processes and verify or contradict the validity of first-level perceptions. The technique provides a tremendous advantage in games such as chess, poker, military intelligence, or business competition.

Perceptual distance gives you a platform from which you can see actions to reactions to reactions. Advanced chess players can often self-reflect out to three or four levels. The technique can render *conscious* perceptual reactions that were *unconscious*.

The collective effects of mass media, quite unfortunately, reinforce a population's superficial, one-dimensional reactions to immediate, first-level stimuli. Aristotle's *laws of identity*, *excluded middle*, and *contradiction* are commercially expedient structures. Their limitations and fallacies remain hidden. Indoctrinated populations remain helplessly vulnerable to verbal or pictorial manipulation in any direction profitable to manipulators.

6 | THE REAL THING — SYMBOLIC REALITIES

The bible should be recognized as mythological, should be maintained in symbolic form and not replaced by scientific substitutes. There is no substitute for the use of symbols and myths. They are the language of faith.

Paul Tillich, *On the Boundary*

A word or image is symbolic when it implies something more than its obvious and immediate meaning. We use symbolic terms constantly to represent concepts we cannot define or fully comprehend.

Carl Gustav Jung, *Man and His Symbols*

Whenever your conscious mind takes anything for granted, tells you something is ordinary, common, insignificant, unworthy of careful attention, go back and take another very careful look. Constantly question your questions and—above all—your answers.

Marshall McLuhan,
University of Toronto seminar

Archetypal literally means "the original form." There have been numerous theories that archetypal symbolic meanings are innate, inherited aspects of genetic heritage. They are found in sight and sound, and in smell, taste, and touch. Archetypal symbols were first discussed in the writings of third-century scholar-priest Saint Augustine. He discovered religious symbols with similar meanings in cultures that had had no known contact over long time periods. Saint Augustine attributed archetypal symbolism to "the hand of God."

Archetypal symbols of one sort or another are common to all cultures and peoples. Symbolic meanings generally involve unconscious perceptual mechanisms and underlie conscious definitions. Humans label consciously, but symbolic significance remains at an unconscious level. Archetypal symbols usually involve the two polarities of human existence—the beginning (reproduction, birth, rebirth) and the end (death, actual or symbolic). These two polarities of human experience have been the major preoccupations of philosophy, literature, art, and religious thought for thousands of years.

Most women adamantly deny that lipstick and rouge are anything but functional products with which they decorate their faces. Cosmetic ad makers know there is a much deeper, more powerful symbolic significance. Women color their lips and faces, so they say, to appear attractive. But what does that mean? Heterosexual men do not use cosmetics. For females, *attractive* relates to sexual or reproductive appeal, fertility, even availability.

During sexual excitation, female genitals become swollen and bright red or purple, as do the facial cheeks. Sexual colorations are less intense and noticeable in men. Lipstick creates a symbolic vulva on the face. Rouged cheeks symbolize the sexual flush. Purple coloration around the eyes also symbolizes the female genitalia. Purple and various shades thereof are called by artists and designers *genital colors*. Women's cosmetics create archetypal genital symbolism, powerfully attractive both to men and to other women— unconsciously, of course. Genital symbolism in cosmetics dates back in human history as far as can be known. Seminal fluid was once used as a body and facial cosmetic.

It did not take much intelligence to realize archetypal symbols could produce enormous profits. Cosmetics manufacturers and their ad agencies elaborate exhaustively on basic archetypal themes. A glance through any periodical provides a moist array of female genital symbolism in eyes, lips, hair, jewelry, clothing, shoes, and food. The exploitation of archetypal symbolic themes fills virtually every ad. Symbolic meanings, however, are repressed by audiences, hidden from themselves by individuals entrapped in the manipulation.

Archetypal auditory symbols include sounds from nature—72 heartbeats per minute, 4/4 time in music; waves at sea and rolling over a beach; wind in trees or on the plains; thunder, rain; bird and animal sounds; human and animal breathing; and many kinds of silences.

Orgasmic sounds are archetypal. A rock music producer became curious about using a tape of male and female orgasmic sounds in an album. A musician-composer, once a musician in a major symphony orchestra, he had built a successful career as a designer of rock groups. He constructed roles and group relationships, costumed and cosmeticized performers, designed staging, and composed, arranged, and orchestrated the music. He had designed rock groups in which the members never met personally. Each recorded separately, and the individual performances were assembled through a studio mixer. Even group photographs were composite, pasted-together assemblages. Emotionally unstable rock musicians were easier to manage individually, he explained.

Once the packaged rock group was assembled, it was sold to a major record company. Several such groups had become internationally famous and financially successful. Success in the popular music industry is defined simply. They made money, lots of money. The producer was an interesting individual—intellectually curious and sensitive to an extraordinary range of conscious and unconscious audio meanings involved with human relationships. He humorously voiced contempt for the performers in his engineering projects. He called them "drug freaks," "not one competent musician if a dozen were melted together," "immature, psychopathic delinquents." The producer's success, however, was displayed in a Beverly Hills mansion and a Rolls Royce.

He decided to insert a tape of orgasmic sounds into an orchestration. His first thought was to hire an actor and actress who could imitate orgasmic sounds. Research suggested, however, that audiences might detect falsity and misrepresentation at this level of perception. For a month the producer and his wife taped their orgasmic sounds. Ingeniously, he used a larynx microphone that amplified a broad range of more subtle sound experiences, concealing the obvious sound characteristics.

The result would probably not have been consciously recognized without explanation. The sounds were strangely unsettling and exciting. They were not sexually stimulating to conscious perception. These sounds had not been experienced consciously by many individuals. Considering the perceptual bias present during orgasm—an event that involves a neurological symphony of feelings—few ever concentrate consciously on the sounds. Unconsciously, however, orgasmic sounds exist in the memories of most humans.

When the orgasmic tape was mixed into the rock music album, the volume level varied—sometimes almost imperceptible, other times deafening. When the completed tape was finally auditioned for a major record company, the producer was awed by the response. Contracts were being typed even before the audition was completed. The producer reported that never in his experience had anyone reacted so strongly, so emotionally to an audition. The man was exuberant. Several weeks later, however, he had second thoughts. He began to worry that the contracts had been signed primarily because of the subliminally embedded orgasmic sounds. The rock group he had invented, at least so he said, was just not that good. In fact, he described it as "quite awful." He finally disclosed to the record company what he had done. They were furious. The contract was canceled.

Two years later, the producer's orgasmic rock album was released by another major record company. The album sold over 10 million copies and spun off rock videos. This time the producer kept the orgasmic tape a secret. Once an audience is told about subliminal embeds in sound, the knowledge changes the way they perceive the music. They become tense, strained, listening carefully to detect the embedded material. Some individuals emotionalize themselves into what could be described as *defensive paranoia* in response to suspected embedded subliminals.

Symbols Evoke Feelings

Symbols circumvent conscious thought and logic. They evoke vague, unspecific feelings. Symbolism constitutes a subliminal technique of communication. Sophisticated, carefully researched, and powerful symbolic communication is basic to commercial manipulation. Symbols directly affect perception, feelings, and behavior. They do not depend upon conscious definitions or explanations.

Gold, for example, is a precious metal as it is perceived to exist in reality. But gold is far more significant to humans in symbolic value. Numerous metals have a greater monetary value and are more rare in nature, but none has a symbolic value more meaningful than gold. At the conscious level, gold is a soft, malleable metal found in relatively pure form in nature. One ounce of gold can be beaten out to 300 square feet. In thin sheets, it transmits green light. Gold does not tarnish or corrode. Because of electrical conductivity, the largest industrial use of gold is in electrical and electronic circuitry. Natural gold is 100% isotope gold—197; atomic number 79; atomic weight 196.967; melting point 1945°F.; specific gravity 19.3; valence 1.3; and the electronic configuration is (Xe) $4f^{14}5d^{10}6s^{1}$. So much for the simple facts, which have little, if anything, to do with the value of gold.

Anything with symbolic value, such as gold, provides a mystique with which humans can be manipulated. Symbol dictionaries are helpful to explore symbolic values (*see* Jobes; Cirlot; and Frazer). Mythology, folklore, and advertising are the means by which symbolic values have been passed along from generation to generation. They are still the best sources for symbolic meaning and significance. The known facts about gold, for example, cannot explain the preference for this metal in jewelry. As an archetypal symbol, the meaning of which appears more or less consistent over thousands of years, gold traditionally has involved religious conviction.

The symbolic meaning of gold includes an identification with solar light, often comparable to the sun, divine intelligence, a fruit of the spirit, supreme illumination, constancy, dignity, an elixir of life, excellence, love, perfection, power, purity, wealth, and wisdom. In the folklore of many cultures, a person is frequently drawn up to heaven by a gold chain that binds heaven to earth. These symbolic or archetypal meanings for gold—interpreted somewhat differently by men and women—have been traced back to the beginning of recorded history. The preciousness of gold has always been in its symbolic value rather than in its functional or monetary use.

The International Gold Corporation ad (fig. 16) appeared in numerous national periodicals. It is a typical example of contemporary manipulation of symbolic values in the pursuit of profit. It is an out-of-focus portrait of a woman wearing a gold collar, necklace, or belt. The details are diffuse, uncertain. Whether the jewelry is around her neck or shoulders is unclear—intentionally unclear. The right background figure is also blurred as the foreground woman's bare shoulder is kissed. The lips, nose, and hair of the background figure appear feminine. The long hair of both models appears differently textured.

The word *GOLD* was printed five times in gold letters across the layout. The fine-print copy, read by approximately 5% of magazine readers, defines the jewelry in the blurred photograph as an 18-karat sculptured-gold collar, "a new direction in dressing, an eloquent way to declare your love. Nothing else feels like real gold." A collar, *gold* or otherwise, is a symbol of bondage, a means to capture, control, or possess an animal or human. The logical explanation of the ad, however, is meaningless and irrelevant, unread by 95% of readers. The ad's objective must be achieved by only three elements in the picture—gold, jewelry, and the two women.

The ad appears unexplainable and unjustifiable as a multi-million-dollar investment at any conscious level of consideration. Published in numerous national magazines, the ad cost IGC several million dollars, not including the $25,000 to $50,000 for the art production. The symbolic concept of *gold* is a powerful force in any of the world's cultures at the conscious level but far more powerful at the unconscious level. Directed at women, the ad stimulates strong—though nonspecific—conscious feelings.

The seemingly inept, out-of-focus ad is only worth the money invested if consumers rush out to their nearest jewelry store and buy. Like most ads, the layout was designed to be read in a few seconds, or less. The ad details may never, at any point, surface consciously in a reader's perception. Attempt to forget, for the moment, how you consciously defined the ad when you first glanced at it. Perception of an ad is a far different perceptual experience in a book about subliminal ad manipulation than in the context of reading *Time* magazine. Search for something special in the picture. Study the ad carefully.

Turn the *GOLD* ad upside down. Try to keep your mind clear and placid. Note your first quick perception of what appears in the inverted picture. Should you have doubts, try the ad on several friends. The subliminal message is quite simple. An 18-karat-gold collar is one way to become pregnant. Pregnancy archetypally symbolizes *the beginning* and *good news*. It is impossible to know whether the collar was a reward for the pregnancy or the pregnancy a result of the gift. In any respect, pregnancy may be the most singularly important event in a woman's life—far too important to corrupt as a manipulative sales gimmick.

Virtually everything perceived by humans is symbolic, functional, or both—usually both. Modern high-technology cultures fantasize that symbolism is an archaic remnant of ancient superstition and medieval alchemy. In the strictly scientific view, such relics from the past have no effect upon modern behaviors. This represents wishful thinking at its worst. Symbolism has, nevertheless, been abolished from serious consideration in higher education, especially in the so-called social and behavioral sciences. Curiously, however, the products of modern science and technology are media-communicated, hyped, promoted, and sold through symbolism. The symbolisms of science often reflect quite unscientific throwbacks to legend, mythology, folklore, and magic.

In ads for computers, electronic equipment, and high-fidelity amplifiers and speakers, units are often arranged in phallic and vaginal relationships. For example, round or elliptical speakers provide female symbols. Amplifiers that drive the speakers are displayed as phallic symbols with their complex control dials and levers. Gender designations can be reversed by design or display. Female symbols in high-tech ads are usually controlled and dominated by male symbols.

Symbolic Leaders

Symbolic leaders are special leaders who function through their stereotypical, fictional meaning or image. They are distinct from organizational leaders who work within societal or institutional structures. Organizational leaders may not mean much as individuals outside their immediate area of expertise or responsibility. Their significance lies primarily in functions. Once in a while, with media support, the two types of leadership merge—often inflicting great mischief upon the world.

Ronald Reagan is an outstanding example. The many movie roles he portrayed as the heroic sheriff, RAF fighter pilot, self-sacrificing athlete, expert narrator of countless air force training films during World War II were still latent in the unconscious memories of anyone who had experienced the films. These roles had nothing to do with Reagan; he was only an actor who played fictional characters. Nevertheless, the roles formed a perceptual background—albeit at the unconscious level—for his entry into politics. During his eight years as president, his only apparent skill was in manipulating acceptance of a continuation of the movie roles. Reagan's ineptness as an executive administrator rapidly became a national disaster, culminating in the discovery that he believed in astrology. Sociologist Orrin Klapp explored the little-known world of symbolic power and authority in his important work *Symbolic Leaders.*

The U.S. is not the only country in which leaders are carefully rehearsed, their words composed by skilled craftsmen, their costumes, makeup, props, and sets engineered by skillful designers. In the developed nations, the lifelong care and feeding of the audience by promotional symbolism extends into economic, political, military, social, and even religious life.

Take the concept of queen, for example, a complex symbolic entity. Unconscious associations include dignity, fertility, motherhood, nobility, wealth, leadership, and tradition. The symbolic queen is traceable back to prehistoric periods. At conscious levels, she may appear little more than an attractive, well-costumed woman.

The chairman of a Canadian university psychology department militantly rejected the idea of symbolic effects upon behavior. Rigorously disciplined in behaviorist empiricism, he religiously denied the validity of unconscious perception. His lengthy, mathematical-statistical analyses of experimental psychology were featured in many academic journals throughout the English-speaking world. His students joked that it was academic suicide to bring up a psychological symptom in his seminars that could not be quantified. "What you see and hear is what you get," he frequently admonished. "That's all there is to it!" He considered symbolism an unsuitable subject for scientific investigation.

Queen Elizabeth II holds a symbolic position as head of state for the United Kingdom of Great Britain and Northern Ireland. In spite of her titles, palaces, wardrobe, and heritage, she holds little power. She exists, is supported and utilized, as a symbol of state. The British Parliament and the prime minister actually govern Great Britain, which considers itself a constitutional monarchy. It is fascinating to observe the symbolic significance of royalty to British and Commonwealth peoples. The queen is deeply loved, revered, worshiped as a celebrity, and honored in a way people in nonmonarchical cultures find difficult to comprehend. Her celebrity status is comparable to media stars and athletic heroes in the U.S., but with the significant additional weight of archetypal symbolism. She represents all things to all people. It is indelicate to attempt a critical discussion of the queen with Anglo-Canadians. Her symbolic significance is one of the remaining remnants of British imperial grandeur, power, and tradition.

In order to become a Canadian citizen, one must swear fealty to the queen. Commonwealth armed forces serve the queen. The queen is toasted at the beginning of formal dinners. Such symbolic devotion amuses French Canadians but is taken most seriously by the Anglos. On one Canadian tour, the queen traveled through Ontario by train. The psychology professor who so passionately denied the significance of symbols waited six hours in a heavy snowstorm with his family to glimpse the queen as her train passed through town. As many observers have noted, the more fiercely individuals defensively reject the idea that they are influenced by unconsciously perceived information, the more intensely subliminals seem to manage their lives.

In his *Letter IV*, Saint Augustine explained that "teaching accomplished with symbols feeds and stirs the fires of love which help humans excel and surpass themselves." Archetypal symbols appear as rich and varied as do life situations. Repetition of certain life events over thousands of years may have engraved these into human predispositions or memory. The most important experiences are, of course, birth, reproduction, and death. These are the basic subjects around which most of the world's religions, philosophies, literatures, arts, and other deeply meaningful experiences focus. Even with modern pretensions to scientific objectivity, these fundamental experiences are still perceived as magical, their specific details and implications usually repressed from conscious awareness. These three fundamental human experiences still carry near universal ritualistic, spiritual, religious, and superstitious significance. Even within the officially atheistic U.S.S.R., solemn ritual ceremonies commemorate birth, marriage, and death. The symbolic significance of these three events appears vital to individual and social human survival. Every known religion, state, and social group has sought to control and utilize these three common human experiences for power or profit. Symbolic values related to these experiences powerfully affect behavior, while conscious awareness of these effects remains repressed.

As an archetypal symbol, birth has little to do with biological sex or reproduction. Unconsciously, birth symbolically relates to such human enigmas as *where did I come from, what was the beginning of existence, feeling, knowing,* and *why do I exist?* The human body and its functions, early in life, become the primary unconsciously perceived reality. Symbolic separation and independence from the mother also appears a basic, universal human dilemma.

Sexual reproduction unconsciously symbolizes, on one hand, a threat to independence and autonomy. On the other hand, however, are the deep symbolic implications of love, bonding, intimacy, search for identity, creativity, eternal life through reproduction, transference, and purification. The unconscious significance of sex within the human psyche extends far deeper than the silly banalities of ad media's pornographic, kick-trip-oriented manipulations.

The most fearsome, private event is death, both in reality and in symbolic terms. Death symbolizes the conclusion of human existence, the ultimate tragedy, the end of feeling, aspiration, expectation, the entrance into the truly great unknown, and—as alluded to in Genesis—"the return to dust."

Some theorists have tried to explain archetypes as genetically inherited information, "racial myths," in the terms of psychologist

Erich Fromm. Others, such as anthropologist Claude Lévi-Strauss, explored the possibility that brain physiology collects information within a matrix that provides common symbolic significance.

Whatever the theory, and there are many, the literature of symbolism, mythology, and folklore provides a rich and fascinating exploration of a vital aspect of human experience. How the brain processes and stores nonverbal, unconscious, symbolic meaning may well be unknowable in any definitive sense. The mental processes involved may not lend themselves to factual or statistical-mathematical ways of knowing. Much about how the human brain functions may well be unknowable, except through theoretics. Nevertheless, humans are highly manipulable by almost anyone with some understanding of symbolic value systems.

The music video entitled "Valerie," by rock star Steve Winwood, thoroughly exploits archetypal symbols. In the lower left quadrant of the TV frame, one minute and forty-five seconds into the video, a cigarette appears to float, rocking back and forth, unrolls to flat cigarette paper, rolls again into a cigarette, the cigarette magically lights, transposes into a wooden match, the matchhead flames, and burns rapidly to the end. Cigarettes, subliminally, relate to death and self-destruction; the match lights, burns completely, and the flame is extinguished like the life of the smoker.

In another segment, one minute and fifteen seconds into the video, the letters *S-E-X* appear sequentially, then a large *X* appears, followed by several hooded, ghoulish figures, followed by the skull and crossbones in several designs, followed by a valentine heart, and finally a circle, symbol of unification—*love* and *death* subliminally invoked to sell a record album. All the video audience consciously perceives, if indeed they conciously perceive anything, are flickers of light in the lower left quadrant of the frame and Winwood singing in the right half of the frame.

Shortly after the "Valerie" video was released, the album it came from, *Chronicles*, was one of the top three best-sellers in the U.S.

Interpret Rather than Define

Archetypal symbolism is also drawn from nature, human struggles against nature, and common biological processes. Similar symbolic representations appear often in dreams, daydreams, fantasies, art forms, myths, legends, and folklore. Bluebeard's secret room, which his wives were forbidden to enter, symbolized his mind. The swan, because of its unusual reproductive behaviors, is symbolic of hermaphroditism, bisexuality, or gender ambiguity. The lion is symbolically the king of beasts because of its prodigious sexual appetites. Symbolism, however, is rarely simplistic. Symbols can be interpreted on a variety of levels, depending upon who uses them, when, and the context. Interpreters of symbolic meaning should distrust simple ready-made definitions. Symbols must be interpreted rather than defined.

Ad media purposely utilize symbolism to sell products, ideas, and personalities. The most intensely exploited, visible area of symbolic manipulation surrounds human reproduction. Sexuality is clearly the area of human experience most vulnerable to manipulation, exploitation, and the eventual development of neurotic and psychotic behaviors. This appears especially true in the acquisitive value systems of Western societies, but probably all humans share a similar vulnerability.

The Oscar Mayer sliced meat ad (fig. 13) is typical of archetypal symbolism applied to merchandising and consumer manipulation. The ad was widely and expensively published in national men's magazines such as *Esquire* and *Gentleman's Quarterly* (*GQ*). The Italian-style beef slices on the left are styled to form a male genital, the cracked black pepper ham slices on the right form a somewhat smaller genital, though perhaps, as the copy explains, "more sharp and peppery." Remember, these symbols were directed at male unconscious perception. The female genital is symbolically represented in the center by smoked chicken breast slices. A recessive area has been subtly painted on the roasted chicken, suggesting female genitalia around the visceral cavity opening. Few macho males could resist the expectational fantasy of two men and a woman intermixing their genitalia. The Oscar Mayer ménage à trois reflects a sexual extravaganza, with male homosexual implications.

Symbolic imagery circumvents conscious, critical thought. It involves not only pictures but also words and numbers. The three symbolic representations in "Select Slices" unconsciously convey spiritual synthesis, childbirth, conflict resolution, harmony, and unity—all associated with heaven or the Trinity. Had the artist utilized a two-, four-, or five-part arrangement, unconscious meanings would have changed. The "select" consumer who unconsciously identifies with the Oscar Mayer ad never consciously considers the expensive artwork significant.

The simple ad layout effectively optimizes the return on Oscar Mayer's media investment. The genital symbolism, in addition, is enhanced by the copy, which tells us that each meat is 95% fat-free. It would be far more medically important if the prospective consumers were 95% fat-free. U.S. readers have been trained to mindlessly accept, trust, and consciously ignore media. Any critical evaluation would quickly reduce the ad's effectiveness.

Almost any erect, long, stiff object can be deliberately engineered into a phallic symbol adaptable to mass-communication media. Audiences are rarely aware of what is going on. Awareness, of course, immediately puts the audience back into control, cancels or at least diminishes the ad's potential to modify behavior. For symbols to motivate sales, they must be consciously perceived as functional or logical. In ad media, phallic symbols are regularly developed from walking sticks, broom handles, fish, neckties, bananas, candles, flagpoles, skyscrapers, lampposts, whales, trees, obelisks, towers, lighthouses, space rockets, weapons, chimneys, cannons, elephant trunks, birds, swords, lances, spears, ejaculating champagne bottles, keys, cigarettes, cigars, automobiles, airplanes, electric guitars, microphones, thumbs and fingers—the list is endless.

Vaginal symbols are as rich in variety as the phallic. Female genitalia can be insinuated by almost any elliptical opening—a skin crevice under an arm, knee, elbow, or the rim of a glass or cup. In the Chivas Regal ad (fig. 7), the phallic bottle penetrates the elliptical rim of the whiskey glass. Similarly, the rim on the dip cup in the McDonald's ad (fig. 14) has been penetrated by the symbolic seminal fluid dripping from the Chicken McNugget. Betty Crocker's Super Moist cake mix (fig. 6) even carried the symbolic vagina into an anatomical replica—and got away with it, almost.

Casual examination of ads reveals an imaginative assortment of deliberate genital symbols. Curiously, the male genitalia ads appear directed at male consumers, the female genitalia ads at females.

Through trial and error, advertisers became convinced ads sell far better via this seeming contradiction. Psychological explanations are tentative. Arguments have been made that such ads appeal to latent homosexuality in both men and women, and that by increasing the taboo nature of the stimuli, consumers become more involved, responsive, and vulnerable. To the ad huckster, it really doesn't matter as long as the ad sells.

Magic Alive in Media

In a thirty-second TV ad for Wishbone salad dressing, subliminal techniques and symbolism combine into a powerful mind massage. The brand label "Wishbone" alludes to magic, belief in resurrection, and, in Hebrew tradition, an indestructible tree and its inner, hidden, inviolable heart. Subliminal meanings are often hidden in video superimpositions—one scene fades as a new scene emerges. Subliminals are easily concealed in this transition. Unless the transition is taped and viewed one frame at a time, the flimflam remains hidden from consciousness. The Wishbone TV ad is a technological masterpiece.

The transition begins with a voluptuous model swimming in a tropical lagoon (fig. 17). As she shoots up from the water, arms and legs apart, the scene transfers to a head of lettuce held by two female hands. The thumbs holding the lettuce appear to press on the model's genital area (fig. 18). As the swimsuit model fades, the lettuce is split in half, symbolically as though a birth had occurred (fig. 19). Emerging from the V-split lettuce head, now appears the symbolic Wishbone bottle (fig. 20). The bottle design includes a male phallic upper portion and an elliptical female bottom—the symbolic unity of male and female in a romantic tropical setting. The scene changes to a head shot of the model, who appears to be licking the female portion of the bottle (fig. 21). As the bottle fades, the model's tongue appears as a tomato in her mouth (fig. 22). The four transitions occur sequentially in less than ten symbolically powerful seconds. Every detail records perceptually at unconscious levels. Tomatoes (also called love apples) and lettuce are symbolic of birth, spring, resurrection, abundance, fertility, fecundity, and regeneration of life. Tomatoes symbolize love; lettuce symbolizes spring and a renewal of life.

Birth, reproduction, and finally death provide strong, underlying archetypal themes for numerous ads. The Seagram's Crown Royal broken bottle (fig. 15) is an example of a subliminal death appeal, inviting the drinker to self-immolate and destruct. Castration is another archetypal death symbol. The death wish is one of the most well-articulated theories in psychological literature—an innate compulsion to seek death, either actually or symbolically.

Numerous ads for alcohol and tobacco were illustrated in earlier studies of subliminal perception. A castrated penis, skulls, and nightmare monster faces appeared in a Johnny Walker ad (see Key, *The Clam-Plate Orgy*, figs. 6–16). The word *cancer* was embedded in a two-page Benson and Hedges cigarette ad (see Key, *Media Sexploitation*, figs. 41–42). Bizarre skulls, scorpions, dead birds, and sharks were embedded in Bacardi and Calvert ads (see Key, *Subliminal Seduction*, figs. 16–17). All these expensively manufactured images are archetypal symbols, personifications of death and self-destruction. They were expensively engineered, tested, and applied as marketing techniques. They sell, or are believed by the advertisers to sell. They have made a great deal of money for advertisers. What the ads accomplished for defenseless consumers can be perceived in public-health statistics.

Someone should be looking into death-wish or self-destruct compulsions evident in U.S. armament strategies. If archetypal death-wish symbolism successfully sells cigarettes, alcohol, and rock music, why not MX missiles, B-1 bombers, and other hardware in the armament pork barrels? The distinct possibility exists that both superpowers are simply acting out their collective death wish in unconscious conspiracy against themselves.

Human history has been a story of incredible survival skill in constant confrontation with suicidal behaviors. No human society has ever been continuous. Sooner or later, all have managed to self-destruct. Yet, they have continued to proliferate. Until quite recently, it was impossible to kill on the scale necessary to destroy everything. Human ingenuity finally triumphed. Suicidal potentialities today provide humans with their own final solution. Mutually Assured Destruction (MAD) is not merely a theory. It is a reality, only minutes away from the press of a button or a phone call. And, in the face of MAD, world leaders along with their scientific sycophants still mumble that there is no such thing as a human death wish.

When the final stupidity occurs—and it is reasonable to assume it will—the act will appear logical, rational, justifiable, and to some the fulfillment of destiny or biblical prophecy. Further, until the last few individuals painfully vomit themselves to death from radiation poisoning, the argument over whose fault it was will passionately continue. Millions of dollars are regularly invested in research into massive destruction; virtually nothing so far has been invested in the study of human survival.

No one has, as yet, made serious long-term investigations into the eventual effects of ad-media flimflam upon human personality, mental health, behavior, and survival. The U.S. blindly allows the commercial establishment to inflict avaricious self-interest upon the entire population. Virtually no one appears to hear the faint ticking of our time running out.

7 | CAUSE AND EFFECT—
THE GREATEST ILLUSION
OF ALL

What we cannot think, we cannot think; we cannot
therefore say what we cannot think.
Ludwig Wittgenstein, *Tractatus Logicophilosophicus*

If I do not know I know, I think I do not know.
R. D. Laing, *Knots*

Only childish people imagine that the world is what
we think it is.
C. G. Jung, *Analytical Psychology*

Humans exhibit an inherited predisposition to believe that for every effect there is a known or knowable cause. The common myth holds that some single or multiple occurrence precedes a particular event, without which the event would have been impossible. With the occurrence, the event becomes inevitable. The cause-and-effect expectation functions at both conscious and unconscious levels within individuals.

Should people have difficulty in isolating a cause, they will, as a general practice, invent one with words, usually by a verbal generalization. *Rain today (effect), the weather again (cause)*. "Weather," an enormously complex abstraction, is largely *unknown*, perhaps even *unknowable*. Contrary to popular fictions, weather is a random, unpredictable phenomenon. An expectation that coincidence is unlikely to be accidental is likewise an aspect of this innate, hereditary perceptual pattern. *Can you believe that lawyer was just accidentally in the hospital when the ambulance arrived?* What has been called the "when-then connection" is a basic ingredient in what is considered common sense.

Attempts to explain or account for coincidence appear common to all peoples, though there are variations in the way they attempt to handle the question. The Chinese, for example, evolved a different approach from the straight-line, simplistic cause-and-effect reasoning of the West, often attributed to Aristotle. Chinese logicians noticed certain types of events appear to cluster at certain times. Chinese theories of medicine, philosophy, and even architecture were based on a science of meaningful coincidence. Chinese theories did not question what causes what. They inquired instead into what "likes to occur" with what. Both Asiatic and Western systems, however, sought verbal solutions to the question of coincidence. Both systems produced verbalized fictions that attempted to explain events in reference to known, unknown, and unknowable causation.

Common sense is based on the simple proposition that the effect of a cause must follow that cause. *Effect* cannot precede *cause*. The proposition can be stated, *After this, therefore because of this!* Unfortunately, experience often contradicts what is assumed common sense. Vicious circles of human conflict, in which the sequence of events is nonlinear, are the most frequent example. The effect, in a nonlinear conflict, feeds back and reinitiates its own cause. Marital conflicts often focus and turn upon themselves in a vicious circle. The starting point is forgotten and, even if remembered, no longer matters. The seventy-year conflict between Soviet communism and Western entrepreneurial economics is another circular, self-perpetuating conflict, as are the Catholic-Protestant struggle in Northern Ireland, the Lebanese Christian-Moslem warfare, and the Arab-Israeli conflict. Once established, circular, self-sustaining sequences continue indefinitely, evolving outside and beyond beginning and end, cause and effect. Throughout human history, common sense has often—if not usually—shown itself uncommonly senseless, often murderously so. Commonsense defensive strategies rationalize, disguise, and attempt to dismiss contradictions. Humans persist in reasoning only at a level of the seemingly obvious. Repression, forgetting that we have forgotten, takes care of the other loose ends—paradoxes, contradictions, and exceptions.

The anatomy of cause and effect is rarely examined carefully. If we do, or do not do, *this*, then *that* is certain to occur. If we do not invest $100 million fighting communism in Nicaragua, the U.S. will soon be invaded by Soviet forces. Silly propositions such as this are acted on each day by millions of people and, most embarrassingly, by high government officials. Such simplisms are nonsense, rhetorical propaganda, and usually recognized as such by those who promote them. Considering human gullibility, especially as it has been conditioned and channeled by the ad media, such cause-and-effect reasoning provides effective strategies of persuasion and manipulation. It exploits human weakness, fear of the unknown, paranoia, insecurities, doubts, and all of the other emotional instabilities. Fear of the unknown or unknowable usually drives humans into the greedy hands of seers who pretend to know the future. Prophecies and inside knowledge strangely serve only the self-interests of prophets.

For every effect, were the real world as logical as words appear, there must indeed be a cause. There could even be multiple causes. Further, there are quite likely unknowable causes or causes that cannot be verbally defined. The worst possible scenario involves situations with a combination of multiple unknown and unknowable causes—the most common situation humans encounter. Also, perceptions of causation can be unconsciously motivated. Simplistic cause-and-effect rationalization could constitute mankind's most dangerous myth. When *causality* is linked with *objective reality* fantasies to create a finality—an ultimate conclusion not to be undone or altered—the connection could be lethal.

That such innate, taken-for-granted mental structures exist—through which disastrous conclusions, evaluations, and analysis are regularly formulated—is generally unknown or, worst of all, repressed. The instinctual human need to draw simplistic cause-and-effect conclusions remains hidden because individuals do not want consciously to know their vulnerability to errors and misinterpretations. In the immortal words of the *Titanic's* brave captain, "Even God could not sink this ship!"

The Flimflam of Because

Scottish philosopher David Hume believed the verbal concept *because* was totally unverifiable and unexplainable as a part of language and thought. One cannot, according to Hume's reasoning, assume an airplane crashed *because* the engines failed, even though such incidents are reported in this way every day in media throughout the world. Such reports only confirm that journalists and readers need to perceive the world in simplistic cause-and-effect relationships. Such reports say far more about the reporters and their audiences than they do about the events described. All that could be stated reliably about the airplane crash, on the basis of perceivable known, unknown, and unknowable fact, is that when the engines failed, the airplane crashed. The actual *cause* or *causes*—known, unknown, and unknowable—are unavailable and could remain so. Hume argued that the verbal concept *because* was, in itself, erroneous, illogical, foolish, mythological, and often highly dangerous. For example, cause-and-effect medicine is simplistic nonsense. Organisms respond as whole, integrated entities—from causes known, unknown, and unknowable.

Simplistic *cause*-and-*effect* assumptions are questionable, even though acted on with apparent success in a practical, commonsense framework. Anyone who keeps track of his or her unsuccessful decisions based on *cause*-and-*effect* conscious assumptions will discover an ego-shattering high score. Humans do not keep such scores, of course. They consciously note a preponderance of wins, repressing or denying the losses. *Cause* and *effect* are also verbally formed after the fact, as a rationalization, rather than before. For example, the popular assumption that the moon's orbit *causes* the rise and fall of tides is false. The complex, only partially understood relationship between the earth and moon suggests that earth's tides actually slow down the moon's orbit. Another false, though profitable, assumption in the U.S. is that industries succeed *because* of consumer preferences. However—as this book points out—consumers are manipulated by the industries in a complex, culturally integrated media system that supplies consumers with the fantasy that they are in control. In experimental psychology, rats are believed to behave in a certain way *because* of experimenters' clever controls, but it is rarely discussed that the limitations of rat behavior mainly determine experimental procedure. The inherent limitations of human assumptions, behaviors, and observations are also virtually never considered a part of scientific method as scores of simplistic, verbal, *cause*-and-*effect* assumptions annually pour forth in the name of science, progress, and profit.

The *because* dilemma appears to be a product of the evolutionary learning of many species as they evolved. Conditioned reflexes are one plausible explanation, but always be careful with cause-and-effect explanations of cause and effect. Whenever events or coincidences repeat frequently enough, an individual expects they will continue. The coincidence can actually be relatively infrequent for a predictive link to become established.

Nobel prize-winning physiologist Ivan Pavlov taught dogs to salivate in the expectation of food when a buzzer was sounded. For the animals, the buzzer became a symbolic representation of food. Humans can similarly be trained to salivate to bells, buzzers, and bugles. They can also be conditioned to salivate to pictures and music in radio and television commercials. Humans will even salivate in a delayed-time response, days or weeks after viewing a TV commercial, when they perceive the brand label in a supermarket (Poetzle effect). Such training easily develops ritual behaviors around the stimulus. Pavlov's dogs behaved much like wolves. Once food was given to the dominant animal, subordinate dogs begged for a share. They displayed ritual whining, tail-wagging, sycophantic slinking, head-lowering, and throat exposure to the dominant animal. The ritualized animal behavior also occurred eventually when only the buzzer sounded. The animals had learned simple cause-effect relationships connecting buzzer, ritual behaviors, and food.

Harvard psychologist B. F. Skinner kept pigeons in a closed environment where food was released at random intervals. The pigeons connected their own movements with food deliveries. The purely random coincidence of food delivery eventually initiated a learning process. When a particular movement was perceived as part of a feeding interval, Skinner's pigeons confirmed their expectations that pellets arrived because of something they had accomplished. Even pigeons had to believe food was a product of acts they had initiated. They could not accept the reality that their food was controlled by outside forces over which they had no influence or control. Events such as a certain wing, body, or claw movement coincidental with the arrival of a food pellet slowly evolved a learned behavior, a cause-effect relationship. The expectation of a connection between their particular movement and food increased and intensified, regardless of what else occurred in the environment.

Skinner described the behavior that appeared to produce food as "a group of crazy pigeons—one circled constantly to the left, another kept spreading its right wing, another moved its head from side to side." These repeated behaviors, of course, eventually appeared to produce food pellets—which would have occurred with or without the behavior. The behavior merely provided the pigeons with the fantasy that they were in control. Cause and effect, for the pigeons, became a self-fulfilling prophecy. Once ritualized behavior becomes established, it is very difficult to change it in either animals or humans.

Anyone who doubts the power of ritualized cause-and-effect expectations can observe them among family or friends. The patterns are discernible around eating, drinking, or reproductive behaviors. We are taught to see consumption of various products—smoking, drinking, eating, costuming, and even TV watching—as *causes* with fantasized *effects*.

After World War II, New Guinea mountain tribes evolved a religious cult that worshiped airplanes. The warplanes that had once brought tribal prosperity had disappeared. Tribal groups constructed shrines from pieces of old airplanes and discarded scrap.

The junk was fabricated to look roughly like airplanes. Eventually occasional planes did fly over, more frequently at some times than at others. The shrines became increasingly elaborate, and cult membership increased as the power and validity of the cult were confirmed. A new religion was born.

Frequent, taken-for-granted ritual behaviors are easily observable—the recitation of Hail Marys, rosary-bead counts, nightly prayers, knocking on wood, reading the daily horoscope, fasting on certain special days, placing the fork on the left side of the plate, word or number magic, carrying a good-luck charm, rarely missing a certain television show, carefully reading the ads, the news, the weather reports, et cetera. Whether in Pavlov's buzzer, in a New Guinea airplane shrine, or attending expensively created ad fantasies, the cause-and-effect symbolism promises sexual gratification, security, good fortune, social acceptability, love, happiness, eternal life. Ads will promise you anything. Chants, incantations, curses, and blessings are as much in daily use today as they were in primitive societies. "Winston tastes good like a cigarette should!"

Verbal Magic

Ernest Cassirer wrote in *Language and Myth* that identification between labels or names and persons or things is the fundamental mechanism of mythmaking. Ali Baba opened the magic door in the mountain with "Open Sesame!" Rumpelstiltskin was defeated in his work for the devil when the princess learned to pronounce his name. As exhaustively documented by J. G. Frazer in his work *The Golden Bough*, primitive peoples surround themselves with endless word taboos. Like their modern counterparts, they manufacture verbal amulets or prayers to protect themselves from evil spirits, such as, "Ban takes the worry out of being close!" American Indians, whose terror of the dead was intense, never spoke the names of the dead—many of which derived from animals or natural objects. So they constantly had to invent new words for common objects, and their vocabularies became endlessly confused with different names for the same things, along with over 100 tribal dialects and languages. J. P. Harrington of the Smithsonian Institute wrote, "The more wars, the more dead, the more new names, the more dialects, the more foreigners, the more wars, the more dead . . ."

Consciously and unconsciously, humans are still victimized by word magic, ritual behaviors, and immersion in an ocean of fantasized cause-and-effect delusions. Modern, educated individuals think themselves liberated from the darkness of superstition and ignorance. Yet they mindlessly accept words or phrases intentionally designed to camouflage reality. U.S. ad media carefully avoid factual, measurable descriptions of product qualities; they emphasize flattering descriptions of the consumer. A list of magic words and phrases can easily be garnered from any commercial publication. Word magic sells products, people, political ideology, religious faith, and everything else sold in the U.S.

Squeezably Soft Charmin

Be a Pepper

Almost Home cookies

Brawny paper towels

Purina Tender Vittles

Chiquita Pops

Just My Size pantyhose

Fantastik cleaner

The Spirit of Marlboro

The Taste of Merit

An American Revolution—Dodge

I Need to Be Accepted—In Touch cards

Dashingly Suave Cuervo tequila

Nocturnes de Caron perfume

The Friendly Skies of United

Publicity and ad hype provide a pervasive philosophical system that dominates thought and feelings for millions. Consumption, as an end in itself, becomes a substitute for democratic idealism.

The freedom to choose what one wears, drives, or eats replaces meaningful social, economic, or political alternatives. Commercial hypes conceal much of what is corrupt, authoritarian, unjust, and cruelly exploitive. Such hype also muffles and distorts clear perceptions of the rest of the world.

Freedom Is a Datsun!

China/Orient, Personal Pleasures, National Treasures, Pampering, Adventuring, with Royal Viking Line

When You Take on the World, You're Not Alone with American Express

Take Time Out from the Real World to Explore the Reel World Through Moviebreak

Camel Filters, It's a Whole New World!

The Spirit of the Empire, Bass Ale!

Freedom Is a Maxi-Pad!

Revolutionary, The Perfect Pantyhose!

Consciously and unconsciously, contemporary men and women are circumspect about words for fear of supernatural reprisals, every bit as much as their prehistoric or medieval forebears. They act as if words themselves had power to control human affairs. In a tragic sense, words do have power to initiate self-fulfilling prophecies. During numerous U.S. administrations, meetings with Soviet diplomats endlessly disputed definitions of nuclear-weapon disarmament, in a childlike faith that correct verbal formulations would magically bring eternal peace and security. As every diplomat knows, words are largely irrelevant unless there is a will among participants to make agreements work.

Over many centuries, lucky numbers three and seven held superstitious fascination for humans. Seven is mentioned many times in the bible; three symbolizes the Trinity. The devil is associated with 666. God allegedly made the world in six days and rested on the seventh. For many centuries, there were only seven known planets. The seventh son is still believed to possess special talents.

Thirteen is considered so unlucky that many hotels do not number thirteenth floors. Virtually all numbers have, at one period or another, held magical significance. Odd numbers were considered masculine, even numbers feminine. Lucky numbers are used for gambling, licen₋e plates, telephone numbers, or lottery tickets. Consumers often pay extra for lucky numbers.

A brief visit to Nevada or Atlantic City casinos confirms widespread belief in magic numbers. Casino dealers and owners know, of course, that anyone who believes such nonsense is a loser. A frequently heard comment among casino employees is "Luck is for losers!" Publicly, of course, they are paid to tell a different story. Gamblers are always given change with the prayerful admonition, "Good luck!" Were they to have good luck, the casino would lose money.

Throughout evolution, humans—not unlike Professor Skinner's pigeons—insisted nothing happens by itself. Threats loom everywhere, hiding in the dark, invisible to the victims. The need to appease gods, control destiny, explain the unexplainable or unknowable, provided a foundation for cultures, languages, religions, laws, and thousands of superstitions. This constant human need for explanations of *cause* and *effect* made fortunes for ad media. As P. T. Barnum's famous comment held, "There is one born every minute!" Modern ad media took over where Barnum left off, vastly expanding the gullible population.

The uncertainties of science, philosophy, and day-to-day perceived realities can be replaced by unquestioning faith in predestiny, a greater power, prophecy, or even by a heavenly endorsed political ideology. Many national leaders work diligently to have God on their side. The process is also a convenient means of scapegoating, blaming misfortunes upon fate, bad luck, or God's punishment—expedients to escape individual responsibility for failure.

Popular media exploitation of chauvinistic nationalism for power and profit—a major U.S. industry—is fueled by magic words and symbols. Flag ceremonies, national anthems, and endless simplistic cause-and-effect rhetoric camouflage selfishness, exploitation of the helpless, avarice, and vicious behavior that violates all human standards of decent conduct. Patriotism, not unlike religious fanaticism, frequently obscures, diffuses, and represses reality-oriented perceptions of what is going on. Inhuman atrocities have been excused by the platitude, "Someone had to do it!" Human vulnerability to media manipulation persists, proliferates, and grows potentially more devastating each year.

Predicting the Unpredictable

Another aspect of cause-and-effect mythology is *predictability*. Prophecy has been replaced in modern fantasies with predictability—which sounds more scientific. The need to predict has been discussed as a genetically inherited drive system. Nothing in the world is predictable! *Nothing!* Anyone who could accurately predict only one simple thing could eventually obtain or achieve whatever riches or power they desired. Predictability is a myth, a myth constructed out of verbal, mathematical, or statistical identifications, excluded middle options, and ignored contradictions. Myth, of course, universally disregards *macro*, *micro*, and *submicro* levels of perception and the conscious-unconscious perceptual dynamic.

Statistical probability has nothing to do with prediction. Statistics only attempt to describe probable outcomes. They do not—in any way—predict. A major research industry survives on profitable misinterpretations of probability. Every professional gambler has bet on odds 99–1 in their favor—and lost. For a long time, crystal balls, tea leaves, astrological tables, and Ouija boards served the need for prediction. They were cheap and readily available. Predictions almost always reduce tension brought on by uncertainty. Unfortunately, these devices were eventually perceived as unscientific. Tea leaves and the like were replaced by computers, probability statistics, Ph.D. seers, and think tanks. Modern predictions are usually hedged through carefully worded evasions or double meanings. The prediction industry succeeded. Those who took the predictions seriously usually did not. Both the Oval Office and the Kremlin are crowded with predictors who are called economists, security and political advisers, military scientists, population analysts, et cetera.

The use of Aristotelian syllogistic logic is ingeniously applied.

If *this* happens, and *this* happens, and *this* happens, then *this* will happen. Such statements can be elaborated into complex, seemingly logical scenarios. Unfortunately, they are invariably wishful thinking. Predictions are usually impossible to pin down to factual specifics. One point is important. Predictions can contribute to desired outcomes as self-fulfilling prophecies if people can be manipulated to accept them as *truth*. As numerous authors have pointed out, the ultimate function of prediction or prophecy is not to tell the future but to make it.

Such areas as economics, sociology, psychology, anthropology, history, and political, military, and computer science have a laughable history of failed, quickly forgotten predictions. Even the weather service does not reliably predict weather conditions. It forecasts only under certain favorable, highly qualified, probable conditions. Weather is an unpredictable random occurrence. Like newspaper horoscopes, media weather reports are well sponsored and profitable, adding credibility to those who publish and broadcast them. All have the same basic U.S. Weather Service information, but are interpreted in relation to audience variables. Such interpretations have more to do with telling audiences what they wish to hear, in the interest of advertisers, than with the actual weather.

Any attempt to predict the future courts disaster. Knowledgeable people hedge predictions carefully. Should predictions turn out to be *true*, or in a way that can be interpreted as *true*, they validate the predictor. If the prediction was *false*, it is forgotten, ignored, or rationalized verbally. As predictive systems are human perceptual constructions, the system is usually protected when results do not work out.

Once individuals understand and accept the subjectivity of human perception, they acquire enormous power over their lives. They can protect themselves from manipulation or—as many appear to do—go into the business of managing the perceptions of others. Famed publisher Henry Luce ordered his editorial staffs to "disregard the nonsense of objectivity." He told them they were "paid to draw conclusions and conclusions they had damned well better draw." The statement caused a small stir in publishing circles at the time, but was probably courageous. Most of Luce's competition still hustled naïve readers with the mythology of objective truth. Many still perpetuate the myth. Anyone willing to accept the simplism of "unbiased truth" is prepared to believe "McDonald's does it all for you!"

The Managers of Cause and Effect

Environmental catastrophes cast thousands of species into the scrap barrel of extinction. No known species, however, has engineered itself into the ultimate disaster. Species extinction, as far as can be determined, was always the result of external forces—climate, disease, or environmental disasters. Humans may be the exception. Through constructed perceptions of language and culture, superficially considered instruments of education and progress, humans may already have condemned themselves to extinction. They display extreme vulnerability to persuasion, flattery, cause-and-effect fantasizations, and self-fulfilling prophecies. The manipulation of these elements can result in profit and power, though they constitute civilization's Achilles' heel.

Day after day, year after year, decade after decade, the U.S. population is indoctrinated with assumptions and expectations that for every *effect* there must be a *cause*. Each individual ad conveys an inherent, simplistic cause-and-effect assumption. Ads educate about logic and thought processes, as well as values. Causation is also a major preoccupation of news and information sources, books, TV soap operas and sitcoms, rock music lyrics, political oratory, and even university education. It is virtually impossible to find cause and effect qualified as known, unknown, unknowable, or in combinations of the three.

Reality-oriented writing might succeed in an off-Broadway play or in a novel published for an elite readership but could never make it in the fantasy-oriented mainstream. A carefully qualified presentation would destroy commercial broadcast or published media. Audiences have been trained to want simple, direct messages with as few reality distractions as possible. When this cultural orientation translates into the selection of political leadership, the delineation of foreign policy, military expenditures, national security issues, public health and social policies, education, and economic planning and strategies, the society functions at the intellectual level of a John Wayne, Clint Eastwood, or Sylvester Stallone movie. Simple, often violent answers to enormously complex questions are readily available, with multiple-choice answers limited to a handful of simplistic verbal alternatives.

One-dimensional, simplistic, cause-and-effect thinking is one of the most dangerous forces on earth. Through available media technology, ideologues can manipulate any decision or policy to appear as the collective will of the people. Nobel laureate, philosopher, and mathematician Bertrand Russell concluded, "The reason physics ceased to look for causes is that, in fact, there are no such things." The only real certainty within the grasp of human perception is uncertainty.

Uncertainty could become the source of endless human joy, innovation, creativity, excitement, multiple perspectives, and the challenge of intellectual adventure. The only real certainty in human life is death. As long as uncertainty is feared, however, humans will remain submissive pawns in the struggle for profit and power.

The Disregarded Unknowable

In one attempt to study simplistic cause-and-effect reasoning, test subjects were given several simple, interpersonal quandaries. Less than 10% were able to qualify causation as unknown or unknowable. Their self-assurance was awesome as they defined and delineated the cause of every stated effect. Certainty over causation often appeared arrogant. The few who appeared concerned about unknown elements of causation were science- or mathematics-oriented.

Strangely, however, only 1% of the subjects dealt with the notion of the unknowable. North American culture seems to ignore the perceptual reality that much, if not most, of both a *cause* and an *effect* will remain unknowable, at least verbally unknowable. Little of what appears evident about biological, physical, and psychological realities is known and understood or even can be. The perceptual process through which knowing is possible is itself poorly understood. Most of this great unknown is quite possibly unnowable, at least in the terms of knowing that prevail at the moment.

When humans think they think they *know* why events, situations, or actions occur around them, they could be in great peril. The simplistic structure of *cause* and *effect* is everywhere in the illustrations in this book. The basic premise of an ad is universal—buy products, brands, ideas, and people. What you perceive about the benefits (effect) of that purchase usually has nothing to do with the actual brand or product (cause). The principal effect of an ad is actually the promise of fulfillment. It includes endless sensual delights and indulgences of the flesh, fantasy escapes, and self-adulation—"Mirror, mirror on the wall, who is the fairest of them all?"

One frequent consequence of cause-and-effect fantasy is that nothing at all actually happens, the promise remains unfulfilled—the cause is ineffective. No perceivable effect results from cause. Like unfulfilled predictions, a missing effect can be camouflaged by further searching out causes until one is discovered that fits the desired effect.

As a large portion of ads pander to the baser motives, the actual consequences of the effect are frequently the opposite of the promised effect—the loser syndrome. Dr. William Masters, who pioneered research in human sexuality, once commented, "When a person's primary motive in life is to get *screwed,* they usually end up *screwed* in the fullest sense of the word." The promise of getting screwed is the basic motivating premise in ads.

The Tanqueray gin ad (fig. 5) promises subliminally to improve your erection. Unhappily, alcohol is a chemical depressant that accomplishes the opposite—chemically induced castration. The Betty Crocker Super Moist cake mix ad (fig. 6) promises to super-moisten the housewife's vagina. Sadly, however, anyone who consumes enough of the high-fat and -sodium content pastry may gain so much weight real sexual experiences will become few and far between. The Chivas Regal ad (fig. 7) promises to get a man's penis gently stroked, but either by himself or by another man. The promise of Soloflex ads (figs. 10–12) also appears to be adulation of men by other men. Buy *Time*, the cover promises (cause), and save yourself from a sexualized Gaddafi (fig. 9), who murderously wants to KILL (effect). The *Time* issue contained numerous supportive stories on the U.S. military buildup, military enforcement of foreign-policy objectives, and the noble crusade against terrorism—all supported by taxpayer money flowing massively into the coffers of large corporations who advertise.

8 | THE EXPECTATIONS OF STEREOTYPES

My *expectations* of your *expectations* of my *expectations* of your *expectations* should send both of us screaming in opposite directions.

Anonymous

Blessed is he who expects nothing, for he shall never be disappointed.

Alexander Pope, Letter to Gay

The remedy in the U.S. is not less liberty but real liberty—and an end to the brutal intolerance of churchly hooligans and flag-waving corporations, and all the rest of the small but bloody despots who have made the word Americanism a synonym for coercion and legal crime.

Archibald MacLeish, The Nation, Dec. 4, 1937

The primary expectation communicated by ad media is sex. Ads in the women's periodicals focus almost exclusively on sex, escape, food, and more sex. Men's magazines focus on sex, escape, power, dominance, and status—most of which, as in the women's media, ties back into sex. TV is the most pervasive educational force in the U.S. A 1987 study of the three networks by Louis Harris found 65,000 sexual references broadcast annually in ad and program content during prime afternoon and evening hours. Sexual references averaged twenty-seven per hour, including nine kisses, five hugs, ten sexual innuendos, and one or two references directly to sexual intercourse and deviant sexual practices. Clearly, sex sells the ads that sell the products in the commercials.

By contrast, Harris had to use fractions to count hourly references to birth control (less than one-fiftieth per hour), sexually transmitted diseases (one-tenth per hour), and sex education (one-seventeenth per hour). The study found no ads or announcements for contraceptive products or services, except for the very few AIDS announcements. Portrayals of sex were overly romanticized and unrealistic. Few messages appeared about responsibility, sexual behavior consequences, and pregnancy prevention. Nearly eight in ten adults surveyed thought TV should present birth-control material. A typical TV viewer saw nearly 14,000 instances of sexual material annually, but only 165 counterbalanced references to education in sexuality, sexual diseases, birth control, and abortion—a ratio of one in eighty-five. Sex sells purchasing, as well as social, behaviors. Harris studied only the obvious conscious sexual content. Had he investigated the subliminal dimensions, the numbers would have been even more overwhelming. The commercial media clearly control value systems and human expectations in the nation's reproductive behaviors.

Print media offer an opportunity to study the more subtle technology of sexual manipulation. Lights and shadows, line curvatures, skin and hair textures, eye positions, subtle, minute features are meticulously detailed. Human perception is extremely sensitive to the most minute detail in pictures—far more sensitive than anyone has suspected. A single print ad can cost $50,000 for art production and require months to manufacture, and TV ads cost $50,000 to $250,000—all ultimately paid for by consumers. Photographs are rarely published without extensive retouching, even news photos. The final reproduction of a reproduction of a reproduction has nothing remotely to do with the original photograph. Countless details affect the *expectations* with which consumers unconsciously identify. Most of the *expectational* aspect of perception is subliminal.

The Kent ad (fig. 23) appeared on the back cover of *Time* magazine and numerous other national publications. *Time* charges roughly $175,000 for a back cover of their national edition. The model play-acts a successful businessman at his private tennis club. In the left background appears an executive's briefcase and tennis racket, at right gym lockers. A well-pressed suit and tie wait behind the model. He has dried with a rich, textured towel after tennis and shower, and a freshly lit cigarette hangs from his mouth. His nude lower body is out of the picture but is projectively *filled in* by the viewer. Filling in is both a conscious and unconscious perceptual process, long studied by Gestalt psychologists, and viewers are always a part of the perceptual construction in ads. The model's posture is one of display. His eyes look right, seemingly off into space, thoughtful; they have been retouched, the pupils enlarged as they are during emotional or sexual arousal. The artist had also added a touch of dissonance, the priming device for subliminal information. The model's left eye focuses upon a different point in space than does the right. The cigarette does not hang down passively, nor point upward in an erect position. The angle suggests the early stages of arousal, now that work and exercise are done. The model is suntanned, athletic, hair still wet from the shower, his face lightly lined with maturity, an outdoor person. Curly hair identifies with pubic hair. The model's expectations have been subtly engineered into the picture. After he has smoked a Kent, relaxed, and dressed, his immediate expectation is of a sexual encounter. The word *SEX* appears repeatedly embedded in his hair, on his body, in the towel texture. Retouch airbrushing is apparent in facial details—especially the eyebrows, lines under the eyes, and in the line of the right jaw.

The above are subtle details, extremely important to the ad artist, cigarette company, and to the ad's sales potential. Consumers read the ad at a glance or, at most, in several seconds. These details—so expensively incorporated—never consciously register. Male readers can unconsciously react in either of two directions, or perhaps both at the same time. They may identify with the model's apparent expectations: "I am like him, we are the same. I like sex after exercise. Kent is a way to relax. Get it together, anticipating sex." Or they may feel latent, unconscious homosexual attraction toward the model. His neck, breasts, and genitals are displayed to the male reader. As body-building magazine publishers know, and have long studied, men are strongly attracted to the bodies of other men. This attraction can be conscious or unconscious. A similar strategy was utilized in the Soloflex ads (figs. 10–12). The powerful appeal aims at latent or repressed homosexual tendencies shared by most—if not all—men.

The ad was only a momentary experience for most of the over 25 million *Time* readers. The manipulative strategy, however, powerfully affected many individuals—even nonsmokers. To justify the million-dollar investment, enough Kents had to be sold by the ad to produce corporate profit. Had there been the slightest doubt about the ad's sales potential, it could never have been published.

Fantasy expectations are similarly used in ads aimed at women. Like men, women are relentlessly manipulated into product use, brand preferences, and ad identities through appeals to reproductive behavior expectations. These frequently take curious twists. Little is ever what it appears to be. The constant manipulation can evoke great confusion, dissatisfaction, and even conscious physical discomfort.

The Alberto mousse ad shown in figure 24 appeared in *Cosmopolitan* and other women's publications. The expectations communicated by the three models are libidinous. The ménage à trois includes a woman with masculine hair and square, masculine ear decorations. She appears enamored of the male model, lovingly caressing his neck with her right hand; her left hand is hidden from view, but its position is perceptually filled in at the unconscious level. The male model looks invitingly toward the reader as he gently caresses the foreground model's feminine hair. The foreground model stares directly, almost defiantly, at the reader. Her carefully crafted expression is invitational and challenging. "Join us!" her expression reads. "If you dare!" The models are formally costumed for an expensive night on the town. The ménage à trois, or *à quatre* if you include the reader, appears a logical expectation for anyone who purchases a phallic bottle of Alberto

Mousse European styling foam. La mousse, in French, means froth, lather, foam—seminal imagery.

That expensively produced ad was carefully retouched. Facial expressions were constructed, hair lines retouched, the man's right hand painted. If the hand is blocked off, the thumb appears an erect penis, pointing upward, not at either of the two female models, but narcissistically at the male model. The masculine woman's box earring was also painted into the picture. Her *box* hangs from her ear, available to all. The question of *who* does *what* to *whom* in the ménage could keep a *Cosmo* reader fantasizing all night if the details were consciously perceived. They are not. The hours of expensive art production and planning were intended for instantaneous, unconscious perception. Without unconscious perception, ads are a waste of time, resources, and money. The carefully designed expectations of the three models sold thousands of gallons of mousse without anyone catching on to the game. What all this flimflam inflicts upon the personality, emotional health, and real-life expectations of the female reader is awesome.

Ad expectations always remain unfulfilled, except in fantasies. Many ads play specifically to masturbatory fantasies, continually placing new, more bizarre expectations before naïve consumers. Reproductive behavior for many consumers remains at immature fantasy levels throughout their lives. Sexual fantasization operates the ad-media vending machines. Sexual realities, on the other hand, escalate toward a dessert of unfulfilled and unfulfillable expectations.

The Potency of Expectation

The above are typical of the half million ads perceived annually by everyone in the country. It is foolish to assume this constant, deep immersion in fantasy sexualization has no effect on *who* people think they are, *where* they perceive themselves going, and *what* they have become as a nation or culture. Ads condition humans to view others as stereotypes, rather than as individuals. The dehumanized regimentation of expectations for self and others makes real-life relationships into our society's most perishable commodity.

Reality can never compete with fantasy in a world where fantasies control basic value systems.

There exist no purposeless communications between humans. Everything that perceptually transpires—most at the unconscious level—affects human relationships. We interact sensitively and continuously both at conscious and unconscious levels. In the media-dominated culture, interpersonal expectations are modeled on stereotypes.

Interpersonal communication involves an enormous range of tactics and strategies, role assumptions, attempts to maneuver others into complementary or subsidiary roles, and frequent variations in the ways individuals portray themselves. All human behavior, whether from conscious or unconscious motives, is basically *goal-seeking*. Self-interest is involved in even the most altruistic behavior. The question of motives is essential to make sense out of human communication. Ad motives are simple and singular—to sell, to sell, to sell, ad infinitum, at both conscious and unconscious levels. What commercial manipulators try to do can be measured against this single motive. Success or failure is empirically, rigorously, and scientifically measured against effort, expenditures, and sales.

In literature and fine art—on the other hand—motivation is never simplistic. The artist's motives are extremely complex. In one sense, the great artists and writers similarly wanted to sell—their work, abilities, and reputations. But other strong motivational forces appear. Da Vinci, according to Sigmund Freud, reflected his homosexuality in his creative work. Pablo Picasso was a lifelong communist (though a multimillionaire), and through his work runs a strong social commentary on human greed, conformity, and the regimentation of capitalist society. Picasso also had monumental difficulties with women; this is reflected in much of his creative production. The motives behind a Picasso painting are diffuse, complex, often contradictory, and mirror the artist's unique perception of the world and its peoples. Most of what is considered significant art and literature is complex. Perhaps this is why art survives over centuries as meaningful human experience.

Though the technology of ads and public relations is awesome, the strategies brilliant, complex, devious, exhaustively researched, and expensively executed, the motive remains simplistic. The motive is always manipulation in the interest of power and profit, not enlightenment or deeper insight into the human condition.

Expectations in human communication are largely unconscious reciprocal influences. We are all influenced by expectations at levels of perception over which we have little control or awareness. Whenever someone is categorized, labeled, or role-defined—stereotyped—specific behaviors, characteristics, and actions are expected. Various groups are expected to behave in certain more-or-less specific ways within any given cultural system. If they fail to comply, a variety of reactions can be anticipated—surprise, anger, disappointment, fear, even disgust. Should expectations be inconsistently fulfilled, the reaction is unpredictable but will probably be aggressively negative.

Instead of worrying vainly about being liked, loved, or respected, individuals should concern themselves with what others *expect* of them. Expectations rule the future of relationships. Once expectations are consciously known, deliberated, and utilized, individuals achieve more control over situations.

There are usually sanctions applied to perceived violators of conscious and unconscious expectations. Deviants or rule-breakers are punished, sometimes severely (penalties are more restrained if violators have a recognized high status). Most people in any culture seek predictable relationships, where expectations are reliably fulfilled. Deviants are avoided.

In both athletic and intellectual competition, the manipulation of the opponent's expectations is vital to success. In popular sports, skilled players pit brute strength, perseverance, and one-dimensional reasoning against each other until one becomes exhausted, overpowered, and vanquished. Mindless, battering brutality is portrayed endlessly in U.S. athletic arenas.

It is curious that U.S. culture, almost uniquely, features athletic confrontations that test strength, brutality, and blind commitment, cultural throwbacks to early frontier experiences. Even more curiously, our international relationships traditionally rely upon threats, force, a big stick, rather than upon the more sophisticated skills of arbitration, persuasion, compromise, and the deft application of expectation strategies. The U.S. appears to much of the world to be anti-intellectual.

On the other hand, expectation strategies become highly sophisticated among master craftsmen. Attempts to transcribe what is going on in an expectational confrontation become pedantically complex. Such competitive tactics are nonverbal and nonconscious, for the most part. When the strategies function effectively between two skilled opponents, the contest becomes a work of art. The thrusts and parries, attacks and defenses, moves and countermoves operate intuitively and quickly. Players appear to psych out each other's expectations at a subtle, unobservable, unconscious level. Each attempts to draw the other into traps of anticipated actions—a feigned or actual expectation is countered by a feigned or actual expectation. Each player attempts to confuse the other as to whether the next action will be feigned or actual. Intellectually skilled opponents can turn a physical contest into an intense intellectual, aesthetic experience.

A Fifth Dan black-belt karateka described martial arts competition as the sensitive unconscious perceptions of one opponent matched against the unconscious perceptions of another. At this level, the game is far too complex, rapid, and subtle to be consciously deliberated. Humans continuously exchange information of which they are consciously unaware, and that information powerfully affects behavior. Every data exchange narrows the number of possible next moves. Motives and strategies to achieve objectives reduce quickly from the general to the specific. The underlying rules of the game are never explicitly stated, but they could not be more binding and significant if expressed in an exhaustively worded contract.

Expectational Stress

Expectations influence our susceptibility to illness and disease. Virtually all illness is affected by a patient's perception of his life situation. Susceptibility increases greatly as one descends socioeconomic levels—especially for those with limited access to medicine. Illness frequently relates to congested living conditions, poor sanitation and nutrition, more stressful employment, lower expectations of success, and increased utilization of commercial mass media. Illness is not randomly distributed throughout the population. Those most susceptible appear to view their lives as difficult, demanding, and unsatisfactory. Recent changes—death in the family, divorce, employment termination, retirement, et cetera—also sharply increase susceptibility to illness. The sense of having options, and being free to choose among them, significantly reduces stress.

No disease, of course, is caused exclusively by problems of social adjustment. An individual's expectations—adaptation or adjustment—are a major factor, however, in the development of many illnesses, including heart disease, kidney problems, high blood pressure, eclampsia, rheumatic and rheumatoid arthritis, inflammatory diseases of skin and eyes, infections, allergic and hypersensitivity diseases, cancer, and metabolic malfunctions.

Stress, of course, is a product of expectations—what we think of ourselves and what we perceive others think of us. These expectations usually determine whether we endure stress or walk away from it. Numerous stress studies have found biochemical changes—such as endocrine responses—related to stressful demands. In response to stress, the body usually passes through three stages:

1. Initial alarm reactions—antibody levels fall below normal.
2. Body resources mobilize to resist.
3. If stress is not reduced, eventual exhaustion occurs and antibody levels drop below normal.

Perceptions of stress vary widely from one individual to another. Stress itself cannot hurt you. Damage results from your perception of being in a stressful situation; the expectation of being unable to cope increases disease susceptibility. Subliminal influences can initiate or manipulate perceptions of both expectations and stress.

The effect of expectations upon health is demonstrated in experiments with placebos. The placebo is an inert, nonmedicinal substance believed by the patient to be actual medicine. *Placebo* means "to please." Until roughly 100 years ago, nearly all medications and therapies were placebic. They worked, some of the time. Placebo effects involve patient expectations—faith, hope, and anticipation of relief. Many modern pharmaceuticals are merely placebos whose ad hype increases expectations of effectiveness.

In numerous studies, placebos worked 25% to 40% of the time for postoperative pain relief. Placebos, or expectations, alone produce measurable physiological changes. Actual medicinal drug effectiveness is also increased or decreased by patient expectations, and by a medical staff's degree of enthusiasm and optimism.

Expectations have also been related to the occurrence and timing of death. Most elderly people view retirement homes as the end of the line. Mortality, for both men and women, doubles after admission. Psychological withdrawal in Nazi concentration camps was known to have been fatal. Giving up involves a perception of impotence, inability to cope, a diminished will to live—often a self-imposed sentence of death.

Studies of voodoo deaths also demonstrate fatal psychogenic effects from the expectation of death by curse. Cursed subjects often saw their destiny as beyond their control—a loss of volition. Predicted deaths not infrequently came to pass. Negative expectations are also fundamental aspects of suicidal behaviors.

Expectations of success are extremely important. On unfamiliar tasks, self-perception of probable success usually derives from a comparison of self with others. Self-perceptions evoke self-fulfilling prophecies. High expectation of probable success enhances performance; low expectation—or worse, helplessness—produces motivational disaster. Low perceptions of success probably can ensure failure, destroying an individual's will to respond with enough effort and vigor for achievement.

In studies of sexual dysfunction, Masters and Johnson discovered that orgasmic success was frequently based upon self-expectations and perceptions of the expectations of sexual partners. The ability of mothers to breast-feed their infants is strongly influenced by the expectations of self and others. If mothers believe they will successfully nurse infants, they probably will. Should individuals believe others believe they will fail, the belief itself contributes to failure.

When people enter undefined situations or seek unfamiliar goals, they first maneuver to learn how others in the system relate to one another and their respective goals. Status hierarchies, the so-called pecking orders, are extremely important as newcomers assume their entry position. Meta-communication, composite signaling about the meaning of other acts of communication (*see* Bateson, "A Theory of Play") occurs both as a consciously and an unconsciously premeditated effort. Newcomers want to ensure inappropriate evaluations of goal-directed roles do not occur accidentally, through subtle language slips or from inept tactics. Name-, place-, and experience-dropping are used to legitimize both role and information credibility. In effect, they say indirectly, "Believe what I say because of who I am." Humans in virtually all known cultural systems perform similarly in relation to expectations of self and others.

The game appears universal throughout the world. Strategies are both verbal and nonverbal. Denying that such strategies exist is in itself a strategy. Expectations are communicated by subtle postures, vocal tonalities and inflections, minute changes in facial muscles, eye contact or avoidance, costume selection, and, in stressful situations, olfactory stimuli. What appears to transpire at conscious levels may be completely contradicted at unconscious levels, or both levels may reinforce each other.

Individuals carry in their heads stereotypical descriptions of groups that include Russians, Chinese, Japanese, Latins, Arabs, Jews, Christians, Moslems, Buddhists, Catholics, Republicans, Democrats, communists, socialists, anarchists, cowboys; the list is endless. The descriptions are fictional, false, factually meaningless nonsense in terms of the complex realities described by the labels. Much of formal education is directed at discrediting stereotypes. They nevertheless persist. Stereotypes are more intensely manufactured in some cultures than in others.

Cultures train and discipline members to expect that certain characteristics cluster in both individuals and groups. Expectations of others usually include broad categories used to describe the abilities, attitudes, interests, physical features, personality traits, and behaviors consciously perceived—or anticipated—in others. These are beliefs about which characteristics in expectations of personality fit together and which do not. For example, in a news story, an ad, or a soap opera, the moment a character is introduced a hierarchy of stereotypical expectations surface in the audience. One piece of data about an individual or group calls up additional characteristics from the audience's cultural storehouse of stereotypical expectations. Conscious and unconscious perceptions project expectations of behavior and the character-istics that produce such behavior.

The Sincerity Fantasy

A primary cultural expectation communicated by ad media is *sincerity*. Models, newscasters, heroes, and even villains collectively establish a national sincerity stereotype. Media-manufactured sin-cerity illustrates that words and images conceal, as well as inform. Sincerity is verbalized as the ultimate achievement in personality development. Leaders do not actually have to be sincere, but they must appear sincere. To appear consistently sincere requires in-sincerity of the highest magnitude. Untrained, undisciplined, av-erage individuals could not pull it off.

Sincere people, neckties, clothing, endless artifacts, and carefully engineered social situations reinforce our sincerity expectations. Stereotypical expectations of sincerity set up a perceptual ideal for interpersonal relationships. The population is constantly admon-ished, verbally and nonverbally, to be sincere. This is such a cultural preoccupation that it suggests deeply ingrained fear of insincerity. Anyone suspected of insincerity is avoided. If reality-oriented per-ception enters into the evaluation, however, excessively sincere persons would be approached with extreme caution.

Sincerity is generally viewed as an honest, friendly, straightfor-ward, disarming, and transparent posture or image. Perceptual sincerity helps us feel that everything is what it appears to be. Nothing is concealed or camouflaged. Consistency is a unique requirement of sincerity. Inconsistent people must be untrustwor-thy, even if they otherwise seem sincere. Yet one of the few valid generalizations one can make about humans is about their incon-sistency. We constantly change in response to conditioning, events, new information, values, physiological processes, et cetera. Beware of anyone who tries to project consistency as an aspect of sincerity!

Sincerity cannot become a significant social value without an impetus provided by insincerity. The truth inherently conceals the lie. Inverse values may be perceived only unconsciously but are always there—hiding, awaiting an opportunity to surface. For salespeople to misrepresent convincingly, for radio and TV announcers to lie and con, for political leaders to manipulate, they must first learn how audiences perceive sincerity. Numerous college courses teach how to speak and write with *apparent* sincerity, an endeavor performed with calculated insincerity. You can be very sincere about insincerity, especially when money or power is involved.

The stereotypical perception of sincerity is an easy cultural pattern to discover. Any TV commercial illustrates the concept. Smooth, articulate, warm, friendly voices emerge from ingratiating, self-assured actors who smile with the solemn integrity and demeanor of priests or surgeons. Note the carefully selected costumes coordinated with the product and fictional media situation, the posture of self-confidence and casual authority, and above all the constant eye contact. Actors are highly trained, disciplined, well-paid liars. The more convincingly they lie, the higher the pay. A skilled actor could even wind up as president.

In U.S. culture, eye contact is essential to credibility. Someone who looks you directly in the eye is perceived to be telling the truth. In Middle Eastern or Latin cultures, on the other hand, steady eye contact is generally considered rudely aggressive. In the U.S., children first learn to lie with their eyes—a behavior reinforced by media throughout their lives. If individuals learn to maintain steady, unwavering eye contact, they can get away with whoppers that would otherwise be rejected offhand. TV pitchpeople appear to have constant eye contact with each individual audience member. (Of course, what they're really doing is reading the script off the teleprompter in front of the camera lens.)

The ersatz sincerity of the media is rarely challenged. As foreign visitors often comment, Americans are extremely mistrustful of others. We are reluctant to trust even next-door neighbors, yet rarely question the validity of the messages pouring forth from the media.

A U.S. corporation conducted a lengthy search for a vice president to manage an important new subsidiary division. Five finalists were eventually selected by an executive committee. All were men in their fifties with distinguished records of accomplishment and education and enjoyed substantial public and private trust in their integrity. From their vitae, each appeared equally distinguished, accomplished, and capable. Attempting to weigh comparative abilities—at least as they appeared on paper—was difficult, if not impossible. Each was also skilled at playing the expected role as candidate with skill and sensitivity, always deferring to perceived expectations of the committee.

One candidate, far more than the others, looked more suitable for the job—tall, muscular, handsome, gray-haired—the visual archetype of the important executive. He visually conveyed a synthesis of what Gregory Peck, Charlton Heston, and Henry Fonda might have looked like in roles as middle-aged executives. The other candidates' physical appearances were unimpressive by comparison. The committee hired the handsome applicant.

The new vice president successfully established the subsidiary division. At the end of the second year, however, he resigned, and soon founded a competitive corporation of which he was president. He pirated nearly a hundred of the engineers and scientists recruited to join the original venture. Attempting to understand how the disaster had occurred, members of the executive committee painfully concluded that they had been conned by the candidate's clever manipulation of their expectations. They did not explore, of course, why they had permitted the con instead of questioning their own assumptions.

Expectation Management

That kind of disaster is rife in social and economic institutions throughout the world. Once situations or individuals are defined perceptually as *real* (they exist), for all practical purposes *they are real*—until they eventually prove themselves otherwise, as they often do. A far more reliable strategy would postpone definitive evaluations until actual behavior confirmed or denied preliminary impressions. Even after that, continuous evaluation and assumption testing should be maintained.

Expectations influence the behavior both of the person holding an expectation and of the person about whom the expectation is held. It matters little whether expectations are positive or negative. Negative expectations actually encourage deviant behaviors further. Positive expectations move individuals to ignore negative facts, impressions, or risks.

No matter how they are played, human expectations are fictional constructs which can lead to disaster if not constantly probed. Many personnel directors discipline themselves to disregard appearances, while realizing that this is never entirely possible.

To increase the likelihood their expectations will be fulfilled, people communicate expectations with glances, avoidance or establishment of eye contact, name-calling and name-dropping, cooperation, competition, and facial or body movements as small as one-fifth of a millimeter. Verbal and nonverbal behaviors let others know how they are perceived in relation to ourselves. The subtle communication of expectations is documented in experiments dating back at least to 1904. Clever Hans was a world-famous German "talking horse." He appeared to converse by tapping out answers to questions with a forehoof—one tap for *A*, two for *B*, etc. He had, so it appeared, learned the alphabet. A panel of thirteen scientists and experts—members of the Prussian Science Academy and University of Berlin—reported that their studies had ruled out deception and unintentional communication by the owner. They awarded Clever Hans honors and proclaimed the animal a respectable and important scientific discovery.

Several months later the only skeptic on the committee discovered that Clever Hans could not perform without observing his questioners. The horse read—as most horses can—signals humans constantly transmit, over which they usually have no control and of which they are consciously unaware. (This is one of the reasons horses are so loved by their owners.)

Clever Hans's sensitivity to the experts' expectations had produced the remarkable feats of intelligence. The horse stopped tapping his hoof when he sensed it was expected. The experts were completely unaware that they were sending subtle messages of expectation. The Clever Hans phenomenon has been experimentally demonstrated with horses, pigs, dogs, and other animals. Were humans as perceptually sensitive as animals, they might avoid the many disasters to which they blindly submit themselves.

Stigmatized individuals, however, are more apt to be aware of the expectations of others, sometimes only unconsciously. There are three broad stigma areas: ethnic or religious affiliations; character or behavior deviations; and physical impairments.

People often find themselves uncomfortable around stigmatized individuals, and attempt to cover it with patronizing kindness. Patronizing behavior is usually apparent to the stigmatized, but any overt response to the perceived hypocrisy would be interpreted as ungrateful. They end up feeling frustrated and saddled with a fraudulent relationship. Virtually any black, Latin, Arab, Asian, or disabled person living in the U.S. can discuss this dilemma in considerable detail.

The stigmatized often develop self-expectations that conform to the expectations of others. They are aware they are disliked or considered inferior. The stereotypical expectations can evoke behavior that reflects the stereotype, which usually provokes and reinforces further rejection and discrimination, or insincere treatment. The mechanism is perpetual, largely unconscious, and deadly in its potential for destructiveness.

It is impossible to hide expectations from others. Humans perceived by others cannot avoid communicating at many levels. Moreover, everyone is in constant jeopardy of expressing miscues and unintended information. It is never what was said that counts, but what was perceived to have been said. Humans can never opt out of the game unless they are content to live alone on a desert island. It is wiser to attempt to understand the strategies and increase the chance of success. The game cannot be stopped, but it can be won through a knowledge of what is going on.

There are several limitations, however, to how well one can consciously manage complex interpersonal communication. Role-playing to accommodate a certain objective is usually detectable. Though they may initially repress an awareness of fraud, audiences are likely to respond negatively sooner or later. Several national TV commercials were tested with individuals unsighted since birth. Visual perception dominates and suppresses the sensitivity of other senses. The unsighted individuals invariably described the actors as "insincere," "untrustworthy," "feigned," "hypocritical," "false," "dishonest," and "devious." After viewing and hearing the same commercials, sighted people described the actors in positive, complimentary terms.

Both sighted and unsighted heard the same voices. At an unconscious level, the sighted must have perceived what the unsighted consciously perceived. But the sighted repressed conscious awareness of being manipulated and allowed the dominance of pleasing, interesting, visual projection and identification cues. Awareness of deception often surfaces later over issues of trust, honesty, integrity, and confidence.

University classes in such areas as advertising, public relations, marketing, and business are far worse than merely worthless. They offer the student little more than one-dimensional human manipulation as a conscious technology directed at goal (profit) attainment. Such education produces people who cannot communicate effectively. Without respect for integrity, dignity, compassion, love, feelings, frailties, weaknesses, and even folly, effective and meaningful communication must always be questionable. One can bribe, cajole, coerce, argue, manipulate, con, and persuade up to a point, but there always exists the threat of discovery and backlash. Truly effective communication skills are the product of honesty, life experience, and broad, genuine humanistic concerns, not simply a desire for money and power.

The Competition for Oblivion

In a number of studies, individuals with strong competitive tendencies were compared with those who appeared strongly cooperative. It is often blindly assumed that competition is the most desirable pursuit available to humans. The two general personalities had very different views of each other. Cooperators were consciously aware that some individuals were strongly competitive and others strongly cooperative. Competitors, however, appeared unaware of the difference. Competitors compel most people with whom they relate to compete. Further, those who bear mindless allegiance to the ideals of unrestrained competition cannot acknowledge the social and human effects of their obsession.

A person's self-expectations—distinct from the expectations of others—involve perceptions of strength, weakness, and ability, or what is popularly called *self-image*. Self-image has much to do with success. Successful decision-making in a goal-structured situation depends on self-expectations of success. If someone believes he or she will succeed, or that there is a good probability of success, the likelihood is greatly enhanced.

That probability is evaluated by comparisons with others. Most people believe they are a little better than average. Perceptions of "average" are usually derived from peers, friends, neighbors, and relatives—persons with whom one has regular personal relationships. For most, such sources of self-image are probably healthy, and based within perceived realities of day-to-day life experience.

When ad media enter the picture, however, the self-esteem derived from peer associations deteriorates rapidly. Ads are designed to evoke a sense of audience inferiority through comparisons with media personalities—the beautiful people. Even the unbeautiful, the losers, in media often appear winners to the audience by comparison with themselves. Fictional media personalities seem educated, surrounded by interesting, pretty, talented, often wealthy and powerful people, easily able to enjoy the world's indulgences and riches. These superior lives become the audience's fantasized goal, both consciously and unconsciously. The mechanism was designed to encourage the purchase of ad-hyped products—the essential raison d'être of commercial media. The implied promise of ad-generated consumption is equality, acceptance, and participation in the good life of the beautiful media people—an unfulfillable promise and expectation.

Reality, as it is perceived by most people, is quiet desperation—often a grim, quiet struggle for survival against illness, boredom, loneliness, anxiety, despair, and countless real and imagined threats to security and well-being. Media celebrities and the roles in which they are cast rarely appear besieged by such problems. Media fantasies provide audiences with a projective escape, through identification. Ad-massaged audiences are taught to view the world as a place where everybody else seems to be getting it all—everyone, that is, except themselves. Consumption becomes the mechanism of liberation, freedom, the pathway to the good life, the new religion.

Individuals who are deeply integrated into media identifications often abandon their own goals without making any effort to achieve them. Their media-derived pessimism is severely damaging. Some may argue that media characters have always been perceived by audiences as special cases, at least since early Greek drama. Perhaps true, but traditional literary or dramatic characterizations were perceived to embody the broadest range of behaviors, from villainy through heroism, instead of the simplistic stereotypes that now dominate. Today, ad media is our environment, omnipresent, an active part of every hour. Were Karl Marx writing today, it is doubtful he could make a serious case against religion. Ad media long ago replaced religion as the opiate of high-technology societies.

By the age of eighteen, the average North American has seen over 18,000 hours of television, far more than the hours spent in educational pursuits. These passive participants unconsciously absorb an exhaustive brainwashing in what eventually evolves as their cultural system. Only 15% of the U.S. TV audience watches documentaries or other thoughtful programming. Television is dismissed as educationally insignificant, as merely entertainment. The long-term cumulative effects are disregarded.

The media condition audiences for a wide range of maladaptive behaviors. Clinical psychiatrists, psychologists, and counselors are inundated by patients who have come to perceive themselves as losers, who have lost or not developed vital self-esteem, confidence, and individual identities. The young emulate rich rock stars, athletes, actors—anyone who appears to have achieved fame and fortune with little effort, sacrifice, or dedication. "Have fun, get rich, and get laid as often as possible" has become the twentieth-century ad-media philosophy. Ads sell! They manipulate! They also grind up humans into pathetic fantasy-obsessed victims.

Stereotypical Personality Myths

The concept of personality—as defined by individuals, so-called scientific facts, testing, and by groups and cultures—is a monstrous fiction. Personality descriptions are constructed to accommodate conscious and unconscious objectives. Every individual has beliefs (generalizations) about what people are like. Personality descriptions group those human characteristics perceived as *fitting together* and *fitting in* as opposed to those that do not.

Humans apparently possess the innate predisposition to evaluate and judge others based on general impressions of *goodness* or *badness*. Such perceptions are often describable as symbolic archetypes and stereotypes. The assessment of personality stems from generalizations. Personality, however it may be explained at any time or place, lies strictly in the eyes of the beholders and depends on the values currently accepted or rejected by their cultural systems.

Individuals hold personality theories similar to those held by others in their group or culture. When visible styles of dress, manner, and appearance conform to what is considered "average" or "normal" (perceptual fictions) at a particular time and place, these fantasized norms become a basis for personality assessment. Characteristics that serve as evaluation cues include clothes, car, musical taste, walk, education, income, voice quality, posture, color preferences—anything, in effect, subjects do or don't do. But which of the many possibilities in each category is judged "good"? There appear to be no universal standards of *beauty* or *goodness*. They have been everything conceivable at various times and places. Concepts of *beauty* and *goodness* must, in fact, be sold or communicated to achieve widespread acceptance—the important cultural role of ad media.

People often dislike or find themselves hostile to someone after brief, summary exposure. Hostility appears for reasons never specified, unconscious reactions to seemingly casual communication. No individual can be perceived completely without prejudice. When perceptions bias *against*, the individual is avoided. His or her companionship is tacitly assumed unrewarding. Avoidance reinforces dislike, so there is less opportunity to discover positive features. On the other hand, when someone is *liked*, it is rewarding to be around them. More time is spent in evaluation, eventually discovering negative features. Negative aspects are often offset by an initial positive reaction. Or, negative realizations may provoke eventual disillusionment, rejection, and enmity.

Personality assessment is one of the weakest, shakiest notions in a world of many weak, shaky notions. Personality characteristics can be packaged to appear reasonable, natural, even scientific. Anything, however, taken for granted as reasonable, natural, and scientific should—in the interest of survival and adjustment—

trigger bright warning lights. Beware! Most significant new ideas—throughout the history of science, scholarship, art, and intellectual innovation—developed in resistance to ideas or assumptions taken for granted. Often an insight, discovery, theory, or treasured assumption fits so well with what common sense and everyday perceptual experience confirm, it is difficult to believe anyone could ever have thought otherwise. These are often the most dangerous of assumptions.

Public-relations and publicity images are the worst of stereotypical fictions. They are harmful if directed inward as part of self-perception. They are self-exploitive when projected outward as fictional images of leaders, celebrities, friends, or enemies. The population has, over the years, been carefully indoctrinated to accept images (stereotypes) as substitutions for reality-oriented perceptions. Realities occasionally seep through the barriers constructed by perceptual manipulators to preserve their client's fictions. Fantasy images of omnipotence, however, are popularly preferred over complex, often contradictory, human qualities.

Former President Lyndon Johnson used to joke privately that it would be a healthy, sobering experience for the public to view their president at least once annually seated upon a toilet. He explained that the publicity might restrain presidents from being carried away by their PR images, and the public might mature if periodically reminded that its leader, with the nuclear attack codebooks, was only human. In the media-dominated U.S., however, such deflation of media puffery in favor of reality appears unlikely.

All humans are influenced by perceptual biases. They preferentially ignore factual data, exclude from definitions, and interpret from subjective perspectives. The more "objective" they fancy themselves, the more extensive and concealed are their biases. No human is more biased than one who perceives himself unbiased. Without awareness of perceptual limitations—and the biases thereby incurred—humans mistake inference for fact, theory for truth, fantasies for realities, and rely on judgments warped by conscious and unconscious influences. This seems to be an innate aspect of the human condition. It would be preferable to admit fallibility and make the best of it, instead of stumbling on with fraudulent, dangerous, illusions of "objective reality." Our *truths* may yet destroy us!

Moralities Require Deviants

Any behavior perceived as normal will be perceived as abnormal in another context or group standard. Behaviors become deviant more through their perception than through the actual behaviors themselves. When acts are perceived as negative deviations from a group's usual expectations, perpetrators will be punished in some way. High-tech cultures, such as the U.S., the U.S.S.R., and Japan, appear more sensitive to deviation than others, and hence more punitive. Middle-income groups are generally more intolerant of deviation than high- and low-income populations. The poor have nothing to lose and the rich are protected against losing.

In addition, the religiously devout are more intolerant than the religiously indifferent. Religious beliefs are major social instruments for defining deviant behavior. Perceived deviation initiates reaction that isolates, treats, corrects, or punishes deviants. The actual behavior itself may be of little consequence. Notions of perceived normality and deviations from it permeate all known cultures and subcultures.

Many groups demonstrate double standards when they deal with outsiders. Newcomers will be expected to conform rigidly to group expectations, while older group members usually have more freedom. Expected behavior norms rarely apply uniformly to all members of any group. Many groups or cultures actually create deviance by making rules that certain individuals will be compelled to violate. Deviations may have been the original source of group cohesion. Such rule structures provide a group with perceived exclusivity, uniqueness, and validity. Deviation rules often have powerful economic sponsorship that reinforces the status quo.

Rule-making usually involves a cast of fictional, perceptually constructed characters that include rule-makers, enforcers, and of course the very necessary deviants. It makes no sense to create and enforce rules that no one violates. Many groups could not survive without deviants. If deviants do not exist, they must be created. One method of creating deviants is through projective stereotyping.

Rule structures may be formal or informal, conscious or unconscious. Deviation rules almost always include moral characteristics—vital ingredients in group cohesion. In a world where no one violated moral expectations, such expectations would vanish. Perceived morality depends entirely upon perceived immorality. Deviance provides a major mechanism by which humans can invent or construct their friends and enemies, gods and devils, loyalties and disloyalties, loves and hates. Morality, utilized to define deviance, is a perceptual product, the engineering of which is a major media industry in the high-tech nations of the world.

This brings into the game a perception, based on a perception, based on a perception, ad infinitum—all locked together, an Ouroborus. The snake again bites its tail. Deviance perceptions operate without conscious awareness by the players involved.

For the game to be played effectively, however, leaders must have some awareness of the dynamics. Without conscious awareness, it is difficult to manage the deviance mechanism over an extended time. The system can, nevertheless, be operated intuitively, with the risk of abruptly losing control. The system operates only as long as the manipulation remains repressed by group members. The skillful management of deviance threats can be observed in the rhetoric of big-money TV evangelists. Their media money-milking machines entrance their victims, who rarely consciously discover their victimization.

A majority group that ignores deviance is eventually likely to disappear in its present form. It will be absorbed or synthesized into another, more militant group. But if the group enforces rules too rigidly, the opposition is enhanced. Democratic political theories of government are based on the careful management of deviance. It is surprising that so many people in democratic societies remain unaware of the significance of deviance. In the U.S.S.R., Gorbachev's *perestroika* (restructuring) demonstrates an attempt to politically manage deviance after seventy years of suppression and restraint. *Perestroika*, assuming it continues and survives the turmoil, is one of the most important political events in Soviet history.

Deviance is difficult to comprehend when one is trapped in the Aristotelian logic of objective reality. Gorbachev has already discovered that a substantial portion of his population is strongly opposed to *perestroika*. Numerous politicians in both the U.S. and the Soviet Union have made profitable, lifelong careers of communist/capitalist bashing. The mass-communication media are also principal beneficiaries of deviant-bashing.

In the U.S., certain categories of people are expected to be deviant—musicians, actors, homosexuals, communists, socialists, atheists, intellectuals, juvenile delinquents, welfare recipients, ethnic minorities, and criminals—not necessarily in that order. At the top of the list are the alleged mentally ill. Mental illness is usually implied in deviance.

Victims almost never consciously discover the games played with their deviance. The conscious, or for the most part unconscious, rules for deviance are rooted deeply in the history and traditions of groups. These rules are taken for granted by group members and often attributed to the word of God or science—the highest high-credibility information sources available. These traditions have become so much a part of perceived reality, especially in high-tech societies, that violations appear bizarre or perverse. Many of the rules exist in residual attitudes, nonverbal and undefined.

This book and its author will be perceived by many as deviant, to some even dangerously deviant—threatening to life, truth, and reason as they are popularly perceived. During broadcast interviews and lecture appearances, this author has been frequently attacked for being insane, subversive, ungrateful, radical, controversial, threatening, and—the ultimate deviance in the U.S.—for being a communist. A major social institution, the ad-media culture machine, seemed to be threatened. Media provide legitimization and cultural verification for much of society.

A particularly vitriolic attack against this author's books appeared in *Advertising Age* (Sept. 17, 1984), the ad industry house organ. Written by a professor of advertising, the 3,500-word cover story ignored the more than five hundred published research studies confirming the effects upon behavior of subliminal stimuli, the many examples illustrated in the books, and authoritative testimony on the subject by respected scientists, scholars, and government administrators. The critique denied the existence of subliminal perception, attacked this author's sanity and credibility, and denounced this "profitable exploitation" of the defenseless ad industry.

The attack was an attempt to generate public pressure on perceptual deviance. The writer and publisher of the story were presumably aware that one month before the *Advertising Age* story was published, the U.S. Treasury Department's Bureau of Alcohol,

Tobacco, and Firearms had issued new regulations prohibiting subliminal stimuli in alcoholic beverage ads (*see* Appendix). Perceptual deviance has caused, and continues to cause, considerable discomfort and expense to the ad industry.

Deviance Manipulation

Several variables appear to control whether rule-breaking will be denied or ignored by a group. Most groups agree that punishment should fit the crime. The rule-breaker's power, status, and wealth are also important variables. The higher the status of the rule-breakers, the more likely the group will permit them to get away with transgressions. Just consider how Richard Nixon or various television evangelists survived enormous scandals.

The amount of tolerance for deviance usually relates to the amount of outside pressure a group feels. To decrease tolerance, leaders often increase group perceptions of outside threats. This mechanism can be observed in government justifications of military expenditures and foreign interventions. Threats from the U.S.S.R. and others appear to fluctuate depending upon whether Congress or public opinion opposes policies or appropriations.

Moral majorities, as many have noted in recent years, usually turn out to be neither. Perceived social ideals invariably have an underside, the inverse, the reality concealed by the ideal. Law and order advocates often end up convicted criminals. Those politicians who most decry wasteful spending have squandered the public purse at rates vastly exceeding the wastefulness of history's most indulged profligates. The most sincere so frequently turn out completely insincere. Godly pretensions often conceal avarice, criminality, and ruthlessness. Stereotypical labels usually say far more about the labeler than they do about the labeled. Individuals who cannot think around and beyond stereotypical expectations are doomed to ritually repeat the tragedies of the past as they follow their leaders into oblivion.

9 | SELF-FULFILLING PROPHECIES

Why and by what right does one nation or one class of people lock up, torture, exile, flog, kill, and destroy other people, when they themselves are no better (or worse) than those whom they torture?

Leo Tolstoy, *War and Peace*

Our deepest fears reside just behind the everyday and the bland.

John Berger, *The Sense of Sight*

The chief source of disorder in society is the hypocrisy of those who pretend to be virtuous, on the one hand, while all the time behaving contrary to their professed beliefs.

Plato, *The Republic*

Swiss psychiatrist Carl Jung recorded the story of a patient who shortly before a vacation dreamed of falling from a mountain to his death. A week later, the patient actually fell to his death from the mountain in the dream. Coincidence? Most unlikely. Self-fulfilling prophecies (SFPs) are assumptions or predictions that seem to cause an event to occur, thus confirming their own accuracy. The process of fulfilling the prediction can be conscious, unconscious, or both.

If people assume they are not liked, the assumption alone often prompts them to act hostile, defensive, suspicious, and aggressive. These behaviors, in turn, provoke similar reactions from others. Thus, initial assumptions are confirmed. Individuals end up being disliked. People rarely realize the power they possess to victimize themselves through assumptions, convictions, and predictions.

Life, for better or worse, is rarely as simple as it is made to appear. Good causes often have bad effects, and vice versa. The complex contradictions of verbal realities ensure that nothing is what it appears to be on the surface, especially for those with mindless faith in simplistic definitions. Advertisers incorporate the underside of cause-and-effect assumptions into ads at subliminal levels in ways that would frighten consumers if they suspected what was going on. U.S. ad technique has been exported throughout the world. The *Paris Match* ad (fig. 25) appears as a simple cause-and-effect proposition. Brightly colored Eminence shorts will improve your sexual success. The copy translates as, "Dress yourself every morning with colors that sing." The models were photographed, the rest of the page painted. The attractive young man is dominant in the illustration. The man's expression appears macho, self-satisfied, even arrogant as he stares off into space with a beguiling though vacuous smile. He is physically attractive but seemingly carried away with his beauty and self-assurance. A reader might speculate that he spent half an hour combing his hair before the photograph. The surface message is that the colored shorts will make you even more irresistible to women. He appears a man wildly infatuated with himself. His left hand condescendingly rests on the girl's shoulder. Anyone who gullibly believes in the promise of Eminence has set themself up with an SFP for failure in complex, sensitive human relationships.

The young woman model, however, appears much more interesting. She is on her knees, her body hidden beneath the windowsill. The pose establishes a relationship between her head and the man's pelvic area. He is clearly dominant, she submissive. Now, the underside! The blond model is asking the reader not to tell, to keep her secret, her index finger seals her lips, *sssssssh*! What is her secret?

On the reverse side of the page appears a conventional black-and-white ad for electrical appliances—nine of them: a toaster, mixer, warmer, opener, et cetera. This is not very exciting stuff in the colorful world of sexualized ads (fig. 26). With nine items, the ad is cluttered. The sales logic is questionable. Readers are unlikely to waste their time on so familiar a group of products.

Paris Match is printed on thin paper. As the pages are turned, light penetrates from one side to the other. Figure 59 shows the Eminence ad held up to light so the appliance ad bleeds through. We can now understand the young woman's secret—the electric carving knife, hovering above the male's genital area. Both of the see-through ads, directed primarily at males, become highly emotionalized by the subliminal embed. Castration fears are a common denominator that unite male consumers. A verbal logic could be constructed to justify the symbolism, but it would end up as a simplistic cause-and-effect rationale. It is probably wiser to simply acknowledge that the symbolic nonverbal mechanisms work often enough to justify widespread use, such as in the scissors hidden within the *Playboy* logo (*see* Key, *Subliminal Seduction,* pp. 123–25).

From a statistical analysis, there were two chances in the 120 total pages in *Paris Match* that the two ads could have randomly ended up back to back, one chance in nine the knife could appear in the position over the male genital area. It is extremely improbable that the placements could have been a random accident, even less probable when knowledge of subliminal embeds was known to the artists and ad agency involved.

SFPs are well known in the sciences. Science philosopher Paul Feyerabend concluded, "Not conservative but anticipatory suppositions (what we wish to happen) guide scientific research." SFPs are much discussed in psychiatry and psychology but are rarely considered a normal aspect of the daily lives of individuals, groups, and even nations.

Many SFPs are attributable to assumptions derived from ad media. The SFP usually derives from strongly believed cause-and-effect assumptions. In these, the relationship between cause and effect becomes circular and self-reinforcing, rather than linear and open-ended—the Ouroborus again. The SFP is an unconscious mechanism whereby humans unwittingly set themselves up for an outcome that their assumptions actually made possible. These outcomes may be either good or bad for the individual involved, sometimes both. If good, they seem to be the product of a wise decision, lucky guess, or profound insight into the mechanisms of causation. SFPs seemingly involve simple, direct decision-making in which you evaluate the future effects of an act, seeking the most advantageous outcome.

The process appears natural, respectable, logical, and defensible. Cause-and-effect conclusions are rarely questioned. All such decisions consider the future, and eventually prove to have been either correct or incorrect or both for a variety of perceptually constructed rationalizations. The SFP may, at first, have been neither true nor false but *produces* a truth or falsity by its existence as part of the reasoning process.

Curious SFPs occur in people's relationships with the Internal Revenue Service. The income tax laws are infamously contradictory and arbitrary, wide open to interpretation. To comprehend the myriad collection of constantly changing laws requires a full-time staff of skilled professionals. Even superficial understanding is a major effort for CPAs. IRS agents assume that taxpayers cheat and seek to avoid truthful income declarations. Anyone who has endured an IRS audit knows how this preconception influences the investigation. IRS agents probe lifestyles, property, and amusements to estimate income. Contrary to legal doctrine in criminal or civil actions, taxpayers are compelled to prove themselves innocent in the face of an IRS assumption of guilt.

That assumption, or prediction, compels the taxpayer to avoid simple, truthful income declarations. Dishonesty, or perhaps borderline honesty, becomes imperative to escape perceived unfair taxation. The IRS's assumptions actually create the situation predicted. It is irrelevant whether initial assumptions were true or false. What was presumed to be the *effect* turns out to be the *cause*.

The cause produces the dilemma. The prophecy of the situation *causes* the situation of the prophecy.

Most corporate personnel officers can recall situations where employees got the notion they were about to be fired—reacting to insecurity over normal business cycles or to guilt over some real or imagined personal deficiency. By behaving erratically or allowing their work to suffer, they progressively set themselves up for firing, which, indeed became reality.

Michel Foucault's brilliant history of insanity, *Madness and Civilization*, documents an astonishing variety of contradictory definitions for insanity. It demonstrates that insanity is a socially manufactured concept, changing as societies over the centuries sought new ways to deal with deviants. Sanity, on the other hand, was rarely defined. Indeed, sanity may be undefinable. Sanity is tacitly assumed to be those practices, policies, and behaviors commonly accepted by a particular society at a particular time as normal. Normalcy is a fine concept until you recall it was once considered normal to burn witches, heretics, and other deviants at the stake after brutal torture. It is currently considered normal to live minutes away from nuclear devastation. When viewed on an ever-changing historical continuum, much of what is today considered sane or normal would be insane or abnormal at another time and place.

Civilizations have manufactured and enforced countless definitions of insanity and continue to elaborate the idea at an increasing tempo. One modern psychiatric criterion for sanity is the extent of a person's reality adaptation, usually defined as "fitting in," or ability to discriminate between fantasy and reality. Common sense, enforced by judicial statutes, assumes that sanity is an objective reality: real, open to examination, measurement, and comprehension. The psychiatric community argues endlessly over verbal definitions within the general framework of insanity. The framework itself is rarely challenged. It should be! Like personality definitions, insanity labels unjustly evoke self-fulfilling prophecies.

Psychiatric diagnoses, unlike diagnoses in other medical specialties, define, and in so doing create, pathological conditions. The diagnosis or definition becomes part of the illness and creates a series of self-fulfilling prophecies. Once an institutionalized diagnosis is made, a reality is invented in which even normal behavior appears disturbed. After the diagnosis, perceptions that reinforce the diagnosis are manufactured. The process quickly moves beyond the control of patients, diagnosing physicians, family, staff, and hospital administrations. All participate in the construction of a reality that supports the diagnosis. A reporter was checked into a mental hospital to gather material for an article. The staff who saw him writing in a notebook portentously observed on his chart that he "engaged in note-taking behavior."

The process also occurs regularly in day-to-day human relationships where, for whatever purpose, individuals are labeled, categorized, and stereotyped. Hospitals overflow with the poor, aged, and abandoned, often from minority groups, who were admitted merely because they embarrassed, disturbed, shocked, or annoyed someone or some group. Stereotypical diagnostic labels confirm and legitimize the wisdom of society.

Schizophrenia, one of the most frequent mental health diagnoses, supposedly describes a psychosis that includes an inability to discriminate between fantasy and reality. It should be clear from the illustrations in this book that many supposedly normal people cannot discriminate between fantasy and reality. They cannot even differentiate between real and fantasy ice cubes. Clinical diagnoses frequently result in self-fulfilling prophecies with two basic ingredients. Patients experience great discomfort and they accept the diagnosis as the explanation for that discomfort. The clinical diagnosis is a high-credibility verification and authorization for the symptoms and treatment for the symptoms.

The labeled patient becomes entrapped in a labyrinth of clinical expectations, interactions, and maladjustment patterns. These further isolate the patient and evoke further fantasy orientations. These fantasies, of course, further confirm the diagnosis, which evokes further fantasy orientations, which further confirm, ad infinitum. The snake again bites its tail, another Ouroborus.

In December 1985, a schizophrenia study by the Yale Medical School found that over two-thirds of patients diagnosed schizophrenic completely recovered and, thereafter, led normal, productive lives. Yet the *Diagnostic Criteria, DSM III*, of the American Psychiatric Association—the basic reference of definitions on which commitments to mental institutions are based—defines schizophrenia as a permanent disability from which it is virtually impossible to recover. Indeed, the *DSM III*'s long, interconnecting, all-encompassing definition of schizophrenia would lock in anyone so designated for a lifetime career as a mental patient. The Social Security Administration accepts the *DSM III* as a basis for disability determinations.

Paranoia, another popular diagnosis, means social conduct perceived as suspicious, aggressive, hostile, stubborn, jealous, and covetous—adjectives that describe most successful businesspeople. Once the process of social exclusion and regimentation begins, the patient defined as paranoid has a reason for this behavior. Simply being sane in an unsane world reasonably evokes the above paranoid symptoms.

Labeled patients become more and more detached from families and social groups. Strained relationships evoke further stereotypical definitions such as *crank, crackpot, crazy, hopeless*, and finally the ultimate branding, *insane*. The door closes, often permanently. "Common sense" entraps everyone. Whether we are active or passive players in the farce, or audience, this entrapment has the potential to justify the ultimate disaster.

SFPs are well illustrated in Ken Kesey's celebrated novel, *One Flew Over the Cuckoo's Nest*, as well as in actual studies. In a study by psychologist David Rosenhan, eight volunteer pseudo-patients were admitted to twelve mental hospitals in five states across the country. Each patient falsely reported hearing "voices" to achieve admission. The pseudo-patients were diagnosed, with one manic-depressive exception, as schizophrenics. They were instructed to act normally after admission and get out of the hosptial by convincing the staff they were sane. Confinements ranged from seven to fifty-two days, averaging nineteen. When finally discharged, each was designated not as cured, but as schizophrenic and manic-depressive "in remission."

The so-called mental illnesses were just perceptual constructions manufactured by the institutional staffs, whose vested interest was in finding clients to treat. Staff members appeared to believe that anything once named or labeled must exist in reality. They compelled reality, the patient, to conform with their perceptual expectations. In effect, they perceived the world as definitions (words) permitted, conforming perceptions of reality to the definitions rather than fitting definitions to their day-to-day observations of each patient.

The pseudo-patients quickly discovered that there were carefully defined labels for pathological, abnormal behaviors. Normal behaviors, on the other hand, were difficult—if not impossible—to define once diagnostic labels became securely attached to patients. Even if a patient was perceived ready for discharge, they were not considered sane or well, but "in remission." Compliance with the construct was then enforced upon patients. Curiously, a common experience was recognition as *normal* by other patients.

Who Is Really Inside, and Outside?

This experience, where sane people are designated insane, can be reversed, especially when perceptions of prestige, professional integrity, and diagnostic skills are at risk. In another hospital, whose staff was aware of Rosenhan's embarrassing revelations, the staff unanimously doubted such errors could occur in their hospital, clearly demonstrating the blind trust people place in science, authority figures, and institutional integrity.

The hospital was informed that during the following three months, one or more pseudo-patients would attempt admission. Each staff member, including attendants, nurses, psychiatrists, physicians, and psychologists, evaluated 193 patients. Forty-one patients were strongly considered pseudo-patients by at least one staff member. Twenty-three were suspected by at least one psychiatrist. Nineteen were suspected by one psychiatrist and one staff member.

The research group had not sent any pseudo-patients to the hospital during the three months.

In the Rosenhan study, normal behaviors were misinterpreted so they conformed to the label *abnormal*. Such labels produced their own realities, causes, effects, and self-fulfilling prophecies. Psychiatric diagnoses are rarely found later to be in error, in contrast to other medical diagnoses, where errors are commonplace and constantly corrected, usually without stigmatic consequences. Psychiatric labels stick like a tattoo that boldly states: "INADE-

QUATE!" It is almost impossible to prove yourself sane, but relatively easy to be proven insane.

There are many comparable SFPs in daily life. Consider the SFP effects of a judicial label—with a court's godlike judgment of *guilty*—for virtually any crime. Incarceration under the stereotype "criminal" sets in motion an entire complex of SFPs that doubtfully serve society's interests.

Test psychologists, a major industry, absurdly continue to believe that they can test people and animals with scientific objectivity. *Stigmatic stereotypes* with SFP potentials are regularly established through tests by school counselors, personnel administrators, and— the most devastating perpetuator of stereotypical labels—the mass-communication media. In one study, teachers were told that certain students (actually chosen at random) had tested as gifted children. It was observed that the teachers then lavished special attention on those students and this in turn evoked superior performance. On the other hand, "slow learner" labels have actually created and sustained the condition they presumed to describe.

SFPs are uncomfortable to examine. They can threaten self-images of sanity, along with superstitious faith in science, reason, individual autonomy, truth, and God. The discovery that humans create their own realities—or have it done for them by media—can be shattering for those immersed in fantasy, which in some cultures includes almost everyone.

SFPs do not happen only to innocent bystanders. They are utilized deliberately, with specific premeditated intent. For the mechanism to function effectively, however, SFPs must be believed, perceived as factual from a high-credibility source, and presented as a functional aspect of reality. Only then can an SFP have a clear effect upon the present, thereby succeeding.

Stereotypical labels victimize both the person to whom they are applied and the labeler. Whether ethnic, celebrity images, product or brand generalizations, or psychiatric diagnoses, labels dehumanize everyone they touch. They evoke fear, envy, distrust, and the treatment of individuals as dehumanized objects. Dehumanization is actually the planned objective of much celebrity publicity, in which a person is merchandised as a sex object, a supermoral paragon of virtue, or an omniscient economic or religious prophet.

Manipulative images are often constructed for political, religious, business, or military leaders. Anyone who is made to appear too honest, or too anything for that matter, should be instantly distrusted.

The pioneer Menninger Psychiatric Clinic in Topeka, Kansas, discontinued diagnostic labeling of patients. Instead, a system of team evaluations was initiated to develop operational diagnoses and prognoses—tentative definitions, continually changed during treatment programs in response to changing patient needs. As might have been expected, Menninger was criticized for his refusal to cooperate with institutional psychiatry. British psychiatrist R. D. Laing made a similar attempt to circumvent diagnostic labels in his London Tavistock Clinic during the 1960s.

The *Diagnostic Criteria, DSM III,* published by the American Psychiatric Association is a catalogue of absurd and damaging nonsense. It is difficult to find a copy of the *DSM III,* which is often kept on the restricted list in medical-school libraries, concealed from patients and the general public. The secrecy, of course, makes the book irresistible to patients, who eventually will find copies. Indeed, such a dictionary of projective, stigmatic stereotypes does have administrative and legal functions. The *DSM III* has very little to do with the so-called mental disorders and their treatment. If taken seriously, the definitions lock both physician and patient into a system of mutual expectations from which it may be impossible for either to be extricated.

As psychological descendants of Greek drama's Oedipus, who fulfilled a tragic prophecy while attempting to avoid it, we continue to fulfill prophecies through attempts to escape. Societies arm themselves to avoid war, thereby ensuring the inevitability of war. Profitable war industries provide short-term employment and economic benefits. Armaments, however, are a disastrous economic drain in a world of diminishing, finite resources. They exhaust any society's resources, thereby increasing the likelihood of conflict. The investment is more damaging than mere wasted raw materials. A truck will earn its investment back many times during its existence. A tank, missile, or warplane, after a brief period of noneconomic use, becomes obsolete and must be scrapped in favor of an even more uneconomic new model.

The megatonnage in the world's current nuclear-weapons stockpiles is enough to kill 58 billion people—every person now living—twelve times. In a world spending $800 billion annually for military programs, one adult in three cannot read and write, one person in four is hungry. Four times as many war deaths have occurred in the forty years since World War II as during the preceding forty years (*see* Sivard, p. 5).

SFP entrapment is a powerful and deadly quagmire—the source of much of the paranoid fear purposely engineered to fuel the profitable armaments industry. The astonishingly simple mechanism is still invisible to most people because what they perceive as their vested interest profits from repression instead of knowledge. It is actually quite difficult *not to know something*, but always possible if the price is right.

We Think, We Think, We Think . . .

Ads and public relations are especially vicious in their potential to invent reality in the service of products, ideas, profits, or individuals. Surprisingly few appreciate the extent to which they have been systematically engineered, assimilated into thinking they think for themselves. In his autobiography, *Mein Kampf*, Adolf Hitler summarized the ideal character of advertising: "All propaganda must be so popular and on such an intellectual level, that even the most stupid of those toward whom it is directed will understand it. People can be made to perceive paradise as hell, and the other way around, to consider the most wretched sort of life as paradise." Similar conversations can be heard in virtually any ad and PR office. This is what they do for a living.

Once humans believe unquestionably they think for themselves, protective, critical postures relax. They can be conditioned in any direction, into almost any construction of reality. While victims babble to themselves endlessly about freedom of choice, individualism, truth, facts, reality, and even God's will, they mindlessly conform to media-constructed consumption patterns and self-fulfilling prophecies. To protect yourself is actually quite simple. Programmed perceptions of reality can be critically dangerous to your health, but only if they are believed blindly with faith and conviction. *Beware of blind faith in anything or anybody, including yourself.*

There are always three alternatives in knowledge: *you know, you do not know but could,* and—the largest, most important alternative—*the unknowable.* Humans compulsively invent verbalisms, or labels, that substitute for knowledge and sustain the pretense that they know more than they actually do. Institutions perpetuate the nonsense for legal, insurance, funding, or administrative convenience. Media do it to sell, persuade, and manage the perception of markets.

Further, there is the question of behavior adaptation to environmental circumstances. Psychiatric patients often appear sane outside the hospital, but insane within—perhaps owing to their forced adaptation to a strange, depersonalized environment. It is never easy to appear sane in an insane world, as anyone knows who has opposed nuclear weapons, environmental degradation, and the exploitation of victims of poverty, greed, dishonesty, and ideological bigotry.

Another catch-22 appears, however, in this attempt to critically evaluate perceptual constructions with SFP potentialities, to differentiate between fantasy and reality. The destruction of one perceptual construction only results in another construction. The best one can hope for are improved constructions with greater potentials for human kindness, tolerance, survival, and adjustment. Any perceptual construction remains a very tentative view of always changing reality.

Humans detest uncertainty. Uncertainties produce anxieties. To reduce anxiety, if no factual structure is readily available, humans will simply invent one or accept a ready-to-wear media reality structure. People constantly compare themselves with others whom they perceive as similar to themselves. These perceptions, of course, are fictional constructs.

The personal conviction that one can accomplish a goal increases the likelihood of reaching the goal. The perception of volition or freedom to decide among options constitutes a powerful motivating influence, even when—or particularly when—such freedom does not actually exist. Humans strive to impose order, meaning, and structure upon the world they perceive around them. They attempt to control events and relationships in which they are immersed, but the more they perceive themselves in control of options, the less they are actually in control.

To optimize outcomes, always keep as many options as possible open as long as possible, in every situation. Behavior can be viewed as an endless sequence of choices between actions, inactions, alternatives, thoughts, and futures, focused upon the conscious pursuit of a goal. Unconscious potentialities, too, should not be ignored.

The Uncertain Certainty

Self-fulfilling prophecies regularly appear in relationships between nations. They are rarely recognized, obscured by fantasies and delusions emanating from nationalistic or ideological chauvinism, repressions promoted by vested interests, or conscious strategies to manipulate reality in the pursuit of power and profit. Take, for example, the relationship between the U.S. and Nicaragua, where the initially moderate leftist Sandinistas deposed the forty-year-old Somoza family dictatorship. The Sandinistas nationalized numerous U.S. corporations, which had strongly supported and financed the ruthless dictatorship. The list included the infamous United Fruit Company, a subsidiary of the W. R. Grace Corporation, a major supporter and beneficiary of the Reagan political administration.

After the Reagan administration began in 1981, U.S. policy in Central America was to overthrow the socialist-leaning Sandinista party. After the way the U.S. government had supported Somoza, Nicaraguans were antagonistic about further U.S. intervention. The anti-U.S. public opinion was predictable and, had it been adequately handled by diplomatic efforts, would have eventually moderated. Over the following six years, however, the U.S. escalated military and economic pressures upon Nicaragua, an impoverished nation of about three million citizens—roughly equal to the population of the city of Chicago. Nicaraguan hatred of the U.S. increased, as consequently did the power of the Sandinistas.

The stated objective was to prevent Nicaragua from forming communist-bloc alliances. Harbors were mined by CIA-sponsored terrorists, international financial standing was demolished, and borders were subjected to constant attack by U.S.-sponsored insurgents officered by remnants of the hated Somoza National Guard. Each act of aggression and terrorism further united Sandinista leadership and strengthened their authority over the population. The Sandinistas were also forced into greater and greater dependence on communist-bloc alliances, and greater and greater alienation from the U.S. Had the U.S. really wished to save Nicaragua from communism, the money wasted on terrorism, sabotage, and attempts at destabilization could have been used instead to rebuild the Nicaraguan economy, with enough left for every Nicaraguan student to spend a year at Harvard.

U.S. policies—and overt intervention—actually brought about those conditions they were supposedly meant to prevent. One by one, the available options were reduced. Rigid stereotypical definitions of "Marxist-communist revolutionary ideology," coupled with simplistic cause-and-effect fantasies, closed doors on both sides of the conflict.

The Reagan administration propagandized U.S. public opinion with the fantasy that if the Contras were not supported, Central America would soon become a Soviet satellite. This was a factually insupportable cause-and-effect prediction. The SFP, of course, had little to do with communism but was a useful ploy in support of increased defense spending and corporate economic domination of Central America.

Similar self-fulfilling prophecies occurred in the early period of Arbenz's Guatemala, Castro's Cuba, and Allende's Chile. Vietnam, Cambodia, and Laos were, perhaps, the most tragic of U.S. self-fulfilling prophecies. The prediction of a communist takeover was virtually ensured by violent, ruthless U.S. intervention. Once the prophecy became fulfilled, the perpetrators confirmed their extraordinary good judgment for having predicted cause and effect. The final statement, "We told you so," always deleted the qualifier, "because we made it happen!"

Leaders who allege they will initiate change rarely change much of anything. They simply relabel the old with new words or phrases. Any attempt at abrupt socioeconomic-political change inevitably triggers counterreactions. Actual change, or what is perceptually measurable as change, constantly occurs with individuals, groups, and nations. But the enormously complex variables of social change make it utterly unpredictable, completely beyond the ability of anyone to control, understand, or even consciously recognize.

For example, criticism of communism is not a fight against communism. The words cannot lead to change. Words can actually make change more improbable. Criticism produces a defense that actually serves to strengthen the resolve of dissidents. Consider, for a moment, the effects of presidential rhetoric at a time of serious world tensions.

Ronald Reagan throughout his political career slandered the U.S.S.R. at every opportunity. In a widely quoted 1983 speech, he called the U.S.S.R. "the Evil Empire, the focus of evil in our time [alluding to the popular motion-picture fantasy *Star Wars*]. We are being told that we can sit down and negotiate with this enemy of ours, that there is a little right and a little wrong on both sides. How do you compromise between good and evil? How do you say to this enemy that we can compromise our belief in God with his dialectical determinism [philosophical jargon for what Soviets call scientific method]? How do you compromise with men who say we have no soul, there is no hereafter, there is no God?"

Demonstrating the power of stereotypes in U.S. political life, the disgraced former President Richard Nixon frequently admonished, "Communists are rats! When you try to kill a rat, you must know how to shoot straight!" Such statements by Nixon and Reagan had nothing to do with communism, but much to do with the gullibility of the U.S. public to whom they spoke.

Rhetoric like this has served many internal political objectives, not the least of which were increased taxation, military appropriations, and the diversion of public opinion away from real and significant issues. When the 280 million Soviets heard about Reagan's speech—Soviet leadership is far from stupid—they united behind their government. Resolve to oppose the U.S. was strengthened. Such rhetoric, which has continued for well over half a century, actually strengthened communism and the U.S.S.R. leadership's power, and sustained the dangerous status quo between the two nations.

These and similar when-then-because fantasies would be outrageously humorous examples of self-deception were it not that people die needlessly each year as a result. During a conversation about SFPs with a career diplomat, I asked, "If we know about

SFPs, why do we permit ourselves to be manipulated into such situations?" He replied, "Simply because we usually win. We invent and control the SFPs and are powerful enough to put them into motion. Even when we appear to lose, we win. When Castro, for example, appeared to win, he really lost. His presence, forty miles off the coast of Florida, justified continuing increases in U.S. military and economic appropriations. Such funding could never have been pushed through Congress without Castro." There always appears another layer to the perceptual onion.

It provides little consolation that any student of Soviet affairs could discover a rich harvest of SFPs in the U.S.S.R.'s internal and foreign policies of the past half century. It is frightening, indeed, to realize that world leaders are no more sophisticated or even knowledgeable about SFPs than the average man or woman.

Ad-Media SFPs

As manufacturer of cultural value systems, commercial mass media set up the society for a nightmare of unfulfilled and unfulfillable expectations, tragic self-fulfilling prophecies, and a myriad of self-sealing premises. Constant pandering through sensory manipulation devalues, dehumanizes, and mechanistically sexualizes everything that is sold or purchased. The self-fulfilling prophecies of the ad media, however, are the opposite of what they appear. The reverse, or negative, side of the expectation is fulfilled. Ads say little about products or brands. The pitch is based upon flattering, patronizing, idealized descriptions of consumers and what the product has done for them. Consumers are endlessly stereotyped as happy, fulfilled, successful, sexually desirable and available, independent, young, knowledgeable, and emotionally secure—a message of flattery. "Mirror, mirror on the wall, who is the fairest of them all?"

"Narcissus Narcosis" was Marshall McLuhan's description of the media-induced stupor where audiences sit mindlessly before the tube, projecting themselves into the video mirror. Narcissus was the Greek god who fell in love with his reflection in a pool of water. He was eventually destroyed by the wise, noble, kind, good, honest, and beautiful creature who smiled lovingly at him from the reflection. He never discovered he had fallen in love with himself.

The self-flattering platitudes of ad media are constant anesthesia against the intrusion of reality into daily life. The implied cause-and-effect reward for purchases is the healthy, handsome, good life with inexhaustible sexual opportunity and abundant sources of sensual gratification reflected by the highly paid, successful, idealized models—the most beautiful of people. Unfortunately for hapless consumers, these rewards are either nonexistent or unobtainable. Real life, as well as anyone can perceive it, is never this simple or consistent. The large-bosomed model cannot be sexually enjoyed or obtained along with the shoe polish she is employed to advertise. If consumers were really capable of thinking for themselves, as they believe they do, they would avoid any product hyped with large mammary glands as a lie. The only sensual indulgence available through an ad illustration would be a masturbatory fantasy.

Joyous, friendly, social acceptance as a strong, independent man or woman does not magically occur via the purchase of a light beer. Just the opposite is closer to reality. Most beer drinkers, especially those in bars, are lonely, isolated, dependent, insecure individuals. Ad models are paid to seem as though a drink or cigarette enhances their consummate social popularity. These fantasies are usually the opposite of the consumer's reality. That is the reason they work. Ads promise that if you buy the product, it will make up for your deficiencies. Uncertain individuals who fall into the ad trap are often conformists who constantly seek the fantasized adulation and approval conformity supposedly brings. The next time an opportunity arises, watch someone reveal their social apprehensions and dependence with a cigarette as a social prop. During the addiction-withdrawal period, anti-smoking clinics utilize videotapes of patients smoking as reinforcement. Smokers find these tapes emotionally very disturbing. Once the smoker perceives what other people have perceived—the ill-at-ease, dependent, nervous, infantile sucking behaviors involved in smoking—kicking the habit becomes easier.

Stereotypical role models from ads, motion pictures, TV, or rock music—perhaps desirable images on the surface—disintegrate into a nightmare of unfulfillable human expectations on close examination. The media image is a lie, but if not examined too carefully it promises eroticized fantasies vastly more enchanting and narcotizing than anything available in reality.

Consumers eventually discover the fantasies were merely hype, but blame themselves for their deficiencies. The good life never materializes, even after endless product purchases and loyalties. The unfulfilled promise must then be internalized. Consumers slowly acquire the self-perception of losers. Hopelessly entrapped in purchasing behavior syndromes, the well-trained consumer will buy something when depressed, disappointed, frustrated, angry, rejected, lonely, and bored, having been exhaustively trained to deal with problems of emotional adjustment through purchasing. But the expectations the ad promotes are never fulfilled. At best, relief is short-term. Effect becomes indistinguishable from cause— the snake again bites its tail. The well-integrated consumer perceives a world where everyone is getting it all—everyone, that is, except the loyal, generous, trusting, obedient consumer who has metamorphosed into a buying machine. Another product and brand is tried, another lover chosen, another social group discovered, a new hairstyle tried, another job found, another residence purchased, another fantasy pursued, and another, and another, and another . . . Reality perceptions fade and superimpose upon one another further and further into the fantasies of media.

False expectations ensure ultimate disappointment and failure— the diametric opposite of what the ad media presents. To the advertiser, fulfilled consumers are undesirable. Satisfied consumers might withdraw, disengage from the system, stop buying.

The Twentieth-Century Sisyphus

The consumer slowly evolves into a modern Sisyphus, trained to push the heavy boulder of hope for an identity, for purpose, acceptance, happiness, and fulfillment, to the summit of a steep hill. The boulder then rolls, once more, to the bottom. The consumer pushes it again to the top—again, again, and again until the end. The motto of a consumer society reads, "I consume, therefore I exist!" The expectations promoted by the ad media, which lead to the self-fulfilling prophecies, emphasize the shortcomings, deficiencies, and weaknesses individuals perceive in themselves. Negative self-esteem is constantly reinforced. The consumer evolves from loser into superloser.

Drug and alcohol addiction have their roots in ads. For nearly a century, the U.S. population was ad-educated to seek chemical solutions to problems of emotional adjustment. Booze, tobacco, pills, dope—all serve the same objective. There is no reason, the ads teach, to experience the slightest discomfort, depression, or pain. Be happy, well-adjusted, ever optimistic, tranquil, self-assured, socially accepted, and loved—on top of the world. If you cannot get there through alcohol, try tobacco, or pick up analgesics, antidepressants, tranquilizers, or happy pills of several dozen varieties. There is a drink or pill for every minor or major symptom. Once integrated, you do not need the symptom, only an *expectation* of the symptom. Ads introduced, rationalized, validated, legitimated, and authorized chemical-drug consumption at staggering levels. It is a very profitable business, except for users—many of whom end up as addicts.

Every political administration over the past century has, at least in words, taken a strong position against illegal drug usage. It is comparable to being against sin, child molestation, and welfare cheats. Legal drugs, that profitable business, are ignored. Distinction between *legal* and *illegal* is another of the perceptual fictions, but a real vote getter. At unconscious perceptual levels, where ads have their most powerful impact, consumers are propagandized to favor the good life you get from drug-chemical products. *Perceived product benefits*, not legal distinctions, motivate and enrapture consumers. While manufacturers and politicians play games with legalisms, ads milk consumers to accept and integrate drug-chemical consumption into U.S. culture.

As the consumption of *legal* drugs—alcohol, tobacco, and pharmaceutical products—proliferated over the past half century, so did the *illegal* drugs—marijuana, heroin, LSD, and more recently cocaine and crack. Illegal drug consumption in the U.S. is now estimated to be a $220 million daily business by the National Institutes of Health. It is curious no one in public life has noted the parallel increase in consumption of both legal and illegal drugs. Judicial distinctions have nothing to do with psychological distinctions. The death wish is regularly manipulated at the subliminal level by alcohol, tobacco, and pharmaceutical ads. The mere designation *illegal* provides powerful consumption appeal for many individuals. Illegal consumption is romantically perceived as an act of liberation from imposed restrictions, a defiance of authority. During 1986, there were an estimated 4 million cocaine addicts, with 5,000 new users added daily to the population.

The Chivas Regal "What's News?" ad appeared for over five years in numerous magazines—*Time, U.S. News & World Report, Newsweek, Business Week,* et cetera (fig. 27)—at an estimated cost of $4 to $5 million for space. With its copy, "Can you think of anything that gives you a better return on your investment?" the ad objective is to establish Chivas Regal as a complement to business, a large portion of which is supposedly conducted over Scotch. The return on your investment of time, effort, and entertainment will be improved with Chivas Regal twelve-year-old Scotch whiskey. The implied prophecy is success, money, power—approved objectives of business. Who could argue against the logic, truth, and good sense of such an ad, even though placed in a periodical context of frivolous appeals to sensuality, indulgence, and superficial distractions? Chivas drinkers are leaders who appreciate the best. Drinking Scotch smooths the climb to the top, helps ensure success. The prophecy appears clear, at least at one level of perception.

The *Wall Street Journal*, with its daily front-page feature, "What's News?" is an icon of business. The Chivas bottle beside it is open, the contents less than full. Presumably the Scotch on the rocks has just been poured. Curiously, the painted replica of the *Journal*, not the real thing, has been indistinctly lettered, as if out of focus. Except for the words *Business and Finance* and *World*, the lettering is obscured. Take a moment, though, to scan the newspaper image. See if you can read any other words.

The word *sluts* can be perceived in the third line of the headline in the left column. Part of a paragraph in the left-column story is distinct and readable, part undecipherable. One word in the text stands out, *banning*. These appear, at first, isolated and irrelevant words, but they have been carefully crafted into the newspaper replica. The words would never be perceived by a reader consciously. Unconsciously, however, even the smallest, most inconspicuous detail could be very important.

Painted obscurely into the ice cubes and glass are various skulls.

One is in the center left of the glass, anamorphically distorted (fig. 53). Another skull appears upside down under the liquid surface just left of center. Skulls and other dead imagery are common in alcohol ads. They appeal to the death wish.

Just to the right of the anamorphic skull appears a standing, robed figure, wearing a peaked cap (fig. 54). Few people wear peaked caps—Catholic bishops, cardinals, and the Pope. Kneeling before him appears a woman. Her face is surrounded by long hair, her shoulders are bare, her gown having slipped off her shoulders. The waist of her gown appears above her billowing skirt. The woman's right arm extends downward from her exposed shoulder, her forearm extends upward. She appears to be holding something with her right hand pointed at her open mouth.

Fellatio with the Pope in an ice cube: a bizarre subliminal strategy to manipulate consumers into the purchase of Chivas Regal Scotch. Most readers will find the embedded obscenity unsettling, at the very least. Considering the kind of world that has been constructed in the name of unrestrained enterprise, with every neighborhood boasting its so-called "adult bookstore," fellatio in an ice cube may have become a normal expectation.

One additional surprise appears in the Scotch on the rocks. Just to the right of the two figures appears a familiar version of Christ (fig. 55), patiently observing the action in the adjacent ice cube.

Though quite small in proportion to the bottle and glass, inconspicuously located, these images will be perceived instantaneously at the unconscious level by anyone who even glances at the ad. At no point in the perceptual process would meaning and significance emerge in conscious awareness. The obscene and taboo representations have a powerful and enduring unconscious effect on those who perceive the ad for even an instant. This ad would have its most powerful motivating effect upon individuals who have strong inhibitions about sex coupled with conservative religious convictions. The two perspectives often go together.

The real name of the game, of course, is sensual indulgence, the reward for success both in business and quality Scotch. The Scotch provides a transport to the "banned" "sluts" mentioned in the *Wall Street Journal*. The taboo world of sex, death, the Christ figure, the skulls, and self-destruction is an end to the hypocrisy and conflicting value systems of modern life. If the businessman happens to be going that way, as many appear to be, Chivas Regal—as the ad suggests—is the way to go. Chivas delivers!

At one level, the conventional road to success—work, preoccupation with Wall Street, business, and finance. On another level, self-destructive, guilt-ridden indulgence that invariably defeats success or achievement. Anyone in business, government, finance, or the professions today who is perceived a drinker turns on warning lights in the heads of peers and superiors. Contrary to ad misrepresentations, the alcohol drinker is publicly perceived as a pathetic loser, not as a great guy.

Simplistic, verbalized notions of cause and effect, if strongly believed, lead humans toward self-fulfilling prophecies. The SFP, once established, takes on a life of its own, creates its own reality, which would not have developed without the initial cause-and-effect assumptions. SFP expectations often bring about what was most feared and anticipated. Mathematician Nigel Howard offered a counterstrategy to SFPs: "If persons become aware of a theory concerning their behavior, they are no longer bound by the theory. They are free to disobey. The best theory is powerless in the face of antitheory."

10 | THE SELF-SEALING WORLD OF OBJECTIVITY

A truly objective world, totally devoid of all subjectivity, would—for that very reason—be unobservable.

Werner Heisenberg, Nobel Laureate in physics

Any form of *double entendre* reminds us that words, as well as people, are capable of hidden meanings, that the very language we use to communicate with each other is not always completely "sincere." Sincerity actually serves to conceal irony, understatement, wit, and deception.

Martin Evans, *America: The View from Europe*

The great enemy of truth is not the lie—deliberate, contrived, and dishonest—but the myth—persistent, persuasive, and realistic. Too often we hold fast to the clichés of our forebearers.

John Fitzgerald Kennedy,
Yale commencement address, 1962

Much of what is known about human communication was learned in clinical psychology and psychiatry. The most common symptom of known mental disorders is the impaired ability to utilize language effectively. As with many systems, language is revealed more profoundly through malfunctions than through more-or-less normal usage. Language behaviors perceived as normal may actually function quite abnormally in terms of survival and adjustment.

To understand ourselves, we must somehow understand others. But, to comprehend others, we must first learn to understand ourselves. Understanding can only be achieved through language. This law of communication is, of course, a paradox, an Ouroborus. Much, perhaps most, of our verbal and nonverbal language operates without conscious awareness. Even the most minute, subtle behaviors communicate information that defines and modifies relationships. Humans are far more perceptually sensitive than they wish to believe. Important information is constantly exchanged, a process of which neither sender nor receiver is consciously aware. Often, there is an unconscious desire to exclude or not deal with what is actually going on.

Humans can feel or sense, act or react, without words. Thinking, however, requires verbal or mathematical language—syntax, structure, definitions, both stated and implied meanings. These are perceived at both conscious and unconscious levels. To make the process even more complex, there appears no universal language system—one simple system through which everyone can make themselves understood. Languages are enmeshed within the cultural systems from which they evolved. All have similarities, as well as differences. The study of any language-cultural system is a formidable undertaking.

To find out what is going on at any particular moment in a language system—especially the one in which you participate—is extremely difficult. Observers can never be isolated from their observations. Humans are a part of what they perceive, abstract into language, and communicate to others. The relationship between language and the realities language attempts to describe—as it may or may not be consciously perceived—is a matter of more-or-less rather than either/or.

Humans, moreover, live at the mercy of influences they are

unconscious of and over which they have no control, but which powerfully affect their behavior and destinies. Though some may manage relationships more sensitively than others, there will always exist more that is unknown and unknowable than what is selectively perceived as known. Regardless of how cautious they might be, humans influence others and are influenced themselves by unconscious motives and strategies that might be unacceptable if consciously considered.

The most dangerous and destructive of human illusions is the assumption of objectivity—*one reality, one truth, one perspective* from which to perceive the world. Individual perceptions of reality have similarities and differences. Yet linguistically these variations are ignored, smoothed out, and fused together into a simplistic illusion. Objectivity myths become even more threatening when attached to ideological zeal that demands the world be enlightened—whether or not the enlightenment is desired. Objectivity is a myth both in science and everyday life, a fantasy that often controls day-to-day relationships.

Unconscious biases, traditional beliefs, and tacit assumptions strongly influence perceptions and decisions. Bias becomes critical when people convince themselves they are completely objective and have discovered "absolute truth." Objectivity assumptions entangle individuals in unknown and unknowable biases from which, once they are entrapped, it becomes difficult for them to liberate themselves. Conclusions achieved through ignorance, blindness, or indifference to perceptual processes should frighten everyone. As a practical matter, however, biased fantasies, delusions, and mythologies are often compulsively and popularly accepted as the real thing.

Illusions can be highly contagious. Once an explanation from a high-credibility source is believed and accepted, contrary information usually produces defensive, rationalized explanations of the myth. Such explanations become part of *self-sealing conjectures*, found in extremist, fanatical, ideological, religious, or political postures. These are assumptions that cannot be refuted. Refutations will be either ignored or rejected offhand. Conjecture based on fantasy becomes pseudoscientific superstition that can lead to neurotic or even psychotic behaviors among individuals or groups. Irrefutable conjecture has been responsible for a wide variety of tragedies, atrocities, and catastrophes throughout world history. Self-sealing premises lead to absolute certainties in such matters as racial superiority-inferiority, ideological pretensions, and prejudicial views of communists, capitalists, Jews, women, Catholics, Presbyterians, atheists, homosexuals, witches, and others perceived in a culture as deviants. Societies have, at various moments, tragically considered these prejudicial perceptual constructions *sane*, even though they often invoked *insane* behaviors.

Ideological Entrapments

When individuals or groups become committed to self-sealing premises, they are compelled to resist—often fiercely—counterinformation. They compulsively attack their critics. The committed ideologue's perceived simple solutions to complex problems have been achieved at the cost of anxiety and/or frustrated expectations. Psychological investment in the premise is very high. The risk that these solutions may be compromised, sacrificed, or modified becomes a threat to self-esteem, social prestige, and even identity. A self-fulfilling prophecy, predicated upon a perceptually fixed cause-and-effect illusion, has been triggered into action. The entire structure is a perceptual fantasy, a construction having little to do with reality-oriented perception. The self-sealing premise often appears an early symptom of emotional disturbance.

This describes, for example, what has occurred over decades between the U.S. and U.S.S.R. The adversaries are entrapped in self-sealing, self-fulfilling prophecies that sooner or later will probably destroy world civilization.

Ad media relentlessly create viable commercial investments for advertisers, who, in turn, create fantasy worlds where populations are immersed in what they have been persuaded to believe they wish to perceive about themselves. To optimize the returns on marketing investments, societies are divided and subdivided into demographic and psychographic categories, each marketed separately or in combinations. The process creates a tribal mode of self-perception and behavior. Society's perception of itself polarizes between "ins" and "outs"—they're either for us or against us, friends or enemies, moral or immoral. The scenario is acted out daily, in radio, TV, newspapers, and magazines. The tribe refuses to accede to goals that reflect common or mutual objectives. The fearful tribe may, for example, become increasingly resistant to appeals for restrained population growth. It may even race to outpopulate other societies.

The mechanism is currently apparent in antiabortion campaigns masquerading as morality crusades. Antiabortion beliefs are not the issue; they are only the up-front manifestation. Protesters are curiously aligned on a spectrum of issues—religious fanaticism, anticommunism, deviant-bashing, and a sense of being threatened from the outside. They represent a small minority within the U.S. population.

The tribe typically seeks to control internal and external resources politically, militarily, or diplomatically. Justice and liberty decline as the fear of outsiders and deviants intensifies or is perceptually intensified by the media. Threats, both real and fantasized, strengthen group identity. The tribe mobilizes its resources for action. Xenophobia becomes a political virtue. Nonconformists within the tribe are more severely punished and restricted.

The grim history of world civilizations, none of which escaped eventual extinction, provides a chilling chronicle of the tribal process. The tribe sooner or later goes to war, often disastrously for both winner and loser. No nation or society has ever been immune to the process. Tribal behavior may be an unconscious, biologically inherited human predisposition. Those involved, however, rarely discover consciously what is being done to them or what they are doing to themselves and others.

Day-to-day reality perceptions that support traditional cultural perspectives are just perceptual constructions—delusions that must continually be shored up and strengthened. A substantial portion of day-to-day energy and behavior must be devoted toward this end. Self-sealing premises, if they are to be sustained, usually require facts to be adapted to fit reality perceptions, instead of the other way around.

For example, to be anti-U.S.S.R. is to be pro-U.S. in the United States, and vice versa in the Soviet Union. All the nations in between also become entrapped in the system. If you are not for us, you are against us. Such constructions are usually designed by clever people who know better, for naïve people who do not. They are simply a technique of mass manipulation. You cannot trust the U.S.S.R., the U.S., or anyone uncommitted to one or the other. Soviet-bashing competes relentlessly with U.S.-bashing, or vice versa. Never forget the vice versa. All verbal fantasies are reversible, interchangeable, and mutually reinforcing. They are also completely childish—albeit deadly—nonsense.

The Friendly Slot Machine

The slot-machine player is another example of someone adapting facts to fit reality perceptions, a behavior mechanism common to most individuals, groups, or even nations. The mechanism has an ancient, unknown origin in human evolution and may be part of the human genetic inheritance.

Slot machines cannot be beaten. They are inexhaustible, mechanical-electrical, impersonal devices that operate strictly in terms of statistical probability. The casino gambling industry, through clever media manipulations, perpetuates the fantasy that "anyone can win." Only luck is required. Luck, as anyone familiar with the gaming industry knows, is for losers! The empirical, statistical facts of the slot machine are well concealed. An individual's statistical chance of leaving the casino ahead of the game is a small fraction of 1%. No professional gambler would accept odds so stacked against winning. Casinos do not gamble. In a gamble, outcomes are indeterminate. The outcome in a casino is always certain, always the same. Casinos know precisely what they are doing. The hapless, deluded clients actually play to lose. The only question in a casino is the length of time required.

Under the intense, media-managed expectation of winning, the slot-machine player begins to perceive patterns in the fruit displays. There seem to be regular patterns of near wins, combinational frequencies in the cherries, oranges, lemons, and bars. The perceptual fantasy is much like that of Dr. Skinner's crazy pigeons. Near wins become as rewarding as the actual wins that return coins. Players perceptually construct these patterns, invent them, fantasy-project their significance. To encourage and reinforce the process, new slot machines include electronic tunes—symbolic rewards—that play when certain near-win combinations occur. The tunes reinforce or cue the fantasized perceptions—like the electronic, controlled laughter injected into television comedies. When an actual win infrequently occurs, the electronic jingle becomes a virtual symphonic chorus.

The slot machine is the ultimate money-milking machine. Curiously, these machines are perceived by their victims as fair, objective, even friendly adversaries. Some players personalize the machines into which they pump their money with human names or attributions. Anthropomorphic projections are encouraged by casino ads. One large Reno billboard boasted, "The hottest slots in the West!" An attractive model is posed on a table corner next to the slot machine, her legs suggestively spread apart, her genital area exposed.

Entire social, political, and economic systems are similarly organized around near-win reward systems. Product salesmen, ad executives, politicians, and others with something to sell frequently design these reward systems, which operate like the carrot on a stick that keeps the jackass (loser) moving along. Wherever rewards are infrequent, management objectives focus on keeping players in the game.

Military intelligence is similarly designed. We watch them watching us watch them trying to control the cherries, lemons, and oranges they hope will appear to *us* as real information. They, in turn, watch us watching them watch us trying to control the cherries, lemons, and oranges we hope will appear to *them* as real information. Meanwhile, both sides hop about like Skinner's pigeons—one side's absurd actions to the other's absurd reactions. The extremely dangerous trouble in the silly game is the known, unknown, and unknowable fruit that keeps turning up. Each side jiggles their fruit to outwit the other, and ends up outwitting themselves. People who take either the CIA or the KGB seriously also probably believe they can win in Las Vegas, that Coke is the "real thing," or that Wheaties is "the breakfast of champions."

In the slot machine, the fruit and bar patterns are totally random and meaningless. The machines simply follow their programmed, statistical payout rules. Anything else perceived about a slot machine is pure fantasy. Among compulsive gamblers—gambling is highly addictive—the machines appear to possess an inner life and function with predictable regularity. These individuals, committed to self-sealed premises achieved at substantial costs in anxiety and expectations, cannot be persuaded otherwise. Their self-sealing convictions are rewarded often enough by actual or symbolic rewards—just often enough to keep them playing. Actual money rewards, nevertheless, are always a minuscule portion of the players' investment.

The need to search consciously and unconsciously for cause-and-effect patterns, regularities within perceptual environments, lies deep within the circuitry and chemistry of the brain. Individuals, unaware of the infinite variety of perceptual realities or options always available, assume there is only *one* reality, *one* cause, *one* interpretation, *one* option, *one* objective, *one* course of action. Their sealed premises are usually supported by others similarly entrapped.

Anyone who presents alternative options risks being considered evil, insane, or subversive. It is next to impossible to explain to an addicted player how a slot machine operates. Your explanation, no matter how well intentioned, will provoke defensive aggressiveness.

It appears virtually impossible to convince a government bureaucrat that the only way to win the dangerous, prolonged struggle between communism and capitalism—a perceptual struggle constructed for power and profit—is simply not to play the game. This conclusion would drastically rearrange profit and power structures on both sides. The conflict endures because certain groups on both sides are served by it. The consciously perceived, or alleged, reasons for the conflict have nothing to do with what is really going on.

During the course of over 300 research projects this author conducted for private corporations and governments, it became apparent that problem-solving was rarely a simple, objective enterprise. The notion that "truth" resolved problems was naïve in the extreme. Institutions hire expensive consultants and research specialists to confirm or reject decisions, perspectives, and perceived truths already apparent. Many institutions will accept failure or even annihilation before agreeing to reconceptualize their dilemmas and paradoxes. During corporate crises, this author usually attempted to provide at least three—preferably more—alternative solutions to each problem under study, each one more or less equally constructive and applicable. A fourth option was usually added to the basic three at no additional cost: Do nothing! Permit the problem, or the perception of the problem, to work itself out. The fourth option was never acceptable. It was rarely an option anyone was willing to pay for, even though it might have resolved the dilemma. Managements compulsively insisted upon the correct and most profitable solution. Such simplistic perceptual conclusions continue to be responsible for countless failures in business, industry, and government throughout the world.

A perceived structure or pattern easily becomes a self-reinforcing delusion. Once the seemingly reasonable, often "scientific" premise has been accepted, delusions follow, through logical deductions. The self-sealed premise often takes on a life of its own. However, in terms of reality—or reality-oriented perceptions—it is usually not the truth or falsity of a delusion that is important; the delusion succeeds because of its mere existence or apparent rewards.

To manipulate reality on behalf of an objective, mere *suspicion* about an alternative's validity is often powerful enough. In the media competition for consumers or in political candidates' competition for voters, great effort is expended to create credible suspicion about opponents. Even minor doubts, once established, can expand effectively. One big lie, of course, feeds back into another big lie. Reality engineering is a major growth industry. Factual evidence is usually unnecessary, often undesirable. The more exaggerated the story, the more believable it can become if properly legitimized. Fact-oriented perceptions become Silly Putty in the hands of anyone who understands perceptual vulnerabilities and how to exploit them.

People generally cannot believe themselves so easily manipulated and controllable. This is precisely why they are so easy to manipulate and control.

Cultural or ideological systems are engineered like casino slot machines. The conviction that members have free choice or volition, once established, makes them even less aware of contradictions, qualifications, and paradox. A substantial majority of citizens in both the U.S. and U.S.S.R., for example, believe their societies are free, democratic, and concerned with human rights. The question is of itself a conditioning device, though complete nonsense in any reality-oriented perception. Both societies ignore or observe human rights when doing so serves some internal or external objective. The question is a matter of more-or-less, rather than either/or. Facts by the trainload could be generated to validate or discredit the view of either society. Yet each side believes with religious fervor its world is superior. The argument is comparable to two small boys arguing over who has the largest penis and finally over whether the comparisons will be made in the flaccid or tumescent state, or somewhere in between.

Reality Is a Drag

Human history reveals a disturbing human inability to deal with reality-oriented perceptions—to comprehend empirical data, the rhetorical nature of questions, and complex arrays of the conscious and unconscious motives underlying arguments.

It appears far easier for humans to fantasize and project responsibility for decisions on some mystical principle, ideology, fate, secret metaphysical power, God, a prophet of God, or an omniscient, charismatic leader. Humans rarely consider that chance or probability—coupled with a handful of basic human needs and always limited resources controlled by ruling power elites—guide world destinies, have done so throughout history, and will likely continue to do so in the foreseeable future. Morality and justice usually depend upon the power to enforce rather than upon intellectual discourse, and so do perceptual realities.

As discussed, perceptual realities appear to exist on at least three levels: *macro, micro,* and *submicro.* At each level, perceptions can be measured and verified by more-or-less standard scales, calibrations, devices, mathematical relationships, and conscious agreements on these standards. Physical and biological properties can be established by experimental, repeatable, and verifiable proofs or refutations. Very few problems between humans cannot be resolved at this fact-oriented level of reality perception. The nightmares in human communication stem from an inability to agree on meanings, values, evaluations, perspectives, syntheses, and analyses. The rules are completely arbitrary. The fantasy of eternal truth frequently appears. Absurd arguments erupt over what really *is* and *is not*, and once verbally resolved, self-sealing premises take over.

The dilemma of human objectivity has often been portrayed in the arts. Lawrence Durrell's superb *Alexandria Quartet* tells the story of an exotic Middle Eastern woman from the unique, quite different perceptual realities of her lover, husband, physician, friends, and enemies. Japanese filmmaker Akira Kurosawa's masterpiece *Rashomon* also probed subjectivity in the story of a rape told from the perspectives of the four individuals involved. Franz Kafka, the master of paradox, made perceptual variations of reality the basis for much of his literary work. Kafka's novel *The Trial* is one of the most disturbing expositions of perceptual relativity, paradox, and double binds. A man is tried for a crime but never discovers the charges, the witnesses, or the reasons for his conviction. He finally becomes convinced of his own guilt without discovering the nature of his crime.

One of the most discomforting expositions of perceptual reality appeared in the eighteenth-century works of the infamous, though curiously—perhaps insanely—brilliant, French Marquis D. A. F. de Sade. De Sade's writings never clarified for the reader whether they reflected *fantasy* or *reality*, or where one merged into the other. In his most well-known work, *Justine*, he wrote, "The mirror sees the man as beautiful, the mirror loves the man; another sees the man as frightful and hates him; and it is always the same being who produces the impressions." De Sade's attacks on *objective reality* and the conventional wisdoms of his day outraged France. His books were burned. His downfall was ensured by literary treatments of sadism and masochism—the most forbidden of literary themes. (The modern word *sadism* was derived from his name.) De Sade perceived that sadomasochistic potentialities were inherent in most humans. Though history does not verify his actual participation in these bizarre behaviors, de Sade was condemned to live most of his life in asylums.

In spite of reality-oriented information, even from high-credibility sources, humans are persistently reluctant to turn loose traditional reality perceptions. As has often been demonstrated over the centuries, cultures hold to perceptual fantasy constructions until death. In the world's history, few humans have been deterred by force, the threat of force, or even death. In spite of this, nations continue to believe brute force is the best way to control dissent and deviance. In fact, brute force ensures dissent and deviance. Societies persist in this fantasy even when the only conceivable reward is self-annihilation.

Your Asylum or Mine

All behaviors communicate reciprocally. Problems arise when misrepresentations, lies, or misinformation are introduced into the system, consciously or unconsciously, purposefully or accidentally. Since meaningful goals are rarely achieved without trust, awareness of manipulation is often repressed. At the unconscious level, though, lies are difficult to conceal. The manipulated usually know they are being manipulated, at some level of perception.

If a certain deception is perceived only by a small, low-status minority, the majority will consider them deviants—insane or bad. No matter how provable their allegations of deceit, deviants will likely be considered in need of therapy, punishment, or exclusion. In situations where the deceit is demonstrable in terms of reality-oriented perceptions, debriefing or therapy may entail reality distortions to refocus deviant perceptions to fit those of the majority. Should majority behavior be insane, attempts will be made to turn deviant minorities from sanity toward insanity. The process is apparent in educational, military, social, economic, and political institutions—and often appears a normal expectation of daily life.

Majority consensus is an overwhelming social force. Consensus is courted by every power structure in the world and is engineered by mass-media ads and public-relations techniques. The human need to be accepted—no matter how absurd or destructive such acceptance may be—extends deeply into the one basic imperative: *survival and adjustment.* There appears an innate willingness to compromise individual perceptions in favor of what appears—or is constructed to appear—as group consensus. Unfortunately, however, intellectual, social, and economic systems depend for new ideas, growth, and survival upon deviant innovators, not conformists.

The famous *double bind* is another usually conscious vehicle for behavioral disaster. In the double-bind situation, you are damned if you *do* something and equally damned if you *do not*. The double bind is a product of self-sealing premises that usually operate at a nonconscious level.

Anthropologist Gregory Bateson tells the story of a New Guinea tribe that held an annual festival with neighboring tribes during which men dressed as women, wild alcoholic binges ensued, and sexual restraints were unleashed. It was, apparently, quite a party. When well-intentioned Christian missionaries arrived, they perceived the annual orgy as sinful, the work of the devil. They persuaded the tribe to abolish the festival. The tribe soon began murderous conflicts with other tribes. The annual orgy had served to resolve intertribal tensions for many generations. Now tribesmen were damned by the missionaries if the festivals continued and condemned to homicidal conflicts if they did not.

The double bind is a no-win paradox in which astonishing numbers of humans spend portions of their lives, while the problem remains consciously unrecognized. In economically developed nations, some double-bind victims eventually find themselves in mental hospitals. In the underdeveloped world, they often become insurgents.

God's greatest irony was inflicted in the Garden of Eden. He generously equipped humans to enjoy erotic, sensual pleasures and fulfillments. He then capriciously expelled Adam and Eve from the garden and forbade them unrestrained play with their delightful toys under a threat of eternal damnation. The original sin described in Genesis may have been the first double bind. It is still with us.

At least four variations of the double bind regularly appear in human relationships. They are perpetuated by the ad media and have evolved as consciously unnoticed aspects of culture.

Perceptual Validity Questioned

Often individuals or groups make a generally valid reality-oriented perception about their world and are subsequently punished for it by a significant high-credibility authority. This double bind often occurs between husbands and wives, parents and children, employers and employees, media and audiences, leaders and followers. Humans conditioned by contradictory perceptual interpretations find it difficult to behave appropriately. Self-enforced, delusionary perceptions usually prevail.

The media or other authority sources tell you repeatedly they would not lie to you, they always tell you the truth. You then repeatedly catch them in lies, misrepresentations, and deceitful manipulations. Your first option—if you continue to play the game—is to accept the lies as truths, to adapt your perception to their fraudulent reality. Eventually, however, you may become confused and distraught. Repression of the contradictory reality may come to the rescue. Conscious knowledge of the lie disappears from the surface. The second option is confrontation, which is difficult if the liars are parents, mates, presidents, trusted ad media, or other valued information sources—very difficult indeed.

Some individuals reject the high-credibility source of the lie, walk away, and search for other less potentially damaging relationships. Anyone who states he or she would never lie to you has just told a whopper. There are, of course, lies of omission, commission, and interpretation. Individuals lie continuously, even if only to themselves about not lying.

Opting out of the system may be extremely difficult, if not impossible. Unable to disconnect, individuals spend much time attempting to discover how reality should be perceived, from which perspective—the incessant and always unfulfilled search for truth. Tell me, what *is* "love," "truth," "life," "faith," "democracy," "freedom," the best toothpaste, automobile, cigarette, underarm deodorant, et cetera? The search often appears in evangelical and born-again religious ritual: "God told me . . ."

Sanity in an Insane Situation

Another double-bind example often appears in hijack and hostage situations. During confinement, hostages who attempt to cooperate and to understand their captors' perceptions (psychotic though the terrorists may be) are labeled traitors, brainwashed cowards, and weak-willed sycophants upon release. Their behavior and perceptions of their situation, nevertheless, were quite sane, reality-oriented in the interest of survival and adjustment, within a totally insane situation.

Reasonable prisoner behavior appears unreasonable to those outside the situation. Military organizations utilize a debriefing process for released prisoners. Debriefing is a systematic reorientation from a reality/survival perception (sanity, perhaps) consistent with the perceptions of those on the outside. Yet outsiders can never really comprehend the fear, exhaustion, anxiety, hopelessness, and intense desire to survive prisoners must endure in confinement.

Be Grateful!

A third type of double bind occurs when people are expected to feel differently than they actually feel. Guilt and self-condemnation result when people are expected to feel something they do not or when they feel something they are not supposed to. Instead of gaining approval for what they perceive as honest feelings, they are punished. The paradox can be expressed as, "After all I (or we) have done for you! You should at least be grateful, happy, proud, loyal, loving, faithful, sexual, patriotic, devout, trusting, obedient, agreeable" . . . ad infinitum. This paradox, like that of the appropriate-inappropriate behavior of the prisoner or hostage, can result in depression or worse. When individuals feel responsible for behavior over which they have little control, inconsistent with the expectations that surround them, they can become ill. The double bind can evolve into a shattering neurosis from its origin as a normal response to an abnormal situation. The media abounds in such hidden, unconscious entrapments.

Do, but Don't

When significant high-credibility authorities—leaders, employers, parents, spouses, friends, governments, ideological or cultural systems—both *demand* and *prohibit* actions, policies, thoughts, or behaviors, individuals become trapped in a double bind. They can obey only by disobeying. This paradox takes such forms as:

Win by any means, but always be honest!

Do what I say, not what you think you should do!

Truthfulness is always the best policy, but business is business!

Individualism, survival of the fittest, is a basic law of nature. Restrictions upon freedom kill initiative and are un-American. But people should work for common purposes, and stand loyally together. Individuals should not live only for themselves!

Be successful, but the kind of person you are is more important than success!

The family is America's basic, sacred institution, but national welfare depends upon business, so other institutions must conform to business!

Democracy is the basis for freedom and equality, yet nothing would ever get done if left to popular vote. No businessperson or employer would tolerate collective decisions!

Human beings are rational and can be trusted to do the right thing, yet some are brighter than others so you can't wait for them to make up their minds!

Religion and the pursuit of a better life are our ultimate objectives, but we owe it to ourselves to make as much money as possible!

We believe in progress and new ideas, yet the old fundamentals are best. Rapid change must be avoided!

The great challenge of capitalism and/or communism is to escape the rules of that way of life.

Capital and labor are partners, but avoid paying higher wages than necessary.

Education is good, but practical people get things done!

Women are sacred, but not very practical, and inferior in their reasoning power and abilities.

Patriotism and public service are the highest ideals, but individuals must look out for themselves!

Double-bind demands cannot be fulfilled. Consider the commands: "Be spontaneous!" (spontaneity cannot be ordered); "Be sexual!" (physiology is not subject to verbal commands); or "Treat

242

all people as equals!" (an instruction from a superior); "Be permissive!" (to obey is obedience).

Consider the Zen proverb:

> *To think I am not going*
> *To think of you anymore,*
> *Is still thinking of you.*
> *Let me try not to think*
> *I am not going to think of you.*
> *But this, of course, is still*
> *Thinking of you.*

Commercial artists have traditionally played games with audience perceptions of objectivity and reality. Their goals were usually money, profit, fame, status, power, or all of the above. Madison Avenue refined the game with enormous investments and high technology, but they did not invent it. Norman Rockwell, commercial artist par excellence, constructed his creations around every self-sealing premise alive and well among the older, middle-class, WASP, conservative, sentimental, and conformist U.S. population. He knew his audience intimately and exploited their illusions mercilessly.

These illusions of self are not reality-oriented; they may in fact sharply contradict reality perceptions. Rockwell ingeniously constructed a world that never was but one his audience desperately needed to idealize and believe had once existed. Projective fantasies appeal to people whose current reality lacks luster and romance. The fantasy is created by regression, moving back to an idealized past. Of course, in earlier periods, people idealized an even earlier time.

In a sentimental appeal to traditional middle-class values, the world's richest artist (a vital criterion of artistic worth) created an expensive porcelain Mother's Day plate (fig. 28). As every child feels some guilt for leaving mother after maturation, the symbol of motherhood has long been used to manipulate consumer behavior. The sales brochure describes the plate painting—*Mother's Blessing*—as, "A rare Rockwell scene that never will be found among magazine covers, posters, or story illustrations. Its illumination and contrast are reminiscent of Renaissance masterpieces.

But the faces are unmistakably Norman Rockwell. Perhaps the most sensitive Mother's Day art ever issued." The brochure's slick sales hype is designed to extract a sizable fortune from consumers trained to accept uncritically media at face value. The lush ad copy might even evoke tears. Maudlin sentimentality, "corn" in media jargon, is a powerful weapon.

In the Rockwell painting, the mother's left hand rests not on the top but on the back of her daughter's head. In terms of movement, she appears to be directing the child's gaze toward the arms of the boy, presumably her older brother. The brother's hands are clasped in prayer, his eyes closed, his forearms making a V. If the painting is turned on its left side, the boy's forearm looks curiously constructed. Block out all the other details in the painting and carefully study the right forearm in isolation (fig. 56). The erect genital is not as dramatically detailed as in the Tanqueray gin ad (fig. 31), but the motive was similar—to sell, to sell, to sell, to sell . . .

The Bigallo Crucifix with Saints (fig. 29), tempera on wood, was painted circa 1240–70 by an anonymous Italian. The embed, which should be readily apparent, is similar to that in the Tanqueray Gin ad (fig. 31), though not as skillfully crafted; the air brush would not be invented for another seven centuries. The Bigallo Crucifix is presently owned by the Art Institute of Chicago. It is curious how time can add value to something perceived as art. Religious art has always been crassly merchandised throughout the world. It is remarkable that this example survived 750 years, ending up in one of the world's most prestigious museums. The reader should keep in mind this crucifix (a symbol) has nothing to do with Christianity, Catholicism, or Jesus Christ. It was painted simply to sell, and indeed it sold—over and over for three-fourths of a millennium. The icon is presently valued at over half a million dollars. The Bigallo Crucifix is as remote from Christianity as the Rockwell painting. Indeed, both works are travesties—private jokes about human perceptual gullibility. But, they sold, and sold, and sold, and are still selling.

Vertically on the Christ figure's tortured body appears an embedded male genital (fig. 57). The face displays humorously pained resignation, as though he carried the weight of the world (fig. 58). Had the genital been consciously perceived, it is doubtful whether the work would have survived seven and a half centuries.

The artist would have ended his career in a heretic's execution had his repressed embed become conscious among viewers. The saint on the left stares directly at the erect penis with an expression of awe and humility, touched perhaps with envy.

Considering the energy currently expended in the study of human communication, it is amazing that subliminal techniques are so little known to people other than the artists who use them. The reasons such chicanery remains hidden say more about human pretensions and avarice than most wish to deal with consciously. The manipulated are willing victims often because of their expectations of gain.

"We thought we knew what we were doing, but there was that small problem of subliminal motivations and perceptions!" This could become the epitaph of world civilization embedded in the last nuclear fireball.

Sealed for an Eternity

The scattered load of passengers settled into their seats for the three-hour flight from Houston to Los Angeles. The U.S. Air Force major in the next seat smiled warmly as he ordered a dry martini. A large man with a rugged, heavy face and a warm, easy smile, he reminded me of a character from a Norman Rockwell painting.

"Stationed in Los Angeles?" I asked.

"Lompoc, a hundred miles north," he replied.

I noticed the two-and-a-half-inch-long silver missile pinned to his tunic. "Missile commander?" I ventured.

He smiled with a trace of pride and nodded. Over the next two hours, the conversation was warm, cordial, and interesting. We exchanged pictures of our wives, our children, even our houses. Both of us were roughly the same age, with the same level of income and education. I had spent four and a half years in the air force during World War II.

Since the beginning of our conversation, I had wondered about the major's job. I hesitated to draw a subject loaded with security questions into a casual conversation between strangers. But I had never met anyone who spent his working life buried in a vault deep underground, training incessantly for the day he would turn a key that launched multiple-warhead missiles at human populations thousands of miles away. The major brought up the subject.

"I'm going for early retirement next year. Twenty years in the military is enough for one lifetime." He described an executive job offer from an aerospace company.

"Ever regret staying in the air force?" I asked.

"All of us do sometimes," he answered. "But it's been a good life, especially with the missiles. They don't transfer us around like the rest. Family housing and allowances are good, promotions virtually automatic. They prefer men with families—more settled, reliable, more dedicated to the job. They give us plenty of free time."

"What about duty in a control bunker?" I asked, trying to appear casual as I talked toward the subject of his work.

There was only a momentary trace of guarded apprehension on his face after the question. He spoke matter-of-factly. "Not much to it. Really! Once you memorize the procedures, you only have to keep up with changes and new gadgets. All you need is a good memory."

"Ever have any doubts about turning the launch key?" I asked, keeping my voice casual, mildly interested.

"No, none at all," he answered. "If they had any doubts about us, we'd never be assigned to missiles. When word comes down, we launch. Simple as that! Besides, at that point you're so busy there's no time to think about anything other than the job. They train us not to think about people. No sense getting yourself upset. It's just a job. We're only technicians. We do what we're told."

Our conversation rambled on until the plane lost altitude for our L.A. landing. We talked about mundane problems of raising teenagers, the cost of living, and airline dinners. The talk was light, friendly, relaxed, and only a few borderline controversial topics were touched on. We shook hands as we parted at the terminal gate.

For many months after this encounter with the missile commander, I could not get him off my mind. I had run head-on into a cultural double bind. The major would probably be described by his neighbors as an average person, nothing remotely outstanding, spectacular, or unusual about him. He appeared to be a father devoted to his family and children, a good husband in every respect—sober, hard-working, modestly ambitious, an apparently kind, respectable person whose morality, sanity, and loyalty to his country would never be questioned—neither by the major himself, by his employers, nor by the world in which he lives.

The stark contradiction between what society has been indoctrinated to perceive as an outstanding citizen and the horror this one was prepared to initiate on the command of some faceless higher authority—communicated via an unsensing, unfeeling computer—illustrated the central question in human survival today. Individuals in the U.S. and U.S.S.R., and numerous other nations, have been exhaustively brainwashed to hide from themselves the reality of their vocations. This reality lies hidden behind carefully repressed reality associations, technological labels, carefully selected euphemisms, and patriotic slogans: "nuclear deterrent," "keeping the peace," "freedom's guardians," et cetera.

It is not easy to compare U.S. and U.S.S.R. missile commanders to the mindless bureaucrats who ran Nazi death camps. The Nuremberg war-crimes trials, and later Adolf Eichmann's trial in Tel Aviv, revealed a vitally important insight few observers recognized at the time. The SS and Gestapo, by the highest standards of loyalty, honor, and patriotism of their day, were superpatriots. Their dedication and sacrifice were qualities legitimized within German society by an uncritical, self-preoccupied population that benefited—at least in the early years—from repressed reality perceptions. The SS were considered brave, honorable, noble, even deeply religious patriots who served their nation, leaders, ideology, and perceived sacred mission to the end. Patriots such as these exist in every nation, certainly in the U.S. and U.S.S.R. This should frighten everyone, but it will not as long as the world persists in its perception of war criminals not as simple-minded, obedient fools but as special villains or psychopaths.

Paradox invariably confuses the herd mentality trained only to superficially evaluate the obvious. Once the keys have been turned in the missile-control centers, of course, it won't make any difference. The "objective realities" that everyone believed justified the ultimate sacrifice will not be around anymore. No humans will be left to perceive reality as objective. The self-sealing premises will finally have been sealed for eternity.

> *A man who specializes in killing other men—*
> *regardless of ideology—is an assassin!*
>
> Jorge Luis Borges,
> *Fervor de Buenos Aires*

II | THE PERMANENTLY CLOSED MIND

Reality is nothing but the free choice of one of many
doors that are open at all times.

Hermann Hesse, *Steppenwolf*

We must remember that we do not observe nature
as it actually exists, but nature exposed to our methods of perception (ways of seeing). The theories determine what we can or cannot observe.

Albert Einstein, *The Meaning of Relativity*

Skepticism and scientific conviction exist in modern
man side by side with old-fashioned prejudices, out-
dated habits of thought and feeling, obstinate misinterpretations, and blind ignorance.

Carl G. Jung, *Man and His Symbols*

Sophisticated development of persuasion technology over the past half century changed the old rules of human communication. As ad and public-relations industries became more skillful in the management of public opinion, attitudes, beliefs, and value systems, it became increasingly imperative to keep secret and enable the population to repress awareness of what the manipulators were up to. Perceptual management cannot succeed if acknowledged, so perceptual controls at conscious and unconscious levels proliferated. Research into language and culture were successfully sidetracked into intellectually sterile, irrelevant directions. Behaviorism in the social and behavioral sciences fitted well the ideological objectives of commercial media. Behaviorism as a scientific or quasi-religious doctrine ensured the social sciences would exhaust themselves endlessly with trivial, inconsequential research that rarely conflicted with the status quo—the best of all possible worlds. Cognitive psychology, sociology, and anthropology became dominant scholarly perspectives. Behaviorism disavowed the existence of the unconscious, terming it "mentalist." The unconscious has virtually disappeared in North America as a topic of study outside the mass-communications industry.

Media-manipulation technology and passive, muted, trivia-preoccupied social sciences are mutually reinforcing cultural characteristics. As U.S. society became increasingly saturated by commercial, manipulative media, scholars legitimized the fantasy that such manipulation was impossible, that the freedom-loving U.S. was invulnerable to propaganda. The population thought, as it was taught to think, that it thought for itself. Contradiction and paradox in this simplistic logic was dismissed or ignored. Besides, the media bombarded the population with fairy-tale assurances that they never lied, could always be trusted, were free of bias and vested interest and diligently served the cause of freedom and democracy.

Every part of a cultural system is magnificently complementary—like beautiful precision mechanisms in an expensive mechanical watch. Every tiny part and function is inextricably integrated and supportive of every other part and function. Cultures integrate themselves in ways, however, that are often nonlinear, nonverbal, extremely complex and subtle, and most difficult to perceive consciously. There is also a time delay. Values appearing today may not become nationally visible for ten to forty years.

National educational systems usually reflect values of the prevailing socioeconomic systems. If greed, acquisitiveness, selfishness, and self-indulgence are fundamental to the economy, education adapts its focus accordingly. The single most dramatic change in education over the past thirty-five years has been the steady growth of get-a-job courses, coupled with the rapid decline in learn-to-read, -write, -mathematize, and -think courses. Through World War II, U.S. education was viewed as an agent of socioeconomic-cultural change. Essays of distinguished educators from the 1930s and '40s—such as Robert M. Hutchins's *The Higher Learning in America* (on liberal arts education)—today appear as anachronistic idealism out of step with contemporary realities. Today's marketable educational commodity is superficial and simplistic. Self-indulgence and self-aggrandizement are now fundamental philosophical premises. The status quo, the best of all possible worlds, has become the model for change. School systems have become indoctrination centers where students are trained, rather than educated, to fit in, find their place, certainly not to challenge the system or the unknown. The media-cultured, indulgence-demanding U.S. university student is almost unique in the world. Education is still a highly competitive privilege in Asia, Europe, and especially in the U.S.S.R.

A major 1986 study by the Carnegie Foundation for the Advancement of Teaching revealed that over 90% of university students and 88% of their parents saw the primary reason for higher education as careerist—jobs, money, and success. Only 28% of parents and 27% of high school students saw education as a means to pursue scholarship, thoughtful citizenship, and a well-rounded education as a foundation for life experiences. The study was titled *Colleges: The Undergraduate Experience in America*. It revealed that only 19% of humanities students have guaranteed jobs upon graduation, compared with 90% for business majors. Student employment preoccupation is foolish but is used as a recruiting or marketing device by schools. One University of Texas dean commented they could not publish a catalogue course description and title unless it appeared to relate directly to employment. During their lifetimes, university graduates will hold dozens of jobs. Job skills constantly change and rapidly become obsolete. To waste valuable and expensive educational years studying for a job, which often does not exist upon graduation, squanders precious resources and is folly.

Nevertheless, bachelor's degrees in business subjects doubled from 114,865 in 1971 to 230,031 in 1984. BAs in English and literature plunged from 57,026 to 26,419. Various universities dropped such subjects as classical languages, geology, and music education. Many severely curtailed studies in philosophy, languages, literature, and history in favor of such trivia as hotel and restaurant management courses.

The Carnegie study cited numerous shortcomings in the typical undergraduate experience:

1. An absent, limited, or confused view of scholarship, science, research, the traditions of knowledge, and the enrichment of human life from learning.
2. A wide, generalized inability among university students to adequately read, write, and think.
3. Fragmented, disjointed course structures where topical, superficial specializations replace depth of insight.
4. Widespread faculty acquiescence to the legitimization of banal course and curriculum content. Excellence in critical, analytical teaching is generally ignored in favor of conformity, upon which promotions and tenure often hang.
5. A separation and downgrading of required undergraduate education from the narrowly focused courses in the major. General education courses are often taught by the least qualified and most poorly compensated faculty.
6. The objectives of higher education have become confused and degraded. Goals are rarely discussed; if mentioned at all, they are expressed in terms of current employment opportunities—jobs, money, and success.

Similar criticisms of U.S. university education have recently come from such authoritative sources as the Association of American Colleges, the National Institute of Education, and the Office of the U.S. Secretary of Education. Higher education has converted itself into an overly merchandised system of trade schools. Careerist-oriented institutions are generally course-deficient in languages, arts, history, study of social and government institutions, and in the natural and physical sciences, where mere technology is considered science. Studies of moral or ethical issues are virtually nonexistent.

Universities are often cultural captives of the media-dominated marketing culture. Pandering to public approval, ad media view outstanding intelligence as abnormal. Intelligence must be made to appear stupid. Stupidity is often celebrated as outstanding intelligence. The confused, impractical intellectual is a well-published and broadcast stereotype. Moral individuals are likewise regarded as simpletons. Nonentities become models of virtue. Those who struggled toward new truths are viewed as naïve or seditious.

U.S. education certainly has not equipped average citizens to deal with manipulative media technology in their lifelong environment. Just the opposite: Education has conditioned the population to become victims, trained to fit into the commercial culture as passive, obedient consumers. Ad media quietly changed the rules of logic, reason, and the human perception of human perception. Along the way, few attempts were made to probe what was going on. Critics probably would not have been believed, in any event. This was a clever accomplishment, difficult to expose, and very good business. Media sustained the audience's illusions that all was well, that nothing had changed except for the better as everyone became smarter, better informed, more perceptive, more able to think for themselves.

The Well-Washed Brain

In 1989 a person in the U.S. confronted a cultural saturation of almost $150 billion of ad propaganda. This media investment usually increases by 10% to 15% annually. The ad investment in cultural propaganda does not include vast amounts spent for promotion, public relations, and other manipulative media technologies.

No nation in the history of the world has ever been so exhaustively propagandized, in quality, quantity, intensity, and technological innovativeness. The individual who seeks to survive this super con confronts a formidable adversary. After all the brand and product purchase shifting occurs, this massive annual investment supports an integrated, interlocking cultural value system.

For the very few, there may exist the possibility of an isolated tropical paradise devoid of media. Most people simply cannot afford to drop out. They must seek some way to sustain sanity in the media madhouse. Defensive strategies against brainwashing are relatively simple. They would probably work best, however, if initiated during early childhood.

Always Act to Increase the Number
of Options Available

Most individuals have been educated from childhood to decrease the number of options—to seek out *truth*. Any commitment to one single view takes on ideological significance, as sales hype for a toothpaste, a religion, or a political candidate. There are multiple answers to every question, problem, or objective. Seek them out. Find at least three, preferably five, even ten, or more. Opt tentatively for the option that appears most likely to succeed for your desired objective. Be prepared to jettison it in favor of another, at any moment, if disaster threatens.

Remember that the content of any verbal ideology, in purchasing, political, or religious behaviors, remains unrelated to the reality. Ideological premises are usually self-sealing. They conflict with other ideologies. This may not be a matter of life and death when one commits to a brand of soap, but unquestioning, blind commitment to political, military, economic, and religious ideologies has inflicted centuries of devastation on the world. Ideologies are based upon stereotypical views of both self and the world. Stereotypes can refute or confirm any ideological perspective and justify unjust, violent, ruthless, dehumanized behaviors that promise to sustain the ideology.

Curiously, acts that support ideological conviction usually contradict the ethics of the ideology. The determination to save the world from communism and/or capitalism, even if everyone must be destroyed in the process, is one of many such paradoxes. Ideologies offer fantasies of solving the problems of human existence— injustice, greed, inequality, wealth, poverty, etc.—but only fantasies. Simplistic solutions usually intensify the problems they propose to resolve. In the end, the most charismatic leader will pass from power.

Human susceptibility to ideological persuasion is based on an eternally unfulfilled promise of meaning and order, a stereotypical answer to loneliness, boredom, fear, threats of hunger, illness, insecurity, and political, moral, or social chaos. These threats are hyped incessantly in the commercial media. Constant media massage from these threats sustains a compulsive search for questions and answers, cause and effect, and ideological commitment. The media massage sets the latest trend in consumption, entertainment, politics, business, industry, the military, and religions with their related stereotypical promises of reduced anxiety. Freedom is a Datsun, a Maxi-pad, a vote for a political candidate, a contribution to a religious prophet, or whatever else provides profit to some hustler.

Once initiated, the fantasies self-perpetuate. The final goal of every ideology is mythological, a never attainable utopia. Utopias *must* remain unobtainable, out of reach, the carrot on the stick that keeps the jackass plodding along writing checks. Time, the fourth dimension, always continues, every moment marking a change in the conditions that gave meaning to the words and symbols. "Eternal" truths must continually be reinforced, refueled, propped up.

Questions with only yes-and-no, true-and-false, or right-and-wrong answers constitute a language removed from human intelligence. They are traps set for primitives. Verbally constructed dilemmas are not real dilemmas. They are merely manipulations, usually constructed so anyone who answers and commits himself or herself loses. The dilemma manufacturer wins. Ads and the media content they control are crammed full of these ersatz dilemmas. They usually appear resolvable through purchases, allegiances, votes, contributions, prayers, or whatever else you have to offer. Cash is usually preferred.

Instead of creatively searching out unique, fact-oriented solutions to real problems, populations are taught to seek out problems resolvable through the solutions that benefit leaders in government, politics, industry, military, media and their advertisers, or anyone else who can afford to enter the game. They create the problem, then create and sell the answer to the problem.

Once both the leadership and followers become entrapped in mutually reinforcing illusions, self-fulfilling prophecies, and self-sealing premises, behavior and decision-making become tragically predictable and narrowly focused. In competition, anyone who becomes predictable loses.

Avoid Polarization, Assertion, or Negation

Stand outside verbal constructions of excluded-middle opposites. The moment individuals are pulled into a dichotomy, control is lost—if, indeed, they had any control to begin with. A passive rather than an active negation always throws the opposition into confusion. Wait and see! Observe! Think! Compare! Evaluate! Play with alternative options and perspectives! Above all, relax. Act only when it is clearly in your interest to act. Consider one of the most important, always available options: Do Nothing!

Avoid the primitive *yes* and *no*. Try to understand everything that can be understood about multiple options. Probe what is *unknowable*! If there does not appear to be time for reflection, change the appearance of time. Time is a perceptual abstraction stretchable or condensable to suit any objective. Students of hypnosis experiment with time distortion—ten mintues of relaxation can be perceptually expanded into eight hours of deep rest.

Sensitize yourself to stereotypical thinking. Ads and commercial media (including news) are loaded with stereotypes; these are excellent places to study meaningless generalizations. They offer the most simplistic abstractions. They do not, of course, simplify perceivable realities and life processes. Stereotypes or images provide momentary tranquillity. They remove the necessity for thought, reasoning, and critical judgment. They also conceal ticking bombs behind simplistic façades. Stereotypes or images are universally wrong, damaging, self-defeating, and grossly misleading.

The world population comprises individuals, each with a unique assortment of perceivable similarities and differences. All are distinct. No two have the same physiology or psychology. Victims of stereotypical thinking include both the labelers and the victims they label.

Privately Question Assumptions, Most
Especially Those You Most Treasure

Heresy can become an exciting way of life. Heresy, however, is impossible without a "true" doctrine. Without heresy, "true" doctrines congeal and atrophy into hopeless sterility. Heresy is essential for creativity, insight, and progress. Whenever heresy was silenced, great suffering and evil ensued. People are often relieved when heresy is not apparent, when no one is rocking the boat. Peace and quiet tranquilize, though they should be terrifying. Heresy and deviance are the foundations of every democratic system. Almost anyone can learn to love deviants and heretics, though it may not be easy at first.

Ideological perspectives are inherently hypocritical. Hypocrisy that takes the form of a denial of hypocrisy is hypocrisy squared. "Trust me! I would not lie to you!" The American Association of Advertising Agencies ad (fig. 8) is a superb example. Dissent, criticism, or any opposition to an established ideology—such as media ad misrepresentations, public-relations flimflam, and promotional puffery—is vital to a nation's health.

Ideological failures rarely produce insights into the reasons for failure or into the nature of ideology. Instead, failures usually energize the zealot into a frantic search for a new theory that can be converted into another ideology. Thus, the disillusioned communist becomes a right-wing religious fanatic, and vice versa. The only escape appears to be the realization that ideology is a perceptual construction, based on fantasy perceptions and stereotypical generalizations. Ideologies usually avoid confirmable, autonomous, fact-oriented perceptions.

The power of ad and public-relations media converts theories into ideologies and enforces the resultant fantasy constructions. Public resistance to ad media can be developed into a deviant heresy that in the beginning will be attacked by the majority. The prevailing system was legitimized by powerful, high-credibility, mutually reinforcing powers—universities, government bureaucracies, corporations, et cetera. Inherent contradictions were ignored, suppressed, or repressed. The frantic search for burning—though actually trivial—issues and problems sidetracked attention away from realities. Trivia begets trivia. Trivial pursuits—feature stories, game shows, situation comedies, and pap—dominate the world of ad media. Substance is considered a minor-audience throwaway to appease critics. Public broadcasting remains an attempt by commercial broadcasters to rid themselves of a non-profitable, minority audience.

Become a heretic. Human perception will likely remain an on-going intellectual crap game. It is important that humans never completely resolve their perceptual dilemmas. The instabilities, insecurities, surprises, contradictions, and paradoxes might become enjoyable—once consciously recognized. Consider the fun and challenge of fighting the army of pandering pitch artists who sell, manipulate, and exploit human perceptual weakness, along with their political sycophants.

Seeing Must Not Be Believing

Little in human perception is what it appears to be. When abstracted into verbal, pictorial, or mathematical languages, per-ceptions become even further removed from the initial realities perceived. Observers can never be separated from their perceptions, except through verbal fictions. Subjectivity levels in perception and language remain a matter of more or less, rather than either/or. And, finally, no serious consideration of perception can ignore unconsciously induced information—the source of basic predis-positions that underlie conscious perceptions.

These are not new ideas. They date to at least Protagoras and other early Greek sophist philosophers from the fifth century B.C., through Kant in the eighteenth century, and to modern philos-ophers of science such as Korzybski, Russell, Malinowski, Einstein, and Wittgenstein. There is very little new in the world of ideas—or in any other world for that matter. There exist only old concepts window-dressed with new labels, often coupled with promotional hype. Such hype, which supports mechandising cultures, can pre-vail only through ignorance and repression. Individuals culture-trained in simplistic perceptions of the world are easy victims, victims who resist attempts to deal with perceptual processes. They shout vociferously about freedom, as they submit and obey as slaves.

For example, anyone who perceives the Tanqueray emerald (fig. 5) as reality—an actual emerald—displays a perceptual inability to distinguish between fantasy and reality. That audiences have been carefully educated not to make this important discrimination illustrates mind control far more advanced than that conceived by Huxley or Orwell. The media educates its population to prefer fantasy over reality.

Cornell astronomer Carl Sagan compared the U.S. and U.S.S.R. to two men in a room, standing knee-deep in gasoline. Each holds a handful of matches, threatening to light them to punish the other for misdeeds, evil motives, and provocative behaviors. Sagan might have added one additional factor to the story.

The room is pitch dark. Each man passionately claims to serve his vision of objective reality. Each has an arsenal of cultural-linguistic clichés, diagnostic labels, prejudices, stereotypes, objectivity illusions, and self-sealing premises. As sociologist C. Wright Mills wrote in his *The Causes of World War Three*, "It does not matter how small the probability of a nuclear accident is in relation to time. It is statistically demonstrable that as time passes, the probability approaches certainty."

Media's perceptual stranglehold should not surprise anyone capable of independent judgment. Actors remain employable only because they create illusions, fantasies, and credible representations of usually stereotypical characters. The U.S., not so strangely perhaps, elected an actor as president. Never before in the history of the world had a professional actor become a head of state. Many of the world's great leaders were accomplished actors, but not by profession; they rose to leadership as statesmen, administrators, authors, militarists, scholars, or from industry and commerce.

Questions of verbal and visual illiteracy go far beyond merely learning to read and write. The world now faces questions of ethical illiteracy. If there are answers to the dilemmas posed by subliminal manipulation, they appear to lie with the manipulated, not with the manipulators. Laws would have little effect, except possibly to publicize the issue. Humans can, however, be taught in the interest of survival to accept individual responsibility for perceptual constructions. They each have the potential to defend themselves. Further, each can learn to create unique individualized relationships with perceived realities. Each can enjoy illusions, fantasies, and projections to the fullest without fear of being entrapped. The human perceptual process has exciting potentialities, barely understood at this point in time. People can avoid being conned into someone else's self-serving simple answers to complex questions.

Unfortunately, the current language-cultural system conditions people not only to permit themselves to be manipulated but to seek it out. There will always be, it appears, people on the make who have a plausible description of what is beautiful, godlike, fair, humorous, loving, faithful, trusting, sexy, good, and *true*—useful to their own, not their believers', interests.

Fantasy science filled the ideological vacuum when traditional religious, philosophical, and ethical ideals faded. Perceptions of "objective" truth replaced truth based in superstition. Ideologies must be absolute, truth must prove everything. Religious, political, social, or economic ideologies are based on the myth of tomorrow, often extended to eternity, but usually focused no farther than the end of the next generation. When approached by anyone carrying such a package, walk rapidly in the opposite direction.

The basic survival problem for modern civilization is how to get out of the problem and away from self-serving solutions to the problem. This will not be easy. Most perceived solutions soon become the problem, another Ouroborus. Only by stepping outside the circle, the never-ending succession of problem-solution-problem-solution, ad infinitum, can we ever resolve problems. The problem with human existence is, in effect, human existence. Approached from an evolutionary perspective—if this is possible with time apparently running out—awareness of perceptual limitations, frailties, and the heritage of vulnerability must somehow become a part of cultural conditioning. An improved, survival-oriented, humanistic construction would still remain a construction, but hopefully one that would better fit a continuation of civilization and life.

Eight Steps to Survival

At the risk of simplifying thought processes—as varied and unique as individuals who think, or even those who only think they think—here are several steps that could decrease human vulnerability to manipulation by the media.

1. *Relax.* Under the constant pressures of modern media, this must be learned, or re-learned. Techniques range from simple deep breathing to autohypnosis and meditation. Relaxation increases the probability of successful, fact-oriented reality perception. Tension, stress, and anxiety increase vulnerability to manipulation. Stress reduction is the most effective approach to analyzing subliminal stimuli, underlying meaning, and motives.

2. *Delay.* Tentative conclusions are imperative. Time is an abstraction, usually engineered to the advantage of some at the disadvantage of others. Slow down. Give yourself time. Time pressure usually triggers perceptual defenses.

3. *Perceive.* Perceptual analysis of what is perceived—and the abstraction process through which it is described—can improve reality perception. Study your reactions to the reactions of others. Then, study their reactions to your reactions. And, finally, examine your perceptions of their perceptions. Consciously consider the entire perceptual concept of communication. This can be fun! It immediately puts you beyond the reach of most ad and media hype. Compare media fantasy perceptions with reality—the perceivable real world.

4. *Decontextualize.* Invert logical, syntactical thought. Normal expectations often appear quite abnormal when viewed out of context. Try crazy, illogical, upside-down and inside-out perceptions of words and pictures. Experiment with perceptual illogic. Creativity can often keep you out of trouble and provide unsuspected answers concealed in self-sealing premises—both yours and those of others.

5. *Molecularize.* Take apart words and pictures. Look for meaning buried within your perceptions. Examine minute fragments. Everything, even the smallest and least conspicuous,

perceived by humans is significant, especially that which appears insignificant. Look most carefully at perceptions your mind tells you are irrelevant. No insignificant, meaningless human perceptions exist.

6. *Symbolize.* Symbols often carry multiple, unconscious meanings. Everything perceived is symbolic—words, things, pictures, and people. Play with symbols. Look for relationships or structures your conscious mind rejects as silly. Look for multiple meanings, meaning without meaning, meaning within meaning, meaning either under or on top of meaning. Probe deeply and carefully.

7. *Motivate.* Work on motive analysis. Every communication involves motives, especially those we deny. Both motives of the initiator and the audience are important. Motives exist at conscious and unconscious levels. Rank the possible motives involved. Look for impossible or unlikely motives. Keep the question of motives open. Motives can be deep, complex, multiple, interlocking, and often appear contradictory. No communication can be meaningfully evaluated without consideration of motives. The motivation to win may camouflage the motive to lose, or vice versa. Apparent winners may unconsciously seek an appropriate disaster so they can lose spectacularly.

8. *Evaluate.* Make certain you have a clear idea about who is talking to whom, about what and whom. The distinctions humans make verbally, the ideologies they pursue, evaluations they perform, theories they espouse, decisions they announce, principles they propose, and arguments they provoke reveal the inner person. They reveal far more about the individual and his or her ways of perceiving the world than they do about the topics they ostensibly describe. Accept nothing and no one at face value.

The High Cost of Fraudulent Reality Perceptions

The destruction of mythological concepts of objective truth deeply troubles the culturally indoctrinated. Some individuals have even responded to the idea with consideration of suicide. Is life worth living without absolute, objective truth? It both *is* and *has been.* Albert Camus explored suicide as an answer to the disappearance of "objective truth" in his modern parable *The Myth of Sisyphus.* Sisyphus was the duplicitous King of Corinth—a trickster, manipulator, and master thief. He cheated even death by manipulating perceptions of reality. He played off one "eternal truth" against other "eternal truths" for whatever served his immediate purpose, not unlike contemporary religious, economic, and political demagogues. A widely popular figure in Homeric literature—not unlike the generations of popular con artists who followed—the gods finally punished him eternally in Hades. Sisyphus was condemned to roll a huge stone up a hill, painfully and laboriously, only to have it roll down once he reached the summit. Over and over and over and over, for an eternity. Had not the eternal "objective truths" of ancient Greece perished with their civilization, such punishment might be useful today. Imagine ad and media hucksters, self-serving politicians, manipulative preachers, and lying salespersons finally doing an honest day's work.

Questions of objective truth, however, are not simple. Neither are each individual's answers to the questions. Humans somehow survived several million years of evolution with belief systems based upon concepts of objective truth. These truths, however, changed dramatically over the centuries, adapting to new technologies, cultures, languages, economics, and power elites. Human perceptual processes ingeniously designed "objective truths" that both fit the moment and could be verbally manipulated to apply to perceptions of past and future.

Language philosopher Ludwig Wittgenstein explored the ways humans perceptually created words in their own fantasized images, then perceptually created themselves as part of their subjective fantasies. Eventually, they permitted social, economic, political, religious, and cultural media to manage perceptions of reality. In *Philosophical Investigations I* Wittgenstein wrote, "One thinks that one is tracing the outlines of nature over and over again. One is merely tracing around the frame through which we looked at her. A picture held us captive. And we could not get outside it, for it lay in our language and language seemed to repeat to us inexorably."

Self-sealing premises, permanently closed minds sealed tightly against the intrusion of reality or assumption testing, is a formidable end result of ad media-dominated culture. Individuals who "know," absolutely for all time, who they are, where they are going and why, are dangerous both to themselves and to the world in which they live. Self-sealed mentalities also cannot get much fun out of life, for they have little opportunity for creative play and innovation.

A survival corps—organized to retrain battered personalities dominated by self-sealing premises—might be worth the effort to create. Candidates could be selected from high up in government, business, education, and industry. Members of the military could probably be written off as a lost cause.

EPILOGUE

Do not wait for the last judgement,
it takes place every day!

Albert Camus, *The Fall*

The moment anyone accepts an *objective reality*, an *eternal truth*,
they have become vulnerable, manipulable, and eminently exploit-
able. They have ceased to function as an autonomous, creative,
thinking individual, living in an integrated, interdependent world.

APPENDIX

U.S. Treasury Department, Division of Alcohol, Tobacco, and Firearms. "New Rules and Regulations." *Federal Register,* August 6, 1984, pp. 31670–76.

Subliminals

ATF proposed a regulatory section prohibiting the use of subliminal or similar techniques in advertising of alcoholic beverages. ATF stated that subliminal or similar techniques refer to any device or technique that is used to convey or attempt to convey a message to a person by means of images or sounds of a very brief nature that cannot be perceived at a normal level of awareness.

Twenty-two comments were received and a number of witnesses presented oral testimony at the public hearings. Of the 22 comments, representing 52 individuals, all but three supported the proposed prohibition. The main arguments against the proposed regulation were that subliminals were not used in advertising, that the advertising and broadcast industries are self-regulating in this area, and that the Federal Trade Commission (FTC) already prohibits by regulation the use of subliminals.

ATF believes that action is necessary in this area. There is increasing concern by consumers over the very nature of alcoholic beverage advertising. Further, strong precedent exists for ATF action. The Federal Communications Commission (FCC) has declared the use of subliminals to be contrary to the public interest because they are clearly intended to be deceptive. Furthermore, the FCC saw no need to differentiate between subliminal advertising and subliminal program content.

Subliminal or similar techniques can take many forms in advertising. These forms include placing a frame in a film which appears at a speed at which the observer cannot consciously perceive its presence, but subconsciously the word, phrase, or scene is registered. Another and more prevalent form is the insertion of words or body forms (embeds) by the use of shadows or shading, or the substitution of forms and shapes generally associated with the body.

Although subliminals or similar techniques are prohibited by the FTC and voluntary advertising and broadcasting codes, ATF has jurisdiction over the advertising of alcoholic beverages. Subliminals are inherently deceptive because the consumer does not perceive them at a normal level of awareness, and thus is given no choice whether to accept or reject the message, as is the case with normal advertising. ATF holds that this type of advertising technique is false and deceptive, and is prohibited by law. Therefore, ATF is issuing regulations prohibiting the use of subliminals or similar techniques.

BIBLIOGRAPHY

Anderson, Alf L.; Fries, Ingrid; and Smith, Gudmand J. "Change in Afterimage and Spiral Aftereffect Serials Due to Anxiety Caused by Subliminal Threat." *Scandinavian Journal of Psychology* 11:1:7–16, 1970.

Antell, Maxine J. "The Effects of Priming and Subliminal Presentation of Sexual and Aggressive Stimuli on Tests of Creativity," *Dissertation Abstracts International* 30 (1969), 3598B (New York University).

Arnheim, Rudolf. *Art and Visual Perception: A Psychology of the Creative Eye.* Berkeley: University of California Press, 1971.

———. *Visual Thinking.* Berkeley: University of California Press, 1969.

Barber, Paul J. "Experimenter Bias Against Subliminal Perceptions: A Rejoinder." *British Journal of Psychology* 68:281–82, Aug. 1977.

———, and Ruston, J. Phillipe. "Experimenter Bias and Subliminal Perception." *British Journal of Psychology* 66:357–72, Aug. 1975.

Bateson, Gregory. *Mind and Nature: A Necessary Unity*. New York: E. P. Dutton, 1979.

————. "A Theory of Play and Fantasy." *Psychiatric Research Reports* (American Psychiatric Association) 2:39–51, 1955.

Becker, Hal C. *Apparatus for Producing Visual Stimulation*. U.S. Patent #3,060,795, Oct. 30, 1962.

————. *Apparatus for Producing Visual and Auditory Stimulation*. U.S. Patent #3,278,676, Oct. 11, 1966.

Beisgen, Robert T., Jr., and Gibby, Robert G., Jr. "Autonomic and Verbal Discrimination of a Subliminally Learned Task." *Journal of Perceptual and Motor Skills* 29:2:503–7, 1969.

Berger, John. *About Looking*. New York: Pantheon, 1980.

Berger, Peter L., and Luckman, Thomas. *The Social Construction of Reality*. New York: Anchor Books, 1966.

Bliss, Thomas Albert. "Subliminal Projection: History and Analysis." *Comment* (University of California, Hastings College of Law), 5:3:419–41, Spring 1983.

Blum, Gerald S. "An Experimental Reunion of Psychoanalytic Theory with Perceptual Vigilance and Defense." *Journal of Abnormal and Social Psychology* 49:1:94–98, 1954.

————. "Reply to Jennings and George." *Journal of Perceptual and Motor Skills*, 41:957–58, Dec. 1975.

Bradbury, Ray. *Fahrenheit 451*. New York: Ballantine Books, 1953.

Bronstein, Abbot A. "An Experimental Study of Internalization Fantasies in Schizophrenic Men." *Dissertation Abstracts International* 37 (1976), 4665B (Yeshiva University).

Brown, U. P. "Conceptions of Perceptual Defence." *British Journal of Psychology Monographs*, Supplement 35, 1961.

California State Assembly. Bill #100. (Introduced by Assemblyman Philip Wyman, December 10, 1982, passed by the Senate June 21, 1983; law to regulate the practice of embedding subliminal communications in media disseminated to the public.)

Camus, Albert. *The Myth of Sisyphus*. New York: Knopf, 1955.

Candela, Anthony J. *Memory as a Function of Defensive Style and Type of Aggressive Stimuli*. Unpublished doctoral dissertation, New York University, 1975.

Cirlot, J. E. *A Dictionary of Symbols.* New York: Philosophical Library, 1972.

Cohen, Roni O. "The Effects of Four Subliminally-Introduced Merging Stimuli on the Psychopathology of Schizophrenic Women." *Dissertation Abstracts International* 38 (1977), 2356B (Columbia University).

Corrigan, R. E. *Verbal, Visual, and Motor Responses as Indicators of Personal Values in Perception.* Unpublished doctoral dissertation, Tulane University, 1954.

Cowen, Robert C. "Subliminal Warrants Caution." *Leader* Feb. 5, 1981 (reprinted from *Christian Science Monitor*).

Cox, Louis D. "Depressive Symptoms as Affected by Aggressive Stimuli Subliminally and Supraliminally Presented." *Dissertation Abstracts International* 35 (1974), 1402B (College of William and Mary).

De Chenne, James A. *An Experimental Study to Determine if a Task Involving Psychomotor and Problem Solving Skills Can Be Taught Subliminally.* Unpublished doctoral dissertation, Virginia Polytechnic Institute and State University, 1976.

Dixon, Norman F. *Subliminal Perception: The Nature of a Controversy.* London: McGraw-Hill, 1971.

————. *Preconscious Processing.* New York: John Wiley & Sons, 1981.

Eagle, Morris N.; Wolitsky, David L.; and Klein, George S. "Imagery: Effect of a Concealed Figure in a Stimulus." *Science* 151:837–39, Feb. 1966.

Ehrenzweig, Anton. *The Hidden Order of Art: A Study in the Psychology of Artistic Imagination.* London: Paladin, 1970.

Ellenberger, Henri F. *The Discovery of the Unconscious: The History and Evolution of Dynamic Psychiatry.* New York: Basic Books, 1970.

Erdelyi, Mathew H. "Role Fantasy of the Poetzle (Emergence) Phenomenon." *Journal of Personality and Social Psychology* 24:2:186–90, 1972.

Foodman, Allan. "Hemispheric Asymmetrical Brain Wave Indicators of Unconscious Mental Processes." *Journal of Operational Psychiatry* 7:1:3–15, 1976.

Foucault, Michel. *Madness and Civilization: A History of Insanity in the Age of Reason.* New York: Vintage, 1973.

Frazer, J. G. *The Golden Bough: A Study in Magic and Religion.* London: MacMillan, 1967.

Freud, Sigmund. *The Interpretation of Dreams.* New York: Basic Books, 1955.

Friedman, Stanley. "Perceptual Registration of the Analyst Outside of Awareness." *Psychoanalytic Quarterly* 76:1:128–30, 1976.

Fromm, Erich. *Beyond the Chains of Illusion: My Encounter with Marx and Freud.* New York: Pocket Books, 1962.

Garner, David M., and Garfinkel, Paul E. *Anorexia Nervosa and Bulimia.* New York: Guilford Press, 1985.

George, Stephen G., and Jennings, Luther B. "Effects of Subliminal Stimuli on Consumer Behavior: Negative Evidence." *Journal of Perceptual and Motor Skills* 41:3:847–54, 1975.

———. "Effects of Subliminal Stimuli on Dreams: Further Evidence Against the Spence-Holland Theory." *Journal of Perceptual and Motor Skills* 35:251–57, Aug. 1972.

———. "Re-Examination of the Effect of Subliminal Verbal Food Stimulus on Subjective Hunger Ratings." *Psychological Reports* 30:2:521–22, 1972.

Glasersfeld, Ernst von. *A Cybernetic Approach to the Assessment of Children: Toward More Humane Use of Human Beings.* Boulder, Colorado: Westview Press, 1979.

Goodkin, Olivia, and Phillips, Maureen Ann. "The Subconscious Taken Captive: A Social, Ethical, and Legal Analysis of Subliminal Communication Technology." *Southern California Law Review* 54:1077–1140, 1981.

Greenburg, Nathan. "The Effects of Subliminal Neutral and Aggressive Stimuli on the Thought Processes of Schizophrenics." *Canadian Journal of Behavioral Science* 9:187–96, April 1977.

Habermas, Jürgen. *Communication and the Evolution of Society.* Boston: Beacon, 1979.

———. *Legitimation Crisis.* Boston: Beacon, 1973.

Haley, J. *Advanced Techniques of Hypnosis and Therapy: Selected Papers of Milton H. Erickson, M.D.* New York: Grune & Stratton, 1967.

Harrison, Robert H. "Effect of Subliminal Shock Conditioning on Recall." *Journal of Abnormal Pscyhology* 75:19–29, Feb. 1970.

Hart, Larry. "The Effect of Noxious Subliminal Stimuli on the

Modification of Attitudes Towards Alcoholism: A Pilot Study." *British Journal of Addiction* 68:87–90, June 1973.

Hawkins, Del. "The Effects of Subliminal Stimulation on Drive Level and Brand Preference." *Journal of Marketing Research* 7:322–26, Aug. 1970.

Herrick, Robert M. "Foveal Light-Detection Thresholds with Two Temporally Spaced Flashes: A Review." *Journal of Perception and Psychophysics* 15:361–67, April 1974.

Hilgard, Ernest R. *The Experience of Hypnosis*. New York: Harcourt, Brace, Jovanovich, 1965.

Hofstadter, Douglas R. *Gödel, Escher, Bach: An Eternal Golden Braid*. New York: Vintage, 1980.

Holtzman, Deanna. "Recall and Importation on a Word Test Primed by a Subliminal Stimulus." *Dissertation Abstracts International* 36 (1975), 2473B (Wayne State University).

Hull, Ethel J. "Ego States Characteristic of Enhanced Utilization of Subliminal Registrations," *Dissertation Abstracts International* 37 (1976), 1903B (University of Chicago).

Huxley, Aldous Leonard. *Brave New World*. New York: Modern Library, 1946.

Jeffmar, Marianne. "Ways of Cognitive Action: A Study of Syncretism, Flexibility, and Exactness." *Psychological Research Bulletin* 16:1:47, 1976.

Jennings, Luther B., and George, Stephen G. "Perceptual Vigilance and Defense Revisited: Evidence Against Blum's Psychoanalytic Theory of Subliminal Perception." *Journal of Perceptual and Motor Skills* 41:723–29, Dec. 1975.

———. "The Spence-Holland Theory of Subliminal Perception: A Re-Examination." *Psychological Record* 20:495–504, Fall 1970.

Jobes, Gertrude. *Dictionary of Mythology, Folklore, and Symbols*, Parts I, II, and III. New York: Scarecrow Press, 1962.

Jones, Russell A. *Self-Fulfilling Prophecies: Social, Psychological, and Physiological Effects of Expectancies*. New York: John Wiley & Sons, 1977.

Jourard, Sidney M. *The Transparent Self*. New York: Van Nostrand Reinhold, 1971.

Jung, C. E. *Analytical Psychology: Two Essays*. New York: Meridian, 1956.

————. *Man and His Symbols*. New York: Doubleday, 1969.

Kaley, Harriette W. "The Effects of Subliminal Stimuli and Drive on Verbal Responses and Dreams." *Dissertation Abstracts International* 31 (1970), 2284B (New York University).

Kallard, T. *Laser Art and Optical Transforms*. New York: Optosonic Press, 1979.

Kant, Immanuel. *Critique of Pure Reason*. London: Macmillan, 1881.

Kaplan, Rosalind B. "The Symbiotic Fantasy as a Therapeutic Agent: An Experimental Comparison of the Effects of Three Symbiotic Elements on Manifest Pathology in Schizophrenics." *Dissertation Abstracts International* 37 (1976), 1437B (New York University).

Katz, Robert J. "Subliminal Perception and Creative Preconscious." *Dissertation Abstracts International* 34 (1973), 1751B (Texas Technological University).

Kaye, Melvin M. "The Therapeutic Value of Three Merging Stimuli for Male Schizophrenics." *Dissertation Abstracts International* 36 (1975), 1438B (Yeshiva University).

Key, Wilson Bryan. *Media Sexploitation*. New York: Signet, 1977.

————. *Subliminal Seduction: Ad Media's Manipulation of a Not So Innocent America*. New York: Signet, 1973.

————. *The Clam-Plate Orgy and Other Subliminal Techniques for Manipulating Your Behavior*. New York: Signet, 1981.

Kihlstrom, John F. "The Cognitive Unconscious." *Science* 237:1445–52, Feb. 18, 1987.

Klapp, Orrin E. *Symbolic Leaders: Public Dramas and Public Men*. New York: Minerva, 1968.

Kleespies, Phillip, and Wierner, Morton. "The Orienting Reflex as an Input Indicator in Subliminal Perception." *Journal of Perceptual and Motor Skills* 35:1:103–10, 1972.

Kohlers, Paul A. "Subliminal Stimulation in Simple and Complex Cognitive Processes." *Dissertation Abstracts International* 33 (1972), 1269B (New York University).

Korzybski, Alfred. *Science and Sanity: An Introduction to Non-Aristotelian Systems and General Semantics*. Lakeville, Conn.: International Non-Aristotelian Publishing Society, 1933.

Kostandov, E., and Arzumanov, Y. "Averaged Cortical Evoked

Potentials to Recognized and Non-Recognized Verbal Stimuli." *Acta Neurobiologise Experimentales* 37:311–24, 1977.

Kramer, Charles B. "Judicial Recognition and Control of New Media Techniques: In Search of the 'Subliminal Tort.'" *John Marshall Law Review* 14:3, Summer 1981.

Kroger, William S., and Fezler, William D. *Hypnosis and Behavior Modification: Imagery Conditioning.* Philadelphia: Lippincott, 1976.

Kubose, Gyomay. *Zen Koans.* Chicago: Henry Regnery, 1973.

Kurtz, David L., and Brone, Louis E. *Marketing.* 2nd ed. New York: Dryden Press, 1981.

Laing, R. D. *The Politics of the Family.* Toronto: CBC Learning Systems, 1969.

Lasch, Christopher. *The Culture of Narcissism: American Life in an Age of Diminishing Expectations.* New York: Norton, 1979.

Lecky, Prescott. *Self-Consistency: A Theory of Personality.* New York: Doubleday Anchor, 1969.

LeClere, Claude, and Freibergs, Vaira. "The Influence of Subliminal Perception and Symbolic Indices on the Formation of a Concept." *Canadian Journal of Psychology* 25:292–301, Aug. 1971.

Ledford, Bruce R. *The Effects of Preconscious Cues upon the Automatic Activation of Self-Esteem of Selected Middle School Students.* Tucson, Arizona Unified School District, Project #1246, Nov. 1985.

————. *The Effects of Thematic Content of Rheostatically Controlled Visual Subliminals upon the Receiving Level of the Affective Domain of Learners.* Commerce, Texas: Office of Organized Research, Grant 1501-9718, East Texas State University, Aug. 1978.

Leeman, Fred. *Hidden Images: Games of Perception, Anamorphic Art, and Illusion.* New York: Harry N. Abrams, 1976.

Leiter, Eli. "A Study of the Effects of Subliminal Activation of Merging Fantasies in Differentiated and Non-Differentiated Schizophrenics." *Dissertation Abstracts International* 34 (1973), 4022B (New York University).

Lidz, Theodore. *The Person: His Development Throughout the Life Cycle.* New York: Basic Books, 1968.

Lieberman, Harvey J. "A Study of the Relationship Between Developmentally Determined Personality and Associated Thought

Styles and Tachistoscopic Exposure Time as Reflected in Conflict Resolution." *Dissertation Abstracts International* 35 (1974), 5670B (Pennsylvania State University).

Litivack, Thomas R. "A Study of Certain Issues Concerning the Dynamics of Thinking and Behavioral Pathology in Schizophrenics Through the Use of Subliminal Stimulation." *Dissertation Abstracts International* 33 (1972), 918B (New York University).

Lomangino, Louis F. "Depiction of Subliminally and Supraliminally Presented Aggressive Stimuli and Its [Their] Effects on the Cognitive Functioning of Schizophrenics." *Dissertation Abstracts International* 30 (1969), 1900B (Fordham University).

Lorenz, Konrad. *Civilized Man's Eight Deadly Sins.* London: Methuen, 1974.

Lovelock, J. E. *Gaia: A New Look at Life on Earth.* New York: Oxford University Press, 1979.

Lozanov, Georgi. *Suggestology and Outlines of Suggestopedy.* New York: Interface, 1978.

Lusseyran, Jacques. *And There Was Light.* Boston: Little Brown, 1963.

Marro, Anthony. "When the Government Tells Lies." *Columbia Journalism Review* 29–41 March/April 1985.

Martin, April. *The Effect of Subliminal Stimulation of Symbiotic Fantasies on Weight Loss in Obese Women Receiving Behavioral Treatment.* Unpublished doctoral dissertation, New York University, 1975.

Maxwell, Neil. "Words Whispered to Subconscious Supposedly Deter Thefts, Fainting." *Wall Street Journal,* Nov. 25, 1980.

McLuhan, Marshall. *Understanding Media: The Extension of Man.* New York: Signet, 1964.

Mencken, H. L. *The American Language.* New York: Alfred A. Knopf, 1946.

Montagu, Ashley. *Touching: The Human Significance of the Skin.* New York: Harper & Row, 1978.

Murch, Gerald M. "A Set of Conditions for a Consistent Recovery of Subliminal Stimulus." *Journal of Applied Psychology* 49:4:257–60, 1965.

O'Grady, Michael. "Effect of Subliminal Pictorial Stimulation on

Skin Resistance." *Journal of Perceptual and Motor Skills* 43:3:1051–56, 1977.

Orwell, George. *1984*. New York: Harcourt, Brace, and World, 1949.

Oxhandler, Eugene K. "Can Subliminal Stimuli Teach?" *Audio-Visual Communications Review* 7:3:109–14, 1960.

Peirce, C. S., and Jastrow, J. "On Small Differences of Sensation." *National Academy of Science* 3:73–83, 1984.

Poetzle, Otto. "The Relationship Between Experimentally Induced Dream Images and Indirect Vision." 1917 Monograph. *Psychological Issues* 2:1:41–120, 1960.

Postman, Neil. *Amusing Ourselves to Death: Public Discourse in the Age of Show Business*. New York: Viking, 1985.

Reese, W. J. "On the Terms 'Subliminal Perception' and 'Subception.'" *British Journal of Psychology* 62:501–4, Nov. 1971.

Rogers, E. *Diffusion of Innovation*. New York: Free Press, 1962.

Rudolph, James K. "Selective Subliminal Perception Relative to Approach/Avoidance Tendencies." *Dissertation Abstracts International* 31 (1970), 1695A (University of Southern California).

Rulstein, Eleanor H., and Goldberg, Leo. "The Effects of Aggressive Stimulation on Suicidal Patients: An Experimental Study of the Psychological Theory of Suicide." *Psychoanalysis and Contemporary Science* 2:157–74, 1973.

Russell, Bertrand. *Mysticism and Logic and Other Essays*. London: Unwin, 1963.

Schwartz, Marvin. "Testing Specific Hypotheses About Subliminal Perception: A Reply to Shevrin." *Journal of Psychophysiology* 13:27–31, Jan. 1976.

———, and Rem, Michael A. "Does the Average Evoked Response Encode Subliminal Perception?" *Journal of Psychophysiology* 12:390–94.

Severance, Laurence J., and Dyer, Frederick N. "Failure of Subliminal Word Presentations to Generate Interference to Color Naming." *Journal of Experimental Psychology* 101:186–89, Nov. 1973.

Sharp, Heber C. "Effect of Subliminal Cues on Test Results." *Journal of Applied Psychology* 43:6:369–71, 1959.

Shevrin, Howard. "Brain Wave Correlates of Subliminal Stimulation, Unconscious Attention, Primary-and-Secondary Process, Thinking, and Repressiveness." *Psychological Issues* 8:2:56–87, 1973.

―――. "Does the Average Evoked Response Encode Subliminal Perception? Yes!: A Reply to Schwartz and Rem," *Journal of Psychophysiology*, 12:395–98, July 1975.

―――, and Fritzler, Dean E. "Visual Evoked Response Correlates of Unconscious Mental Processes." *Science* 161:295–98, July 1968.

―――; Smith, William H.; and Fritzler, Dean E. "Average Evoked Response and Verbal Correlates of Unconscious Mental Processes." *Journal of Psychophysiology* 8:149–62, March 1971.

―――; Smith, William H.; and Fritzler, Dean E. "Repressiveness as a Factor in the Subliminal Activation of Brain and Verbal Responses." *Journal of Nervous and Mental Disease* 149:3:261–69, 1969.

―――; Smith, William H.; and Fritzler, Dean E. "Subliminally Stimulated Brain and Verbal Responses of Twins Differing in Repressiveness." *Journal of Abnormal Psychology* 76:1:39–46, 1970.

Silverman, Lloyd H. "Drive Stimulation and Psychopathology: On the Conditions Under Which Drive-Related External Events Evoke Pathological Reactions." *Psychoanalysis and Contemporary Science* 72:1:306–26, 1972.

―――. "An Experimental Technique for the Study of Unconscious Conflicts." *British Journal of Medical Psychology* 44:17–25, March 1971.

―――. "On the Role of Laboratory Experiments in the Development of the Clinical Theory of Aggressive and Merging Wishes in Schizophrenics." *Internal Review of Psychoanalysis* 2:1:43–64, 1975.

―――. "Psychoanalytic Theory: The Reports of My Death Are Greatly Exaggerated." *American Psychologist* 31:621–37, Sept. 1976.

―――. "Study of the Effects of Subliminally Presented Aggressive Stimuli on the Production of Pathological Thinking in a Non-Psychiatric Population." *Journal of Nervous and Mental Disease* 131:4:443–55, 1966.

―――. "A Technique for the Study of Psychodynamic Relationships: The Effects of Subliminally Presented Aggressive Stimuli on the Production of Pathological Thinking in a Schizophrenic Population." *Journal of Consulting Psychology* 30:2:103–11, 1966.

————, and Candell, Peter. "On the Relationship Between Aggressive Activation, Symbiotic Merging, Intactness of Body Boundaries, and Manifest Pathology in Schizophrenics." *Journal of Nervous and Mental Disease* 150:5:387–89, 1970.

————, and Goldweber, Arthur M. "A Further Study of Subliminal Aggressive Stimulation on Thinking." *Journal of Nervous and Mental Disease* 143:463–72, Dec. 1966.

————, and Silverman, Doris K. "A Clinical Experimental Approach to the Study of Subliminal Stimulation upon Rorschach Responses." *Journal of Abnormal and Social Psychology* 69:2:156–72, 1964.

————, and Silverman, Stephen E. "The Effects of Subliminally Presented Drive Stimuli on the Cognitive Functioning of Schizophrenics." *Journal of Projective Techniques and Personality Assessment* 31:78–85, Feb. 1967.

————, and Spiro, Robert H. "The Effects of Subliminal, Supraliminal, and Vocalized Aggression on the Ego Functioning of Schizophrenics." *Journal of Nervous and Mental Disease* 146:1:50–61, 1968.

————, and Spiro, Robert H. "Further Investigations of the Effects of Subliminal Aggressive Stimulation on the Ego Functioning of Schizophrenics." *Journal of Consulting Psychology* 31:3:225–32, 1967.

————; Bronstein, Abbot; and Mendelsohn, Eric. "The Further Use of Subliminal Psychodynamic Activation Method for the Experimental Study of the Clinical Theory of Psychoanalysis: On the Specificity of the Relationship Between Symptoms and Unconscious Conflicts." *Psychotherapy: Theory, Research, and Practice* 13:1:2–16, 1976.

————, et al. "A Clinical Application of Subliminal Psychodynamic Activation: On the Stimulation of Symbiotic Fantasies as an Adjunct in the Treatment of Hospitalized Schizophrenics." *Journal of Nervous and Mental Disease* 161:6:379–92, 1975.

————, et al. "The Effects of Aggressive Activation and the Need to Merge on Pathological Thinking in Schizophrenia." *Journal of Nervous and Mental Disease* 148:1:39–51, 1969.

————, et al. "The Effects of Subliminal Drive Stimulation on the Speech of Stutterers." *Journal of Nervous and Mental Disease* 155:1:14–21, 1972.

Silverman, Stephen E. "The Effects of Subliminally Induced Drive Derivations on Ego Functioning in Schizophrenics." *Dissertation Abstracts International* 31 (1970), 2291B (New York University).

Sivard, Ruth Leger. *World Military and Social Expenditures 1986.* Washington, D.C.: World Priorities, 1988.

Skinner, William S., Jr. "The Effect of Subliminal and Supraliminal Words Presented via Videotaped Motion Pictures on Vocabulary Development of Ninth-Grade Students." *Dissertation Abstracts International* 30 (1969), 2430A (Arizona State University).

Smith, G. J. W.; Spence, D. P.; and Klein, G. S. "Subliminal Effects of Verbal Stimuli." *Journal of Abnormal and Social Psychology* 59:2:167–76, 1959.

Somekh, David E. "The Effect of Embedded Words in a Brief Visual Display." *British Journal of Psychology* 67:529–35, Nov. 1976.

————, and Wilding, J. N. "Perception Without Awareness in a Dichoptic Viewing Situation." *British Journal of Psychology* 64:3:339–49, 1973.

Spence, Donald P., and Gordon, Carol M. "Activation and Assessment of an Early Oral Fantasy: An Exploration Study." *Psychological Issues* 8:2:11–28, 1973.

————, and Holland, Bert. "The Restricting Effects of Awareness: A Paradox and an Explanation." *Journal of Abnormal and Social Psychology* 64:3:163–74, 1977.

————, and Smith, Gudmund J. "Experimenter Bias Against Subliminal Perception: Comments on a Replication." *British Journal of Psychology* 68:279–80, Aug. 1977.

Spiro, Robert H., and Silverman, Lloyd H. "Effects of Body Awareness and Aggressive Activation on Ego Functioning of Schizophrenics." *Journal of Perceptual and Motor Skills* 28:575–85, April 1969.

Spiro, Tova W. "The Effects of Subliminal Symbiotic Stimulation and Strengthening Self-Boundaries of Schizophrenic Pathology." *Dissertation Abstracts International* 36 (1975), 5818B (New York University).

Spitzer, Robert L. *Diagnostic Criteria, DSM III.* New York: American Psychiatric Association.

Suckheim, Arnold A.; Packer, Ira K.; and Cur, Ruben G. "Hemisphericity, Cognitive Set, and Susceptibility to Subliminal Perception." *Journal of Abnormal Psychology* 6:624–30, 1977.

Taris, Louis J. *Subliminal Perception: An Experimental Study to Determine Whether a Science Concept Can Be Taught Subliminally to Fourth-Grade Pupils.* Unpublished doctoral dissertation, Boston University, 1970.

Thass-Thienemann, Theodore. *Symbiotic Behavior.* New York: Washington Square, 1968.

———. *The Subconscious Language.* New York: Washington Square, 1967.

Tippett, Jean, and Silber, E. "Self-Image Stability: The Problem of Validation." *Psychological Reports* 17:323–29, 1965.

Trausch, Susan. "This Mama Will Faint If She Wants To." *Boston Globe*, Dec. 14, 1980.

Turnbull, Colin M. *The Mountain People.* New York: Simon and Schuster, 1972.

U.S. House of Representatives, Subcommittee on Transportation, Aviation, and Materials of the Committee on Science and Technology. *Subliminal Communication Technology.* Washington, D.C.: U.S. GPO, 1984.

U.S. Senate, Subcommittee on Alcohol and Narcotics, Committee on Labor and Public Welfare. *Media Images of Alcohol: The Effects of Advertising and Other Media on Alcohol Abuse.* (Testimony of Dr. W. B. Key on the Effects of Subliminal Advertising of Alcoholic Beverages, 173–86.) Washington, D.C.: U.S. GPO, 1976.

U.S. Treasury Department, Division of Alcohol, Tobacco, and Firearms. "New Rules and Regulations." *Federal Register*, Aug. 8, 1984, 31670–76.

Varga, Michael P. "An Experimental Study of Aspects of the Psychoanalytic Study of Elation." *Dissertation Abstracts International* 34 (1973), 4062B (New York University).

Veeder, Gerry E. K. *The Influence of Subliminal Suggestion on the Response to Two Films.* Unpublished doctoral dissertation, Wayne State University, 1975.

Vernon, Jack A., and Badger, David H. "Subliminal Stimulation in Human Learning." *American Journal of Psychology* 72:265–70, June 1959.

Wagner, Jane. *The Search for Signs of Intelligent Life in the Universe.* New York: Harper & Row, 1986.

Wagstaff, Graham F. "The Effects of Repression-Sensitization on a Brightness Scaling Measure of Perceptual Defense." *British Journal of Psychology* 65:395–401, Aug. 1974.

Walker, Peter. "The Subliminal Perception of Movement and the Suppression in Binocular Rivalry." *British Journal of Psychology* 66:347–56, Aug. 1975.

Watson, Georgia B. "Motor Response Latency as an Indicator of Subliminal Affective Stimulation." *Journal of General Psychology* 82:139–43, April 1970.

Watzlawick, Paul. *How Real Is Real? Confusion, Disinformation and Communication.* New York: Vintage, 1977.

———. *The Invented Reality: How Do We Know What We Believe We Know? (Contributions to Constructivism).* New York: Norton, 1984.

———. *The Language of Change: Elements of Therapeutic Communication.* New York: Basic Books, 1978.

Weiner, Norbert. *The Human Use of Human Beings: Cybernetics and Society.* New York: Doubleday, 1954.

Weinstein, Sidney; Weinstein, Curt; and Drozdenko, Ronald. *Advertising on Super-Paper: Effects upon Brain Response, Purchase Intention, and Simulated Purchase.* Danbury, Connecticut: Neuro-communication Research Laboratories, 1984.

Whitehead, Alfred North. *Symbolism: Its Meaning and Effect.* New York: Capricorn, 1959.

Wilentz, Joan Steen. *The Senses of Man.* New York: Crowell, 1968.

Wilson, Edward O. *Sociobiology: The New Synthesis.* Cambridge, Massachusetts: Belknap Press of Harvard University, 1975.

Wise, David. *The Politics of Lying: Government Deception, Secrecy, and Power.* New York: Random House, 1973.

Woodward, Bob. *Veil.* New York: Simon and Schuster, 1987.

Worthington, A. G. "Paired Comparison Scaling of Brightness Judgments: A Method for the Measurement of Perceptual Defense." *British Journal of Psychology* 60:3:363–68, 1969.

INDEX

Abstracting process, 42
Abstraction:
 defined, 68
 language:
  high-order, 111, 128
  perception of, 111, 128
Adaptation levels (AL), 56–58
Adrenal glands, 60
Advertising Age, 42, 203–4
Advertising Council, 257
Advertising and public relations, 58–
  59, 74–75, 203–4, 215, 256. *See
  also* Media technology; *specific
  ads and types of ads*
 background lighting in, 32–34
 cause and effect and, 178–79
 costs of, 57, 119–20, 253–54
 double binds and, 243
 double entendre in, 17–20
 education in, 196
 embedding in, 13–17, 22–31, 44, 48–
  52, 97–98, 123, 162, 207
 figure-ground reversals in, 9–11

introduction of new words and
  meanings into language by,
  112–14
magic words in, 171–72
motivation of, 185–86
newspaper, 104
non-Aristotelian logic and, 118, 120
personality stereotype and, 200
projection in, 87–88
regulation of, 12–13, 18, 125, 142–
  43, 203–4, 267–68
self-comparison with media personalities, 196–98
self-fulfilling prophecies of, 220–26
self-sealing premises of, 230–31
sex and. *See* Sex
sincerity in, 192
subliminal indoctrination in, 28, 30,
  31, 40–41, 42, 47, 48–49, 57, 95,
  97–98, 142–43, 159–62, 207,
  223–26
symbolic values transferred by, 152
"truth in," xi, 141–43

Aggression, 60
Agriculture Department, U.S., Grain Division of, 142
Albee, Edward, 144
Alberto mousse ad, 183–84
Alcohol abuse, 104, 124–25, 223
Alcoholic beverages, ads for, 13, 17, 18, 19, 59, 63, 74, 88, 125, 160, 162, 204, 221, 224–26
  castration themes in, 123
  Gilbey's, 129–30
  regression techniques in, 81
  Seagram's, 23, 81, 121–23, 124, 125, 133, 162
  Tanqueray emerald ad, 14–15, 48–49, 178, 259
Alexandrian Quartet (Durrell), 237
All in the Family, 88
Altruism, 38
American Association of Advertising Agencies (AAA), 18–19
American Medical Association, 18
American Psychiatric Association, 210–11, 214
Animals, 133–34, 194
Anorexia, 30, 62
Anthropomorphic identification, 133–34, 233
Archetypal symbols, 149–51, 152–63
  auditory, 150–51
Arendt, Hannah, 64
Aristotelian logic, xi–xii, xiv, 6, 117–45
  language structure and, 117–47
  law of contradiction, 138–45
  law of excluded middles, 134–37
  law of identity, 121–34
Aristotle, xi–xii, 5, 6
Arizona State University Advanced Optics and Lunar Laboratories, 50–51
Armaments, 214–15
  nuclear missile launch crews, 75–76, 245–47

Art, motivation of, 185
Artificial intelligence, 67–68
Art Institute of Chicago, 244
Association of American Colleges, 252
Atlantic, 103
Auburn University, 51
Auditory archetypal symbols, 150–51
Auditory figure-ground reversals, 11–12
Augustine, Saint, 149, 156

Bacardi and Calvert ads, 162
Background:
  figure reversals, 8–13
  lighting and sound, 31–34
Backward masking, 21
Bakker, Jim, 43
Barnum, P. T., 173
Bateson, Gregory, 239
"Beat It," 19–20
Becker, Dr. Hal, 20, 26–28, 31
Beethoven, Ludwig van, 12
Behaviorism, 250
Behaviorists, 45
Belief systems (ideologies), 38, 254–55, 257, 260. *See also individual belief systems, e.g.*, Capitalism; Communism
  justifying atrocities in name of, 4–5
  objective reality of, 98–99
Bell, Eric T., 115, 126
Benson and Hedges ads, 162
Berger, John, 205
Betty Crocker ad, 16–17, 23, 44, 47, 160, 178
Bigallo Crucifix, 244
Birth, 149, 154, 157, 161, 162
Blind faith, 84, 215–16
Blindness, 101–2
Bonanza, 80
Borges, Jorge Luis, 248
Brain, human, 37–38, 41–42, 98
  perception of. *See* Perception(s)
  study of the, xi–xii, 37, 65–66
  theories about functions of, 66–67

Bulimia, 30, 62
Bullock, August, 9
Business schools, 116
Business Week, 224

Cambodia, 218
Camus, Albert, 263
Canada, 156
Cannistraro, Vincent M., 25
Capitalism, 82, 234
Caraffe, Cardinal Carlo, 3
Carnegie Foundation for the Advancement of Teaching, 251, 252
Carroll, Lewis, v
Carter, Jimmy, 24
Casey, William J., 25
Casinos, gambling, 73, 232–33
Cassirer, Ernest, 170
Castration themes in advertising, 123, 162, 207
Castro, Fidel, 220
Catholic scholastic philosophers, Aristotelian logic used by, 6
Cattell, James, 67
Causes of World War Three, The (Mills), 259
Cause and effect, 164–79, 230, 234
  the managers of, 176–77
  nonlinear conflicts, 165–66
  prediction, 174–76
  self-fulfilling prophecies and, 206, 207, 208, 221, 226
  the unknowable, 177–79
  verbal concept of "because," 167–70
  verbal magic, 170–74
Celebrities, media coverage of, 99–100
Censorship, 42–43
Central Intelligence Agency (CIA), 25, 217
Change, constant state of, 145, 218–19
Chariots of Fire, 32
Chauvinistic nationalism, 173–74
Chevrolet Nova ad, 132–33

Chicago Tribune, 118
Chile, 218
China, People's Republic of, 43
Chinese, 165
Chivas Regal ads, 17, 160, 178, 224–26
Christian Science Monitor, 28
Chronicles, 158
Cigarettes and cigarette ads, 63, 74, 75, 87, 182–83, 221
  as archetype symbol, 158
  castration themes in, 123
  death imagery in, 124, 162
Circular conflicts, 165–66
Civil Aeronautics Board, 142
Civilized Man's Eight Deadly Sins (Lorenz), 94
Clever Hans, 194
Coca-Cola, 22, 126
Colleges: The Undergraduate Experience in America, 251
Columbia Journalism Review, 102
Commerce Department, U.S., 122
Common sense, 112, 165, 166
Communication, 228, 236. *See also* Language
  of expectations, 194–96
Communication schools, 116–17
Communism, 4, 82, 202, 219–20, 231
  in Nicaragua, 217, 218
Competition, 196
Computers to translate languages, 111
Conditioned reflexes, 168
Conformity, 74, 136, 201, 221, 238
Conscious perception, 42–43
Consistency, 84, 140–41
  sincerity and, 191
Contradiction(s), 166, 206, 250
  in cultures, 105–6
  law of, 138–45
Control, need to, 45–46, 216–17
Cooperation, 196
Cosmetics, 149–50
Cosmopolitan, 183, 184
Cruz, Juana Inéz de la, 128

Cuba, 87, 218, 220
Cultural values, 38
Culture, 4, 55, 228, 250
    description of, 55
    perception and, 69, 70, 74
    psychological theories and, 65

Darwin, Charles, xiv
Da Vinci, Leonardo, 185
Death, 72, 149, 157–58
    expectation and, 189
    imagery of, in ads, 124–26, 158, 162, 223–26
Decontextualizing, 261
Défense de la France, 101
Defense Department, U.S., 30
Defensive paranoia, 151
Defensive strategies, 254–58, 261–62.
    See also Perceptual defenses
    avoid polarization, assertion, or negation, 256
    increase number of available options, 254–56
    privately question assumptions, 257–58
Definition of words, 120, 127
Delaying reaching conclusions, 261
Denial, 70, 84–85
Dependency, 79–80
De Sade, Marquis D. A. F., 237
Deviant behavior, 136, 201–4, 209, 221, 238, 257
    degree of tolerance of, 204
Dewey, John, 67
Diagnostic Criteria, DSM III, 210–11, 214
Dichotomy. *See* Excluded middles, law of
Discoveries, 136
Disease and stress, 187–88
Dixon, Norman, 24, 36
Do, but don't, double bind, 241–43
Double binds, 237, 238–45
    cultural, 246–47
    do, but don't, 241–43

feeling differently than you're supposed to, 241
questioning validity of one's perceptions, 239–40
sanity in an insane situation, 240–41
Double entendre, 17–20
Downy fabric softener ad, 71
Dreams, 39–41
Drive-related behavior, 46–47
Drugs:
    abuse of, 63, 105, 124–25, 223
    castration themes in ads for, 123
    death imagery in ads for, 124
    illegal addictive, 63, 223, 224
    pharmaceutical, 63, 74, 110, 223
    placebo effect, 188–89
Durrell, Lawrence, 237

Eating disorders, 30, 62
Education in the United States, 116–17, 125, 196, 251–53
    in advertising, 196
    labeling of children, self-fulfilling prophecies and, 213
Effect. *See* Cause and effect
Ehrenzweig, Anton, 3, 12
Eichmann, Adolf, 247
Einstein, Albert, 67, 93, 249, 255
Eisenhower, Dwight D., 53
Either/or assumptions, 134–37
Elizabeth II, Queen, 156
Embedding, 13–17, 22–31, 44, 48–52, 97–98, 123, 139–40, 162, 207, 244–45
    of orgasmic sounds, 150–51
    regulation of, 12–13, 18, 125, 142–43, 203–4, 267–68
Emotional response, 43–44
Epimenides or "liar" paradox, 143–44
Epinephrine, 60
Esquire, 159
Eternal truth, 137, 229, 236, 263
    search for, xvi, 5, 97

Ethics, 28, 259
Euclid, xiv, 120
Evaluation, importance of, 262
Evangelists, TV, 43, 145, 202
Evans, Martin, 227
Exceptions, 166
Excluded middles, law of, 134–37, 256
Exclusivity, 138–39, 145
Exorcist, The, 60
Expando-Vision, 29
Expectations of stereotypes, 180–204
  degree of tolerance of deviant behavior, 204
  management of expectation, 193–96
  morality and deviants, 201–4
  personality myths, 198–200
  potency of, 184–87
  self-comparison to ad personalities, 196–98
  sincerity fantasy, 191–93
  stress and, 187–89
Eye contact, truth-telling and, 192

Falwell, Jerry, 43, 145
Fantasy, 70, 237, 243
Fantasy formation, 82–83
Fatal Attraction, 75
Federal Communications Commission (FCC), 14, 30, 142, 268
Federal Trade Commission (FTC), 142, 268
Feeling differently than you're supposed to, 241
Fellatio, 225
Feyerabend, Paul, 207
Figure-ground reversals, 8–13
  auditory, 11–13
Filling in parts of a picture, 182
Fine art, motivation of, 185
Flexner, Abraham, 67
Flight and fight reactions, 60–61
Folklore, 152, 154, 158
Food advertisements, 16–17, 23, 44, 47, 58, 62, 124

Food and Drug Administration (FDA), 142
Foucault, Michel, 209
Frazer, J. G., 170
Freud, Sigmund, xiv, 35, 124, 185
Fromm, Erich, 157–58
Fundamentalists, 40, 43

Gaddafi, Muammar, 23–26, 44, 73, 133, 179
Gambling casinos, 73, 232–33
General Mills Corporation, 16
Genesis, 239
Genitalia, 244–45
  castration themes and, 123, 162, 207
  cosmetics and, 149–50
  subliminal, in advertisements, 14–17, 18, 40, 48, 49, 154, 159–62, 178
Gentlemen's Quarterly (GQ), 33, 159
Georgia Institute of Technology, 50
Georgia State Crime Laboratory, 50
Gestalt psychologists, 182
"Gifted," children labeled as, 213
Gilbey's gin ad, 129–30
Glickman, Dan, 30, 31
Goal-seeking behavior, 185
Gödel, Escher, Bach (Hofstadter), 67–68
Gödel, Kurt, 143–44
Gold, symbolism of, 152–54
Golden Bough, The (Frazer), 170
Gordon's gin ad, 88
Great Britain, 156
Greece, ancient, 143, 263
  philosophers of, xi, 5–6, 113, 258
Greek language, ancient, 118
Ground and figure reversals, 8–13
  auditory, 11–12
  perceptions of genius, 11–13
Guatemala, 218
Guilty, labeling as, 213

Hamurabi Code, xiv
Harlow, Bryce N., 53

Harrington, J. P., 170–71
Harris, Louis, 181
Hayakawa, S. I., 118
Health, effect of expectations on, 187–89
Heisenberg, Werner, 109, 146, 227
Heresy, 257–58
Hesse, Hermann, 249
Higher Learning in America, The (Hutchins), 251
Hijackings, behavior of victims of, 240–41
Histories, 81
Hitler, Adolf, 86, 215
Hobbes, Thomas, 124
Hofstadter, Douglas, 68
Home computers, 29
Homosexuals, ads directed at, 20, 33–34, 178, 183
Hostage situations, 240–41
Hospital waiting rooms, subliminal indoctrination in, 27
Howard, Nigel, 226
Hughes, Emmet John, 53
Human Use of Human Beings: Cybernetics and Society, The (Weiner), 67
Hume, David, 167
Hutchins, Robert M., 251
Hypnosis, xiv, 24–25, 256
posthypnotic suggestion, 40, 45–46

Identity, laws of, 121–34
fallacy of identification, 121–24
fantasy versus reality, 125–26
times, places, and situations, 129–34
verbal abstractions, 127–29
Ideologies. *See* Belief systems
Ideologues, 96, 229
Idioms, 110
Iks, 39
Illness and stress, 187–88
Inconsistency, 84, 140–41, 191

Indians, American, 170
Indoctrination, subliminal. *See* Advertising and public relations; Media technology, subliminal; Perception(s)
Inherited predispositions, 38
manipulation of, 38–39
Innate behaviors, 38
Insanity, 209, 211–13, 216, 238. *See also* Mental illness
Intelligence, 67, 99
artificial, 67–68
basis for evaluating, xiii
Internal Revenue Service (IRS), 208
International Gold Corporation, 153
Introjection, 70, 85–86, 89–90
Iran-Contra affair, 102
Isolation (exclusivity), 138–39, 145
Isolation technique, 70, 73–79

Jackson, Michael, 19–20
Janson, Maris, 32
Jargon, 110
Johnny Walker ad, 162
Johnson, Lyndon, 102, 200
Johnson, Virginia, 189
Judgmental values, 56–58
Jung, Carl Gustav, 148, 164, 206, 249
Justice, sense of, 38
Justine (de Sade), 237

Kafka, Franz, 237
Kamp, Dr. Charles, 30
Kant, Immanuel, 258
Kennedy, John F., 227
Kent ad, 182–83
Kesey, Ken, 211
Khomeini, Ayatollah, 24
Klapp, Orrin, 155
Koestler, Arthur, 66
Korzybski, Alfred, 118, 258
Kovach, Bill, 103
Kurosawa, Akira, 237

Labeling. *See* Stereotypes
Laing, R. D., 137, 164
Language, 4, 66
abstractions, perception of, 106–9, 111
Aristotelian logic and, 117–47
attempts to objectify, 109–11
computer translation, 111
innovation in, 112–14
meanings of words. *See* Meanings of words
reality and, xii–xiii, 111, 113, 228
rhetoric, 219
verbal behavior, 52–56
Language and Myth (Cassirer), 170
Laos, 218
Latin, 109, 110, 132
Law and order advocates, 204
Laws, Aristotelian. *See* Aristotelian logic
Leaders, symbolic, 154–57
Leakey, Dr., xiii
Ledford, Dr. Bruce R., ix–xvi, 51
Leky, Prescott, 146
Letter IV (Augustine), 156
Levi-Strauss, Claude, 158
Liberal arts education, 116, 251, 252
Libya, 23–26
Lies. *See* Lying
Light(ing):
background, 32–34
low-intensity, and low-volume sound, 22–31
Literature, motivation of, 185
Lorenz, Konrad, 38, 94
Love, 72
Low-intensity light and low-volume sound, 22–31
Luce, Henry, 175
Lucky numbers, 172–73
Lusseyran, Jacques, 101–2
Lying, 192. *See also* Truth
by governments, 100, 102–4
Lysenko, Trofim, 65

McDonald's ad, 47, 160
MacLeish, Archibald, 180
McLuhan, Marshall, ix, xiii, 88, 106, 148, 220
Macro level of perception, 107, 108, 236
Madness and Civilization (Foucault), 209
Magic words, 170–74
Mailer, Norman, 64
Malinowski, Bronislaw, 258
Mark III-B Programmable Subliminal Audio Processor monitors, 26
Mark III Video Subliminal Processor, 26–27
Marro, Anthony, 102, 103
Martineau, Pierre, 118
Marx, Karl, xiv
Masters, Dr. William, 178, 189
Masturbation, 19–20, 184
Mathematical paradoxes, 143–44
Mathematics, 119–20
Mathematics-based languages, 117
Meanings of words, 52–53, 110–11, 120, 127–28
contextual variations in, 110
introduction of new, 112–14
Media technology, subliminal, 3–90, 113–14, 250
areas of human behavior on which effects of can be measured, 36–44, 47–63
adaptation levels or judgmental values, 56–58
conscious perception, 42–43
dreams, 39–41
drive-related behavior, 46–47
emotional response, 43–44
memory, 41–42
perceptual thresholds, 48–50
psychopathology, 59–63
purchasing behavior, 58–59, 60
verbal behavior, 52–56
double entendre, 17–20
embedding. *See* Embedding

Media technology, subliminal (*cont'd*)
  figure-ground reversals, 8–13
  lighting and background sound, 31–34
  low-intensity light and low-volume sound, 22–31
  perceptual defenses and, 44–45, 69–90
  sophistry and, 6–7
  susceptibility to, 23, 55–56, 74, 94–95, 215–16
  tachistoscopic displays, 20–22
Mein Kampf (Hitler), 86, 215
Memory, 41–42, 60
Menninger Psychiatric Clinic, 214
Mental illness, 203, 228
  insanity, 209, 211–13, 216, 238
  self-fulfilling prophecies and, 209–13, 214, 216
Merit cigarettes ad, 87
Metacontract, 21
Metropolitan Life Insurance weight tables, 62
Micro level of perception, 107, 108, 236
Milky Way ad, 47
Miller, James Nathan, 103
Mills, C. Wright, 35, 259
Molecularizing your perceptions, 261–62
Moos, Dr. Malcolm, 53
Morality, 38, 202, 203
Mother's Blessing, 243–44
Motivation analysis, 262
Mozart, 11–12
Mutually Assured Destruction (MAD), 162–63
Myth of Sisyphus, The (Camus), 263
Mythology, 82, 124, 152, 157–58, 229

Narcissus, 220–21
Narcosynthesis, xiv
National Association of Advertising Agencies, 143
National Institute of Alcohol Abuse and Addiction, 18

National Institute of Education, 252
National Institute of Mental Health, 58
National Institutes of Health, 18, 223
Nazi Germany, 39, 76–77, 78, 101, 189
Nervous system, 60
Neuro-Communication Research Laboratory, 50
New Guinea, 169–70, 239
New Orleans Medical Association, 27
Newsday, 102
News information system, 99–100
Newspapers, advertising in, 104
Newsweek, 17, 33, 224
Newton, Sir Isaac, xiv, 120
New York Times, The, 103
New York University, 31
Nicaragua, 217–18
Nixon, Richard, 102, 204, 219
Nonconformity. *See* Deviant behavior
Nonlinear conflicts, 165–66
Norepinephrine, 60
Normal versus deviant behavior, 201–2, 209, 212
Northern Ireland, 156
Noxema ad, 88
Nuclear missile launch crews, training of, 75–76, 245–47
Numbers, lucky, 172–73
Numerical objectivity, 77–78
Nuremberg trials, 247

Obesity, 62–63
Objective reality, 95–104, 167, 200, 237
Objective truth, 5, 6, 260, 262–63
Objectivity, 77–78
  self-sealing world of, 230–48
Office of U.S. Secretary of Education, 259
One Flew Over the Cuckoo's Nest (Kesey), 211
Opinions, 38
Options, increase number of available, 254–56

Oscar-Mayer ads, 40, 159–60
Osman-Kord, Ltd., 50
Ouroborus, 143, 202, 208, 228, 260

Packaging advertising, 47
Paper stock, subliminally embedded, 50–52, 139–40
Paradoxes, 143–45, 166, 202, 208, 210, 228, 237, 247, 250, 260
  do, but don't, double bind, 241–43
Paranoia, 211
Paris Match ad, 206–7
Patriotism, 173–74, 247
Patronizing behavior, 195
Pavlov, Ivan, 168
People magazine, 100
Perception(s), 37–38, 215, 258–60
  conscious and unconscious inputs, 10
  consciously examining your, 261
  defined, 68
  of geniuses, 11–12
  instantaneous, 14, 37, 68
  isolation of, xiii
  limitations of conscious, 204
  macro level of, 107, 108, 236
  micro level of, 107, 108, 236
  multidimensional, 12
  perceived reality as a, 145–46
  peripheral, xiv
  self-reflexiveness, 146
  sophists and relativism of, 6
  of space, 112
  submicro level of, 107, 108, 236
  total, 14, 37, 68
Perceptual bias, 100–102, 113, 151, 200, 229
Perceptual defenses, 44–45, 69–70. *See also* Defensive strategies
Perceptual overload, 73
Perceptual rigidity, 74
Perceptual thresholds, 23, 48–50
Perestroika, 202
Peripheral perceptions, xiv

Personality myths, stereotypical, 198–200
Phallic symbols, 160. *See also* Genitalia
Philosophical Investigations I (Wittgenstein), 263
Physician waiting rooms, subliminal indoctrination in, 27
Piaget, Jean, 99
Pica, 62
Picasso, Pablo, 185
Placebo effects, 188–89
Plato, 5, 113, 205
Playboy, 17, 45
  logo, 207
Poetzle, Otto, 39, 40
Poetzle effect, 168
Poindexter, John M., 25
Point-of-sale advertising, 47
Polarization. *See* Excluded middles, law of
Politicians:
  lying by, 100, 102–4
  rhetoric of, 219
  self-fulfilling prophecies and, 219–20
  symbolic, 154–56
Politics of Lying, The (Wise), 103
Pope, Alexander, 180
Pope Paul IV, 3
Postal Service, U.S., 142
Posthypnotic suggestion, 40, 45–46
Pound, Ezra, ix
Predictability, 174–76
Proactive Systems, Inc., 28–29
Projection, 70, 85–89
Projective characterizations, 88–89
Propaganda, xvi, 39, 94, 215
Prophecies, 166, 174
  self-fulfilling, 189, 205–26
  ad-media, 220–26
  armaments and, 214–15
  in foreign relations, 217–20
  mental illnesses and, 209–13, 214, 216
  uncertainty and, 216

Protagoras, 5
Prussian Science Academy, 194
Psychological theories, 65
Psychopathology, 59–63
Psychopaths, 77
Public-opinion surveys, 56
Public relations. *See* Advertising and public relations
Purchasing behavior, 18, 40, 50, 58, 69–70, 170, 220–23
  studies of, 50–51, 58–59

Quantification as isolation technique, 77–78
Quantum mechanics, 119
Queen, symbolic, 155, 156
Quick cuts, 21

Rapid-eye movements (REM), 39
Rashomon, 237
Rat behavior, experimental research with, 106, 168
Rationalization, 72, 168
Reaction formation, 72–73, 85
Reaction shots, 22
Reader's Digest, 16
Reagan, Ronald, 25, 43, 102–3, 155, 219, 259
Reagan administration, 217–18
Reality, 236–38
  fantasy versus, 125, 133
  language and, xii–xiii, 111, 113, 228
  objective. *See* Objective reality
  perceived. *See* Perception(s)
Rebirth, 149
Regression, 70, 79–82, 243
Regulation of advertising, 13–14, 18, 125, 142–43, 203–4, 267–68
Relativity, 119
Relaxation, 261
Religious fundamentalists, 40, 43
Religious idealism or fanaticism, 83, 204, 225, 229, 231
  intolerance of deviants, 201

Repression, 14, 20, 70, 71–73, 83, 96, 98, 125, 166
  criterion for, 39–40
  national cultures and, 48–49, 71
Reproduction, 149, 157, 162
Rhetoric, 217
Roberts, Oral, 145
Robertson, Pat, 43, 122–23, 145
Rock music:
  archetypal symbols in, 150–51, 158
  introjection and, 89–90
  projection and, 89
  stereotypical role models in, 221–22
Rockwell, Norman, 243–44
Rosenberg Self-Esteem Scale, 51
Rosenhan, David, 211, 212
Rosenthal, Robert, 3
Rubinoff, Lionel, 35
Rule structures, 201–2
Russell, Bertrand, 177, 258

Safety indoctrination, subliminal, 27
Sagan, Carl, 259
Sandinistas, 217–18
Sandburg, Carl, 139
Sanity in an insane situation, 240–41
Schizophrenia, 210–11
Schrödinger, Irwin, 93
Science and Sanity (Korzybski), 118
Sciences, 119–20
  verbal/pictorial-oriented, 120
Scientific facts, 78–79, 109
Scientific method, xii
Seagram's ads, 23, 81, 121–23, 124, 125, 133, 162
Securities and Exchange Commission (SEC), 142
Self-destruction, 124–26, 158, 162–63, 224–26
Self-esteem, 51
Self-expectations, 195
Self-flattery, audience, 104–6, 221

Self-fulfilling prophecies, 189, 205–25, 230
  ad-media, 220–26
  armaments and, 214–15
  in foreign relations, 217–20
  mental illnesses and, 209–13, 214, 216
  uncertainty, 216
Self-image, 196–97
Self-reflexiveness, 146
Self-sealing premises, 229–48, 264
Sensory perception, 107
  bias in, 38, 101–2
Sex, 244–45
  in advertisements, 181–84, 206–7, 221, 225
    aimed at homosexuals, 20, 33–34, 178, 183
    castration themes, 123, 162, 207
    genitalia, subliminal, 14–17, 18, 40, 48, 49, 154, 159–62, 178
    "SEX" embedded in paper stock, 50–52, 139–40
SFPs. *See* Self-fulfilling prophecies
Shakespeare, William, 138
Shevrin, Dr. Howard, 30–31
Shultz, George P., 25
Silverman, Dr. Lloyd, 31
Sincerity fantasy, 191–93
Sisyphus, 263
Sivard, Ruth Leger, 137
Skinner, B. F., 65, 67, 169, 232, 233
Slot machines, 232–34
"Slow learner" label, 213
Smithsonian Institute, 170
Smoking and smoking ads, 63, 74–75, 87, 182–83, 221
  castration themes in, 123
  death imagery in, 124, 162
Social Security Administration, 211
Soloflex ads, 33–34, 178, 183
Somerset Importers of New York, 14

Somoza family, 217
Sophists, 5–6, 37, 258
Sophistry, 6–7
Sound:
  background, 31–32
  low-intensity light and low-volume, 22–31
Soviet Encyclopedia of Science, 118
Soviet Union. *See* U.S.S.R.
Star Wars, 219
State Department, Office of Intelligence and Research, 25
Statistical probability, 174, 232
Status hierarchies, 189–90
Stay Trim diet gum ad, 87–88
Stereotypes, 82–83, 100, 131–32, 254, 256
  expectations of, 180–204
    degree of tolerance of deviant behavior, 204
    management of, 193–96
    moralities and deviants, 201–4
    personality myths, 198–200
    potency of, 184–87
    self-comparison with media personalities, 196–98
    sincerity fantasy, 191–93
    stress and, 187–89
  projective, 86–89
  self-fulfilling prophecies and, 210, 213–14
  stigmatic, 213
Stigmatic stereotypes, 213
Stigmatized individuals, 195
Stimulus-response-reward system, 113
Stimutech, Inc., 29
Stone, I. F., 100
Strange loops, 144
Strategic Air Command, 76
Stress, expectational, 187–91
Subaru ads, 87
Sublimation, 70, 83
Subliminal media technology. *See* Media technology, subliminal

Subliminal Seduction (Key), x

Subliminal Sex® T-shirts, 9–10

Subliminal techniques, 8–34. *See also* Advertising and public relations; Media technology, subliminal; Perception(s); *specific techniques*

Submicro level of perception, 105, 106, 236

Success, expectations of, 189, 196–97

Suicide, 124, 162

Suspicion, 235

Swaggart, Jimmy, 43, 145

Symbolic Leaders (Klapp), 155

Symbols and symbolism, 9, 106, 108, 126, 127, 133, 148–63

archetypal, 149–51, 152–63

dictionaries of, 152

examining, 262

feelings evoked by, 152–54

interpretation of, 158–61

language abstractions and, 106–9, 127–29

symbolic leaders and, 154–57

Syncretistic illusions, 8–9

Synthesia, 12

Taboos, 83, 225

word, 170

Tachistoscopic displays, 20–22

Tanqueray emerald ad, 14–15, 48–49, 178, 259

Teenagers:

manipulation of, 12–13

projection in rock music and, 89

suicide among, 124

Teicher, Howard R., 25

Texas Chainsaw Massacre, The, 60

Thanatos, 124

Theft, subliminal indoctrination to prevent, 27, 28

Thorndyke, Edward, 67

Thriller, 19

Tillich, Paul, 146

Time delay in influence of subliminal perceptions, 40, 42

Time magazine, 14, 17, 33, 129, 182, 224

Gaddafi cover, 23–26, 44, 73, 133, 179

Tobacco. *See* Smoking and smoking ads

To be (the verb), 131–32, 133, 140

Tolstoy, Leo, 205

Translation of language, computer, 111

Treasury Department, Bureau of Alcohol, Tobacco, and Firearms, U.S., 142, 267–68

"New Rules and Regulations," 13, 18, 125, 142, 203–4

Truth, 52, 79, 99, 129, 137, 254. *See also* Lying

"in advertising," xi, 141–43

eternal, xvi, 5, 97, 137, 229, 236, 263

media's view of, 6–7

objective, 5, 6, 260, 262–63

search for, xvi, 5, 97

unbiased, 106, 176

TV evangelists, 43, 145, 202

TV Guide, 16

Two-valued assumptions, 134–37

Tyler, David, 28, 30

Unamuno, Miguel de, 140

Unbiased truth, 106, 176

Uncertainty, 216

United Fruit Company, 217

United Kingdom, 156

United States, 247

Central American policy of, 217–18

education in, 116–17, 125, 196, 213, 251–53

history of, 81

need to control in, cultural, 45–46

projection in, 87
Southeast Asian policy of, 218
U.S.S.R. and, 77, 82, 84, 172, 230, 231–32, 235–36
Vietnam and, 78, 218
U.S. Congress, House Committee on Science and Technology, 30–31
U.S. Defense Department, 30
U.S. Department of Agriculture, Grain Division of, 142
U.S. Department of Commerce, 122
U.S. News and World Report, 17, 224
U.S. Secretary of Education, Office of, 252
U.S. State Department, Office of Intelligence and Research, 25
U.S. Treasury Department, Bureau of Alcohol, Tobacco, and Firearms, 142, 267–68
"New Rules and Regulations," 13, 18, 125, 142, 203–4
University of Berlin, 194
University of Kansas Medical School, 139
University of Michigan Medical School, 30
University of Texas, 251
Unknowable, the, 177–79, 216, 256
U.S.S.R., 43, 65, 157, 204, 219, 247
lie-detection technique, 30–31
media's visibility in, 116
need to control in, cultural, 45–46
perestroika in, 202
projection in, 87
propaganda in, 94
quantification in, 77–78
self-fulfilling prophecies in, 220
U.S. and, 77, 82, 84, 172, 230, 231–32, 235–36

Vaginal symbols, 160–61. *See also* Genitalia

"Valerie," 158
Value systems, 146
either-or, 135
Veblen, Thorstein, 99
Verbal behavior, 52–56
Verbal splits, 135–36
Vietnam, 78, 218
Village Voice, 47
Voltaire, 71
Von Glaserfeld, Ernst, 93
Voodoo deaths, 189

Wall Street Journal, 50, 224, 225
Wars, regression fantasies about, 80
Washington Post, 25
Watzlawick, Paul, 64
Weaponry, 214–15
nuclear missile launch crews, training of, 75–76, 245–47
Weather predictions, 165, 175
Weight control, subliminal indoctrination for, 27, 29
Weiner, Norbert, 67
Weinstein, Dr. Sidney, 50
"When-then connection," 165
Whitehead, Alfred North, 115
Who's Afraid of Virginia Woolf?, 144
Wilson, Edward, 38
Winwood, Steve, 158
Wise, David, 103
Wishbone ad, 161–62
Wittgenstein, Ludwig, 164, 258, 263
Woodward, Bob, 25
Words, 133, 218–19. *See also* Language
accuracy of, as to times, places, and situations, 129–31
coining of, 110
colloquialisms, 110
definitions of, 112, 127
idioms, 110
jargon, 110
magic, 170–72

Words (*cont'd*)
   meaning of, 52–53, 110–11, 120, 127–28
   new, 110, 112–14
World Health Organization, 19
World Military and Social Expenditures
   (Sivard), 137

W. R. Grace Corporation, 217
Wrigley's chewing gum, 10–11
Wundt, Wilhelm, 67

Xenophobia, 231

Yale Medical School, 210

CPSIA information can be obtained at www.ICGtesting.com
Printed in the USA
BVOW08s1003200815

414162BV00002B/2/P